# THE SUNDAY TIMES

## The UK's 100 Best Restaurants

# THE SUNDAY TIMES

## The UK's 100 Best Restaurants

51 Black Swan, Oldstead

52 Artichoke, Amersham

53 The Harrow at Little Bedwyn, Marlborough

54 The Ritz Restaurant, The Ritz, London W1

55 Roka, London W1

56 La Petite Maison, London W1

57 Wiltons, London SW1

58 The Castle Terrace, Edinburgh

59 Trinity, London SW4

60 The Crown at Whitebrook, Whitebrook

61 Morston Hall, Morston

62 The Sportsman, Whitstable

63 Kai Mayfair, London W1

64 Club Gascon, London EC1

65 Koffmann's, The Berkeley, London SW1

66 Hakkasan, London W1

67 Seafood Restaurant, Padstow

68 Yauatcha, London W1

69 Murano, London W1

70 Auberge du Lac, Brocket Hall, Welwyn

71 Gauthier Soho, London W1

72 Martin Wishart, Cameron House, Loch Lomond

73 La Trompette, London W4

74 Number One, Balmoral Hotel, Edinburgh

75 21212, Edinburgh

# THE SUNDAY TIMES

## The UK's 100 Best Restaurants

1   Andrew Fairlie, Gleneagles Hotel, Auchterarder

2   Gidleigh Park, Chagford

3   The Ledbury, London W11

4   Waterside Inn, Bray

5   One-O-One, Sheraton Park Tower, London SW1

6   Le Manoir aux Quat' Saisons, Great Milton

7   Midsummer House, Cambridge

8   Restaurant Martin Wishart, Edinburgh

9   Le Gavroche, London W1

10  Mr Underhill's, Ludlow

11  L'Enclume, Cartmel

12  Marcus Wareing, The Berkeley, London SW1

13  Umu, London W1

14  Hambleton Hall, Hambleton

15  The Fat Duck, Bray

16  Pied à Terre, London W1

17  Purnells, Birmingham

18  The Square, London W1

19  Simon Radley, The Chester Grosvenor, Chester

20  Texture, London W1

21  Restaurant Sat Bains, Nottingham

22  Restaurant Nathan Outlaw, The St Enodoc Hotel, Rock

23  Theo Randall, InterContinental Hotel, London W1

24  The Kitchin, Edinburgh

25  The Greenhouse, London W1

# THE SUNDAY TIMES

## The UK's 100 Best Restaurants

76   Pétrus, London SW1

77   J Sheekey, London WC2

78   Benares, London W1

79   Hélène Darroze, The Connaught Hotel, London W1

80   Vetiver, Chewton Glen, New Milton

81   Scott's, London W1

82   The Walnut Tree, Llandewi Skirrid

83   Assaggi, London W2

84   Morgan M, London EC1

85   The Seahorse, Dartmouth

86   The River Café, London W6

87   Amaya, London SW1

88   Tyddyn Llan, Llandrillo

89   Wheelers Oyster Bar, Whitstable

90   The Glasshouse, Kew

91   Hibiscus, London W1

92   The Vanilla Pod, Marlow

93   Roka, London E14

94   Nobu, London W1

95   Yashin, London W8

96   La Bécasse, Ludlow

97   Angelus, London W2

98   Jin Kichi, London NW3

99   Alain Ducasse, Dorchester, London W1

100  Gordon Ramsay, London SW3

# Eat Well

If issues such as climate change, animal welfare and treating people fairly matter to you, look out for the SRA Sustainability Ratings next to restaurant listings.

The Sustainable Restaurant Association (SRA) is a not for profit body helping restaurants achieve greater sustainability. To help diners, it has developed Sustainability Ratings to assess restaurants in 14 key focus areas across three main sustainability categories of Sourcing, Environment and Society.

Harden's has partnered with the SRA to include its Sustainability Ratings, setting a new benchmark for the industry and giving diners the information to identify those restaurants doing great things. For example, sourcing seasonably and supporting local producers is important, as is using high welfare meat and dairy and ensuring fish stocks aren't endangered. Cutting down on food waste and ensuring energy and water efficiency are more ways for restaurants to be sustainable. And the most sustainable restaurants really engage with the communities around them.

Sustainability is an ongoing process: there's always room to improve and there's no final destination. By choosing a sustainable restaurant, you can be sure that your meal isn't costing the earth.

> *Food connects us with our landscape, our soil, our heritage, our health and what kind of society we are creating for tomorrow. Chefs, restaurateurs and diners can make the difference by embracing sustainable values and in doing so create a better food chain. We hope diners will consider these ideals when choosing to dine out.* – **Raymond Blanc OBE, President of the SRA**

> *We're proud to support the SRA, and hope that by adding SRA Sustainability Ratings to the restaurants we include, we can help set diners' expectations as to which of their choices will ensure the trade thrives for decades, and hopefully centuries to come.* – **Harden's**

More than 50% = Good Sustainability
More than 60% = Excellent Sustainability
More than 70% = Exceptional Sustainability

## PLACES PEOPLE TALK ABOUT

These are the restaurants outside London that were mentioned most frequently by reporters (last year's position is shown in brackets). For the list of London's most mentioned restaurants, see page 29.

For the list of London's most mentioned restaurants, see page 29.

**1**   **Manoir aux Quat' Saisons** (2)
*Great Milton, Oxon*
**2**   **Fat Duck** (1)
*Bray, Berks*
**3**   **Waterside Inn** (3)
*Bray, Berks*
**4**   **Hand & Flowers** (10)
*Marlow, Bucks*
**5**   **Seafood Restaurant** (4)
*Padstow, Cornwall*

**Manoir aux Quat' Saisons**

**6**   **Hind's Head** (6)
*Bray, Berks*
**7**   **Northcote** (5)
*Langho, Lancs*
**8**   **Chapter One** (8=)
*Locksbottom, Kent*
**9**   **L'Enclume** (17=)
*Cartmel, Cumbria*
**10**   **Gidleigh Park** (7)
*Chagford, Devon*

**Gidleigh Park**

**11**   **The Kitchin** (8=)
*Edinburgh*
**12**   **Hambleton Hall** (20)
*Hambleton, Rutland*
**13**   **Sportsman** (16)
*Whitstable, Kent*
**14=**   **Hix Oyster & Fish House** (12)
*Lyme Regis, Dorset*
**14=**   **Pipe & Glass Inn** (-)
*Beverley, East Yorkshire*

**Pipe & Glass Inn**

**14=**   **Magpie** (17=)
*Whitby, N Yorks*
**17**   **Yorke Arms** (19)
*Ramsgill-in-Nidderdale, N Yorks*
**18**   **Simpson's** (-)
*Birmingham, W Midlands*
**19**   **Porthminster Café** (-)
*St Ives, Cornwall*
**20**   **Vineyard at Stockcross** (11)
*Stockross, Berks*

**Porthminster Café**

## TOP SCORERS

*All restaurants whose food rating is ❶; plus restaurants whose price is £50+ with a food rating of ❷.*

| | | |
|---|---|---|
| **£220+** | The Fat Duck *(Bray)* | ❶❷❸ |
| **£180+** | Waterside Inn *(Bray)* | ❶❷❸ |
| **£160+** | Le Manoir aux Quat' Saisons *(Great Milton)* | ❶❶❷ |
| **£130+** | Gidleigh Park *(Chagford)* | ❶❶❷ |
| **£120+** | Andrew Fairlie *(Auchterarder)* | ❶❶❷ |
| **£100+** | Midsummer House *(Cambridge)* | ❶❷❸ |
| | Restaurant Nathan Outlaw *(Rock)* | ❶❷❸ |
| | Restaurant Sat Bains *(Nottingham)* | ❶❷④ |
| | Lucknam Park *(Colerne)* | ❷❶❷ |
| | Winteringham Fields *(Winteringham)* | ❷❷❸ |
| | Bath Priory Hotel *(Bath)* | ❷❷④ |
| **£90+** | Number One *(Edinburgh)* | ❶❶❸ |
| | Restaurant Martin Wishart *(Edinburgh)* | ❶❷❸ |
| | Dining Room *(Easton Gray)* | ❶❶④ |
| | Paris House *(Woburn)* | ❶❶④ |
| | L'Enclume *(Cartmel)* | ❶❸④ |
| | Restaurant Coworth Park *(Ascot)* | ❷❶❶ |
| | 21212 *(Edinburgh)* | ❷❷❷ |
| | Martin Wishart *(Loch Lomond)* | ❷❷❷ |
| | Simon Radley *(Chester)* | ❷❷❷ |
| **£80+** | The Three Chimneys *(Dunvegan)* | ❶❷❸ |
| | Mr Underhill's *(Ludlow)* | ❶❶❷ |
| | The Kitchin *(Edinburgh)* | ❶❶❷ |
| | Yorke Arms *(Ramsgill-in-Nidderdale)* | ❶❶❷ |
| | Hambleton Hall *(Hambleton)* | ❶❷❷ |
| | Bybrook Restaurant *(Castle Combe)* | ❶❷④ |
| | Drakes *(Ripley)* | ❶❷④ |
| | The Hambrough *(Ventnor)* | ❶❷④ |
| | The Samling *(Windermere)* | ❷❷❶ |
| | Longueville Manor *(Jersey)* | ❷❶❷ |
| | Gilpin Lodge *(Windermere)* | ❷❷❷ |
| | The French Horn *(Sonning-on-Thames)* | ❷❷❷ |
| | Morston Hall *(Morston)* | ❷❸❷ |
| | The Latymer *(Bagshot)* | ❷❸❷ |
| | Kinloch Lodge *(Sleat)* | ❷❷❸ |
| | Holbeck Ghyll *(Windermere)* | ❷❸❸ |

| Restaurant | Score |
|---|---|
| La Bécasse *(Ludlow)* | 2 3 3 |
| Harry's Place *(Great Gonerby)* | 2 0 4 |
| The Pass Restaurant *(Horsham)* | 2 0 4 |

**£70+**

| Restaurant | Score |
|---|---|
| Simpsons *(Birmingham)* | 0 0 2 |
| Fraiche *(Oxton)* | 0 2 2 |
| Purnells *(Birmingham)* | 0 2 2 |
| The Harrow at Little Bedwyn *(Marlborough)* | 0 2 2 |
| Lasan *(Birmingham)* | 0 2 3 |
| The Albannach *(Lochinver)* | 0 2 3 |
| The Box Tree *(Ilkley)* | 0 3 4 |
| Burgh Island Hotel *(Bigbury-on-Sea)* | 2 2 0 |
| Samuel's *(Masham)* | 2 2 0 |
| Seafood Restaurant *(Padstow)* | 2 2 2 |
| The Peacock *(Rowsley)* | 2 2 2 |
| Tyddyn Llan *(Llandrillo)* | 2 2 2 |
| Buckland Manor *(Broadway)* | 2 3 2 |
| Michael Caines *(Chester)* | 2 3 2 |
| Monachyle Mhor *(Balquhidder)* | 2 4 2 |
| The Crown at Whitebrook *(Whitebrook)* | 2 0 3 |
| Artisan *(Hessle)* | 2 2 3 |
| Bohemia *(Jersey)* | 2 2 3 |
| Fischers at Baslow Hall *(Baslow)* | 2 2 3 |
| Read's *(Faversham)* | 2 4 3 |
| Elephant Restaurant & Brasserie *(Torquay)* | 2 3 4 |
| Hand & Flowers *(Marlow)* | 2 3 4 |

**£60+**

| Restaurant | Score |
|---|---|
| Le Champignon Sauvage *(Cheltenham)* | 0 2 |
| Driftwood Hotel *(Rosevine)* | 0 2 0 |
| Braidwoods *(Dalry)* | 0 0 2 |
| The Castle Terrace *(Edinburgh)* | 0 0 2 |
| The Neptune *(Old Hunstanton)* | 0 2 2 |
| The Peat Inn *(Cupar)* | 0 2 2 |
| Caldesi in Campagna *(Bray)* | 0 0 3 |
| Loves *(Birmingham)* | 0 2 3 |
| Lumière *(Cheltenham)* | 0 2 3 |
| Northcote *(Langho)* | 0 2 3 |
| The Walnut Tree *(Llandewi Skirrid)* | 0 2 3 |
| The Seahorse *(Dartmouth)* | 0 3 3 |
| The Vanilla Pod *(Marlow)* | 0 3 3 |
| 5 North Street *(Winchcombe)* | 0 2 4 |
| Cotto *(Cambridge)* | 0 2 4 |
| Sienna *(Dorchester)* | 0 2 4 |
| The West House *(Biddenden)* | 0 3 4 |

| | | |
|---|---|---|
| Hotel Tresanton *(St Mawes)* | | ②②⓪ |
| Plas Bodegroes *(Pwllheli)* | | ②②⓪ |
| Artichoke *(Amersham)* | | ②⓪② |
| Green Inn *(Ballater)* | | ②⓪② |
| Bluebells *(Sunningdale)* | | ②②② |
| Café 21 *(Newcastle upon Tyne)* | | ②②② |
| Crab & Lobster *(Asenby)* | | ②②② |
| Darroch Learg *(Ballater)* | | ②②② |
| Hipping Hall *(Kirkby Lonsdale)* | | ②②② |
| Plumed Horse *(Edinburgh)* | | ②②② |
| Seafood Restaurant *(St Andrews)* | | ②②② |
| The Feathers Hotel *(Woodstock)* | | ②②② |
| The Star Inn *(Harome)* | | ②②② |
| Portmeirion Hotel *(Portmeirion)* | | ②③② |
| Kinloch House *(Blairgowrie)* | | ②⓪③ |
| Isle of Eriska *(Benderloch)* | | ②②③ |
| Lavender House *(Brundall)* | | ②②③ |
| Little Barwick House *(Barwick)* | | ②②③ |
| Miller Howe Restaurant & Hotel *(Bowness-on-Windermere)* | | ②②③ |
| Thackeray's *(Tunbridge Wells)* | | ②②③ |
| Casamia *(Bristol)* | | ②③③ |
| Feversham Arms *(Helmsley)* | | ②③③ |
| Hintlesham Hall *(Hintlesham)* | | ②③③ |
| The Olive Tree *(Bath)* | | ②④③ |
| JSW *(Petersfield)* | | ②②④ |
| Van Zeller *(Harrogate)* | | ②②④ |
| Alimentum *(Cambridge)* | | ②③④ |

| | | |
|---|---|---|
| **£50+**   The Pipe & Glass Inn *(Beverley)* | | ⓪②⓪ |
| The Old Passage Inn *(Arlingham)* | | ⓪⓪② |
| Estbek House *(Sandsend)* | | ⓪②② |
| Freemasons at Wiswell *(Wiswell)* | | ⓪②② |
| Great House *(Lavenham)* | | ⓪②② |
| Jeremy's at Borde Hill *(Haywards Heath)* | | ⓪②② |
| Paul Ainsworth at Number 6 *(Padstow)* | | ⓪②② |
| Roger Hickman's *(Norwich)* | | ⓪②② |
| Tanners Restaurant *(Plymouth)* | | ⓪②② |
| The Dining Room *(Ashbourne)* | | ⓪②② |
| The Oystercatcher *(Portmahomack )* | | ⓪②② |
| The Butcher's Arms *(Eldersfield)* | | ⓪②② |
| Black Swan *(Oldstead)* | | ⓪③② |
| Restaurant Tristan *(Horsham)* | | ⓪③② |
| Chapter One *(Locksbottom)* | | ⓪②③ |
| Apicius *(Cranbrook)* | | ⓪②③ |

| | | Score |
|---|---|---|
| | Chez Roux *(Inverness)* | ❶❷❸ |
| | Gamba *(Glasgow)* | ❶❷❸ |
| | Ode *(Shaldon)* | ❶❷❸ |
| | The Old Inn *(Drewsteignton)* | ❶❷❸ |
| | The Oyster Shack *(Bigbury)* | ❶❷❸ |
| | Verveine Fishmarket Restaurant *(Milford on Sea)* | ❶❷❸ |
| | The French Table *(Surbiton)* | ❶❷④ |
| | McCoys at the Tontine *(Northallerton)* | ❷❷❶ |
| | Silver Darling *(Aberdeen)* | ❷❷❶ |
| | Grain Store *(Edinburgh)* | ❷④❶ |
| | The Mason's Arms *(Knowstone)* | ❷❶❷ |
| | Brockencote Hall *(Chaddesley Corbett)* | ❷❷❷ |
| | Cringletie House *(Peebles)* | ❷❷❷ |
| | Smith's Brasserie *(Ongar)* | ❷❷❷ |
| | St Petroc's Hotel & Bistro *(Padstow)* | ❷❷❷ |
| | The Sir Charles Napier *(Chinnor)* | ❷❷❷ |
| | Two Fat Ladies at The Buttery *(Glasgow)* | ❷❷❷ |
| | Ubiquitous Chip *(Glasgow)* | ❷❷❷ |
| | The Crab at Chieveley *(Newbury)* | ❷❸❷ |
| | The Feathered Nest Inn *(Nether Westcote)* | ❷❸❷ |
| | Terravina *(Woodlands)* | ❷❶❸ |
| | The Arundell Arms Hotel *(Lifton)* | ❷❷❸ |
| | The Black Rat *(Winchester)* | ❷❷❸ |
| | The Hind's Head *(Bray)* | ❷❷❸ |
| | The Wensleydale Heifer *(West Witton)* | ❷❷❸ |
| | Tony Tobin @ The Dining Room *(Reigate)* | ❷❷❸ |
| | Wedgwood *(Edinburgh)* | ❷❷❸ |
| | La Chouette *(Dinton)* | ❷❸❸ |
| | Ondine *(Edinburgh)* | ❷❸❸ |
| | Second Floor Restaurant *(Manchester)* | ❷❸❸ |
| | The Three Lions *(Stuckton)* | ❷❸④ |
| | The Hardwick *(Abergavenny)* | ❷④④ |
| | Gourmet Spot *(Durham)* | ❷❸⑤ |
| **£40+** | Porthminster Café *(St Ives)* | ❶❷❶ |
| | Bilash *(Wolverhampton)* | ❶❶❷ |
| | Guildhall Tavern *(Poole)* | ❶❶❷ |
| | Rogan & Co *(Cartmel)* | ❶❶❷ |
| | The Ambrette at Rye *(Rye)* | ❶❶❷ |
| | Wild Thyme *(Chipping Norton)* | ❶❶❷ |
| | Anokaa *(Salisbury)* | ❶❷❷ |
| | El Gato Negro Tapas *(Ripponden)* | ❶❷❷ |
| | Kota *(Porthleven)* | ❶❷❷ |
| | Les Mirabelles *(Nomansland)* | ❶❷❷ |

| | | |
|---|---|---|
| The Lime Tree (Manchester) | | 0 2 2 |
| The Nut Tree Inn (Murcott) | | 0 2 2 |
| The Parkers Arms (Newton-in-Bowland) | | 0 2 2 |
| The Sportsman (Whitstable) | | 0 2 2 |
| Wheelers Oyster Bar (Whitstable) | | 0 3 2 |
| Fat Olives (Emsworth) | | 0 0 3 |
| Fishers Bistro (Edinburgh) | | 0 2 3 |
| Gingerman (Brighton) | | 0 2 3 |
| Maliks (Cookham) | | 0 2 3 |
| Pea Porridge (Bury St Edmunds) | | 0 2 3 |
| Rick Stein's Café (Padstow) | | 0 2 3 |
| Riverford Field Kitchen (Buckfastleigh) | | 0 2 3 |
| Sojo (Oxford) | | 0 2 3 |
| The Ambrette (Margate) | | 0 2 3 |
| The Grassington House Hotel (Grassington) | | 0 2 3 |
| The Pony and Trap (Newtown, Chew Magna) | | 0 2 3 |
| Maliks (Gerrards Cross) | | 0 3 3 |
| Le Langhe (York) | | 0 4 3 |
| The Feathers Inn (Hedley On The Hill) | | 0 2 4 |
| J Baker's Bistro Moderne (York) | | 0 4 4 |
| £30+ | Xian (Orpington) | 0 0 2 |
| | Food by Breda Murphy (Whalley) | 0 2 2 |
| | Valley Connection (Bury St Edmunds) | 0 0 3 |
| | Colmans (South Shields) | 0 2 3 |
| | Loch Bay (Waternish) | 0 2 3 |
| | Mourne Seafood Bar (Belfast) | 0 2 3 |
| | Mother India (Glasgow) | 0 3 3 |
| | My Sichuan (Oxford) | 0 4 3 |
| | Ebi Sushi (Derby) | 0 2 4 |
| | Magpie Café (Whitby) | 0 2 4 |
| £20+ | Hansa's (Leeds) | 0 0 3 |
| | Graveley's Fish & Chip Restaurant (Harrogate) | 0 2 3 |
| | The Company Shed (West Mersea) | 0 4 3 |
| | Karachi (Bradford) | 0 3 4 |
| | McDermotts Fish & Chips (Croydon) | 0 0 2 |
| | Bukhara (Preston) | 0 2 3 |
| | Anstruther Fish Bar (Anstruther) | 0 4 4 |
| £10+ | Vegetarian Food Studio (Cardiff) | 0 0 4 |
| | This & That (Manchester) | 0 3 5 |

Andrew Fairlie at Gleneagles Hotel

## ABERAERON, CEREDIGION 4–3C

**Harbourmaster** £47 ④❷❷
Quay Pde SA46 0BT (01545) 570755
"A heavenly location, right on the quay,
overlooking the picturesque harbour" adds lustre
to this well-known seafront restaurant-with-
rooms; both bar and restaurant are "relaxed" (if
sometimes "crowed and noisy") venues, serving
"tasty" fish-centric fare.
/ **Details:** www.harbour-master.com; 9 pm; no Amex.
**Accommodation:** 13 rooms, from £110.

**The Hive On The Quay** £43 ⊤
Cadwgan Pl SA46 0BU (01545) 570445
A waterside café where the food is tipped as
"very good" ("and the service is great too…
even when you arrive in motorbike gear").
/ **Details:** www.thehiveaberaeron.com; 9 pm; closed
Mon & Sun D; no Amex.

## ABERDEEN, ABERDEENSHIRE 9–2D

**Silver Darling** £59 ❷❷❶
Pocra Quay, North Pier AB11 5DQ
(01224) 576229
"Watching the boats come and go" adds to the
ambience at this well-established fixture, which
has an "awesome" waterfront location (in the old
harbour control building); "a consistently superb
fish-based menu" adds to the all-round (if pricey)
appeal. / **Details:** www.silverdarlingrestaurant.co.uk;
9 pm; closed Sat L & Sun; children: +16 after 8 pm.

**La Stella** £56 ⊤
28 Adelphi AB11 5BL (01224) 211414
A "cosy" spot, tipped for "fresh seafood cooked
to perfection"; "it's good for lunch or dinner", and
"booking is essential".
/ **Details:** www.lastella.co.uk.

## ABERGAVENNY, MONMOUTHSHIRE 2–1A

**The Angel Hotel** £46 ❸④❸
15 Cross St NP7 5EN (01873) 857121
This former coaching inn is especially noted for
"an afternoon tea to die for", but it's often hailed
as an "impressive" destination all-round; the only
problem is that it's "too popular" – "the staff
often seem rather stressed".
/ **Details:** www.angelhotelabergavenny.com; 10 pm.
**Accommodation:** 35 rooms, from £101.

**The Hardwick** £58 ❷④④
Old Raglan Rd NP7 9AA (01873) 854220
"Delicious food, carefully cooked and presented"
is still the backbone of reports on Stephen
Terry's "outstanding" gastropub (with rooms);
since the recent expansion, though, a vocal

minority have been "disappointed" – the place
now "lacks any wow-factor", they say, and they
claim it's "overpriced" too.
/ **Details:** www.thehardwick.co.uk; 10 pm; no Amex.
**Accommodation:** 8 rooms, from £150.

## ABERYSTWYTH, POWYS 4–3C

**Gwesty Cymru** £42 ❷❷❸
19 Marine Ter SY23 2AZ (01970) 612252
"The top-quality place in town" – this upmarket
seafront hotel has a snug (slightly "cramped")
restaurant and bar serving a "very well-cooked"
menu that "makes good use of fresh Welsh
fare". / **Details:** www.gwestycymru.com; 9 pm; closed
Tue L; no Amex; children: 5. **Accommodation:** 8
rooms, from £85.

**Ultracomida** £30 ❷❷❷
31 Pier St SY23 2LN (01970) 630686
"A really delicious tapas bar, just off the prom!'"
– attached to a deli, this "interesting place to
eat" features an "excellent range of meats";
dishes are consumed "at large communal
tables". / **Details:** www.ultracomida.com; 9 pm;
Mon-Thu & Sat L only, Fri open L & D, closed Sun.

## ACHILTIBUIE, ROSSSHIRE 9–1B

**Summer Isles Hotel** £75 ⊤
IV26 2YG (01854) 622282
This remote hotel (named after the islands it
overlooks) attracted limited feedback this year;
one repeat-visitor reported "a poor meal at this
once-superlative destination", but the majority
still acclaim its "seriously good" cuisine, and
"superb" wines.
/ **Details:** www.summerisleshotel.com; 25m N of
Ullapool on A835; 8 pm; Closed from 1st Nov - 1st Apr;
no Amex; no jeans; children: 8+.
**Accommodation:** 13 rooms, from £155.

## ALBOURNE, WEST SUSSEX 3–4B

**The Ginger Fox** £44 ❷❸❸
Muddleswood Road BN6 9EA
(01273) 857 888
Eight miles from Brighton, the country outpost of
that city's 'Ginger' empire is a "useful" gastropub,
with an "interesting" and "inviting" menu, and at
"reasonable prices" too.
/ **Details:** www.gingermanrestaurants.com; 10 pm,
Sun 9 pm.

## ALDEBURGH, SUFFOLK 3–1D

**Aldeburgh Fish And Chips** £15 ❷④⑤
225 High St IP16 4BZ (01728) 454685
"Reason in itself to head to Aldeburgh" – so say
fans of this "wonderful" chippy, where "the
queue stretches right around the block when the

tourists are about"; a meal "tastes best overlooking the sea" (sitting on the harbour wall). / **Details:** 8 pm; no credit cards.

**The Lighthouse**     **£42**   ❸❸❸
77 High St IP15 5AU   (01728) 453377
For a "casual" meal, this "happy and buzzy", "brasserie-style" operation is "always fun", and it has long been the best-known place in town; most reporters feel the food is "unfailingly good" too, but not everyone is quite convinced.
/ **Details:** www.lighthouserestaurant.co.uk; 10 pm.

**Regatta**     **£42**   ❸❸④
171-173 High St IP15 5AN   (01728) 452011
"A charming and friendly seaside restaurant which never disappoints" – it rarely dazzles either (which no one seems to see as much of a negative), but it can get "very noisy".
/ **Details:** www.regattaaldeburgh.com; 10 pm.

**The Wentworth Hotel**     **£40**   ❸❷❷
Wentworth Rd IP15 5BD   (01728) 452312
"A delightful, old-fashioned family hotel", overlooking the sea; no one pretends it's a foodie haunt, but its "gentle and efficient" service and "wholesome" cuisine ("strong on fish") invariably impress reporters, and prices are "very sensible". / **Details:** www.wentworth-aldeburgh.com; 9.30 pm; no jeans or trainers. **Accommodation:** 35 rooms, from £157.

**The Marquis**     **£65**   ❸❸④
Alkham Valley Rd CT15 7DF
(01304) 873410
On most accounts, this popular small restaurant-with-rooms (a former pub) "punches well above its weight"; not everyone's impressed, however, with the odd sceptic finding the whole experience too "uneventful" for comfort.
/ **Details:** www.themarquisatalkham.co.uk; 9.30 pm, Sun 8.30 pm; closed Mon L; children: 8+ D.
**Accommodation:** 10 rooms, from £95.

**Treehouse**

**Alnwick Castle**     **£42**   ⊕
Denwick Ln NE66 1YU   (01665) 511350
Tipped for its "truly magical" setting – a "stunning" venue in a (real) tree house of which Walt Disney himself would have been proud; the food and service may be a bit of a side-show, but they rarely disappoint; for a stroll afterwards, the Duchess's garden isn't bad either.
/ **Details:** www.alnwickgarden.com.

**Caracoli**     **£29**   ❷❸❸
15 Broad St SO24 9AR   (01962) 738730
Imagine a rather smarter version of Carcluccio's, and you have something like this "popular coffee shop and deli" (one of three branches locally), where "superb" coffee and "original" sandwiches are just part of a formula that's "really fresh and exciting". / **Details:** www.caracoli.co.uk; 2.30 pm; L only; no Amex; no booking.

**Baraset Barn**     **£45**   ⊕
1 Pimlico Lane CV37 7RJ   (01789) 295510
Tipped for its "general attention to detail", a large and airy gastroboozer, in a former tithe barn, which continues to be an all-round crowd-pleaser. / **Details:** www.barasetbarn.co.uk; 9.30 pm; closed Sun D; no Amex.

**Amberley Castle**     **£85**   ❸❸⓿
BN18 9LT   (01798) 831992
As picture-perfect a medieval castle as you could hope to find, this is certainly "a great destination for romance"; some reporters find the food "excellent" too, but there's also a feeling that "you're paying for the beautiful surroundings as much as you are for the food".
/ **Details:** www.amberleycastle.co.uk; N of Arundel on B2139; 9 pm; no jeans or trainers; booking: max 6; children: 12+; SRA-53%. **Accommodation:** 19 rooms, from £315.

**Doi Intanon**     **£35**   ❸❷❷
Market Place LA22 9BU   (01539) 432119
"Best Thai in the south Lakes!" – this "very friendly" operation is highly rated for its "good, very fresh food", and as a "really enjoyable" destination all-round.

**Drunken Duck**     **£53**   ❷❸❷
Barngates LA22 0NG   (01539) 436347
"A lovely upmarket gastropub experience, in the heart of the Lake District"; it impressed most reporters this year with its "unbeatable location", "excellent" food, "very good" wine list, plus "especially good microbrewery beers".
/ **Details:** www.drunkenduckinn.co.uk; 3m from Ambleside, towards Hawkshead; 9 pm; no Amex; booking: max 10 (D only). **Accommodation:** 17 rooms, from £95.

**Lucy's on a Plate** £43 🅣
Church St LA22 0BU (01539) 431191
*"As close as you can get to feeling you're eating in someone's house" – this "welcoming" bistro has long been particularly tipped for its "wonderful" cakes and puds; reports of late, though, have also included the odd let-down.*
/ **Details:** www.lucysofambleside.co.uk; 9 pm.

**Zeffirelli's** £33 ❸❸❷
Compston Rd LA22 9AD (01539) 433845
*"A good pizza 'n' pasta restaurant attached to a three-screen arthouse cinema" – this "unique" Lakeland institution is universally praised by reporters for its "value-for-money" charms; "it's 100% veggie, but you probably wouldn't immediately notice".* / **Details:** www.zeffirellis.com; 10 pm; no Amex.

**Artichoke** £65 ❷⓿❷
9 Market Sq HP7 0DF (01494) 726611
*"Just getting better and better after its extension" – Laurie Gear's "friendly" Old Amersham restaurant continues its phoenix-like recovery since its destruction by fire in 2008; it's a "smart, comfortable and characterful" place, with notably "interesting" cuisine – the tasting menu in particular is "exquisite".*
/ **Details:** www.theartichokerestaurant.co.uk; 9.15 pm, Fri & Sat 9.30 pm; closed Mon & Sun; no shorts.

**Gilbey's** £48 ❸❷❸
1 Market Sq HP7 0DF (01494) 727242
*The food "doesn't quite excite", but reporters are pretty much unanimous that they "would return" to this "efficient" and "cosy" restaurant, owned by a scion of the eponymous gin dynasty.*
/ **Details:** www.gilbeygroup.com; 9.30 pm, Sat 9.45 pm, Sun 8.45 pm.

**Anstruther Fish Bar** £24 ⓿④④
42-44 Shore St KY10 3AQ (01333) 310518
*"Fantastic, consistent and reasonably-priced fish 'n' chips" – no wonder the Smith family's famous institution, near the harbour, is "always busy".*
/ **Details:** www.anstrutherfishbar.co.uk; 10 pm; no Amex; no booking.

**Applecross Inn** £38 ❷❸❸
Shore St IV54 8LT (01520) 744262
*"Miles from anywhere", but even so this famous inn "manages to be incredibly busy, and deservedly so"; "fish to die for" is the highlight – "the only complaint is the huge portion sizes!"*

/ **Details:** www.applecross.uk.com; off A896, S of Shieldaig; 9 pm; no Amex; need 6+ to book.
**Accommodation:** 7 rooms, from £90.

**Kilberry Inn** £51 🅣
Nr Tarbert PA29 6YD (01880) 770223
*An obscurely-located restaurant-with-rooms that, say fans, "never disappoints" – it's tipped for its "fresh" and "lively" cuisine, nicely offset by an "eclectic range of unusual wines".*
/ **Details:** www.kilberryinn.com; 9 pm; closed Mon; no Amex. **Accommodation:** 5 rooms, from £195.

**The Old Passage Inn** £54 ⓿⓿❷
Passage Rd GL2 7JR (01452) 740547
*This "very good fish restaurant" doesn't just boast a "unique" location on the banks of the Severn – Mark Redwood's "sophisticated" cuisine is "exemplary"; 'bore breakfasts' a speciality.*
/ **Details:** www.theoldpassage.com; 9 pm; closed Mon & Sun D. **Accommodation:** 3 rooms, from £80.

**The Town House** £45 ❸❷❷
65 High St BN18 9AJ (01903) 883847
*The "splendid ceiling" (from 16th century Florence!) is a talking point at this "delightful" (if "cramped") restaurant-with-rooms, overlooking the castle; "by offering an excellent set menu, it is thriving".* / **Details:** www.thetownhouse.co.uk; 9.30 pm; closed Mon & Sun. **Accommodation:** 4 rooms, from £95.

**Ascot Oriental** £44 ❷❷❸
London Rd SL5 0PU (01344) 621877
*"The best out-of-town oriental restaurant I've encountered!" – Konrad Liu's stylishly-housed pan-Asian "always maintains high standards", and makes a slightly surprising find in its rural location.* / **Details:** www.ascotoriental.com; 10.15 pm.

**Restaurant Coworth Park**
Coworth Park £90 ❷⓿⓿
Blacknest Rd SL5 7SE (01344) 876 600
*John Campbell has gone, but this doesn't seem to have had any great negative impact on the "beautifully balanced" cuisine at this swanky "boutique-style" country house hotel – "a stunning venue in every respect".*
/ **Details:** www.coworthpark.com; 9.45 pm; closed Mon & Sun D.

### ASENBY, NORTH YORKSHIRE 8–4C

**Crab & Lobster** £ 65 ❷❷❷
Dishforth Rd YO7 3QL (01845) 577286
*"An eccentric interior packed with junk-shop rejects" isn't the only notable feature of this "quirky" and "cluttered" thatched pub – its "seriously good" fish-based menu makes it "perfect for seafood-lovers, as well as for a date"; "the lunchtime deal is unbeatable for quality and value" too.*
/ **Details:** www.crabandlobster.co.uk; at junction of Asenby Rd & Topcliffe Rd; 9 pm, 9.30 pm Sat.
**Accommodation:** 14 rooms, from £160.

### ASHBOURNE, DERBYSHIRE 5–3C

**The Dining Room** £ 59 ❶❷❷
33 St. John's St DE6 1GP (01335) 300666
*"By far the best food for miles around"; this tiny (six-table) husband-and-wife operation is a "charming" spot, where the "great and innovative cooking" punches "far above the establishment's perceived weight".*
/ **Details:** www.thediningroomashbourne.co.uk; 7 pm; D only, closed Mon–Wed & Sun; no Amex; booking essential; children: 12+. **Accommodation:** 1 room, at about £120.

### ASHBURTON, DEVON 1–3D

**Agaric** £ 56 ❶
30 North St TQ13 7QD (01364) 654478
*A village-restaurant-with-rooms that's "always welcoming", and tipped for its "very impressive" cuisine; room-and-dinner packages offer "excellent value".*
/ **Details:** www.agaricrestaurant.co.uk; 9.30 pm; closed Mon, Tue, Sat L & Sun; no Amex.
**Accommodation:** 5 rooms, from £110.

### ASHTON UNDER LYNE, GREATER MANCHESTER 5–2B

**Indian Ocean** £ 26 ❶
83 Stamford Street East OL6 6QH (0161) 343 3343
*The local subcontinental tip – "a lot smarter than most of the local Indians, and the food's better too, if not by quite the same margin"; it's very "popular" too.*
/ **Details:** indianoceanonline.co.uk; 11 pm, Fri-Sat midnight, Sun 10.30 pm; D only.

### ASTON TIRROLD, OXFORDSHIRE 2–2D

**The Sweet Olive** £ 49 ❶❷❷
Baker St OX11 9DD (01235) 851272
*"Basically French food, but actually more varied and interesting than you get in France!" – this*

Gallic-run country restaurant (and bar) is undoubtedly *"the best in the area"*, and it pleases all who comment on it.
/ **Details:** www.sweet-olive.com; half a mile off the A417 between Streatley & Wantage; 9 pm; closed Feb.

### AUCHTERARDER, PERTH AND KINROSS 9–3C

**Andrew Fairlie**
**Gleneagles Hotel** £ 128 ❶❶❷
PH3 1NF (01764) 694267
*"The ultimate gastronomic experience!";* Andrew Fairlie's *"extremely polished"* operation won the survey's highest food rating this year, thanks to his *"original"* cuisine that creates *"an amazing experience every time";* it's a cossetting, dark-walled chamber at the heart of this famous Edwardian golfing hotel.
/ **Details:** www.andrewfairlie.com; 10 pm; L only, closed Sun; children: 12+; SRA-74%.
**Accommodation:** 273 rooms, from £320.

**Jon & Fernanda's** £ 46 ❶
34 High St PH3 1DB (01764) 662442
*Run for over a decade by an ex-Gleneagles couple, this high-street hidden gem is tipped for its "excellent menu at reasonable prices".*
/ **Details:** www.jonandfernandas.co.uk.

### AVIEMORE, HIGHLAND 9–2C

**Mountain Cafe** £ 30 ❶
111 Grampian Rd PH22 1RH (01479) 812473
*"Mountainous views, and mountainous portions of home-baked cakes too!" – especially in an area which is "something of a culinary desert", this cafe above an outdoor clothing shop is a tip well worth knowing about; more substantial dishes reflect the chef's Kiwi origins.*
/ **Details:** www.mountaincafe-aviemore.co.uk; L only; no Amex.

### AXMINSTER, DEVON 2–4A

**River Cottage Canteen** £ 39 ❷❷④
Trinity Sq EX13 5AN (01297) 631715
*"We visited because of the Fearnley-Whittingstall connection… and were not disappointed!" – this rustic canteen is generally hailed as a "great informal place to meet", even by those who find the food "a bit hit-and-miss", or portions rather on the "mean" side.*
/ **Details:** www.rivercottage.net; 9 pm; closed Mon D & Sun D; SRA-84%.

value". / **Details:** www.piedaniels-restaurant.com;
10 pm; closed Mon & Sun D.

---

| AYLESBURY, BUCKINGHAMSHIRE | 3–2A |

**Hartwell House**     **£76**   ❸❸❸
Oxford Rd  HP17 8NR  (01296) 747444
*"Superb food and wine in a lovely setting"; this
(National Trust) country house is – for the most
part – as "luxurious" a find for today's traveller
as it once was for Louis XVIII in exile.*
/ **Details:** www.hartwell-house.com; 2m W of
Aylesbury on A418; 9.45 pm; no jeans or trainers;
children: 4+. **Accommodation:** 49 rooms,
from £260.

---

| AYLESFORD, KENT | 3–3C |

**Hengist**     **£48**   ❷❷❸
7-9 High St  ME20 7AX  (01622) 719273
*"When it's good, it's very hard to beat!", say fans
of this chic (arguably to the point of "camp")
country restaurant; the food can sometimes
seem "inconsistent", but even many critics "keep
going back".* / **Details:** www.hengistrestaurant.co.uk;
10 pm; closed Mon, Tue L, Wed L, Thu L & Sun D.

---

| BAGSHOT, SURREY | 3–3A |

**The Latymer**
**Pennyhill Park Hotel**    **£86**   ❷❸❷
London Rd  GU19 5EU  (01276) 471774
*For most reporters, Michael Wignall's "fantastic"
cooking is all part of the formula that makes
visits to this grand country house hotel (and spa)
a "very special" event; if there is a criticism, it is
that the style of this 'Exclusive' hotel can
sometimes seem a touch "corporate".*
/ **Details:** www.pennyhillpark.co.uk; 9.15 pm, Fri &
Sat 9.30 pm; closed Mon, Tue L, Sat L & Sun; booking:
max 8; children: 11. **Accommodation:** 123 rooms,
from £315.

---

| BAKEWELL, DERBYSHIRE | 5–2C |

**The Monsal Head Hotel**   **£40**   ❶
DE45 1NL  (01629) 640250
*It's not just the "dramatic" Peak District location
(overlooking a huge railway viaduct) which
makes this former coaching inn well worth
seeking out; it is also tipped for its "very good
local produce, well prepared".*
/ **Details:** www.monsalhead.com; 9.30 pm, Sat & Sun
9 pm; no Amex. **Accommodation:** 7 rooms,
from £90.

---

**Piedaniels**     **£45**   ❸❶④
Bath St  DE45 1BX  (01629) 812687
*"If you like traditional French cooking, this is
excellent!", say fans of the Piedaniels'
"comfortable" barn-conversion; sceptics feel its
culinary style is a little "stuck in the past" but,
"for lunch or midweek", it's undoubtedly "great*

---

| BALLATER, ABERDEENSHIRE | 9–3C |

**Darroch Learg**    **£61**   ❷❷❷
56 Braemar Rd  AB35 5UX  (01339) 755443
*A small country house hotel, hailed by most
reporters as offering a "wonderful all-round
experience", including cuisine which "makes
excellent use of local produce, particularly game
and fish"; even big fans, though, have discerned
the odd "jaded" note in its recent performance.*
/ **Details:** www.darrochlearg.co.uk; on A93 W of
Ballater; 9 pm; D only, ex Sun open L & D; no Amex.
**Accommodation:** 12 rooms, from £140.

---

**Green Inn**     **£62**   ❷❶❷
9 Victoria Rd  AB35 5QQ  (01339) 755701
*Fans of this "friendly" family-run restaurant-with-
rooms find simply "nothing to fault", and they
say it's a destination that's "always enjoyable" –
"if anything, the cooking gets better every year!"*
/ **Details:** www.green-inn.com; 9 pm; D only, closed
Mon & Sun; no Amex; no shorts.
**Accommodation:** 3 rooms, from £60.

---

| BALQUHIDDER, PERTH AND KINROSS 9–3C |

**Monachyle Mhor**    **£71**   ❷④❷
FK19 8PQ  (01877) 384622
*With its splendid menu of "Scottish dishes with a
twist", the Lewis family's "stunningly-located"
restaurant-with-rooms, in the Trossachs National
Park, can make a "perfect get-away"; now, if they
could just do something about the occasionally
"chaotic" service...* / **Details:** www.mhor.net; take
the Kings House turning off the A84; 8.45 pm.
**Accommodation:** 14 rooms, from £185.

---

| BARNET, HERTFORDSHIRE | 3–2B |

**Savoro**     **£41**   ❸❷❸
206 High St  EN5 5SZ  (020) 8449 9888
*"A fantastic neighbourhood restaurant" (part of
a small hotel); "reasonably-priced", "relaxed" and
"pleasant", it strikes some reporters as "the best
place in the area, and by some way".*
/ **Details:** www.savoro.co.uk; 9.45 pm; closed Sun D.
**Accommodation:** 11 rooms, from £75.

---

| BARNSLEY, GLOUCESTERSHIRE | 2–2C |

**Barnsley House**    **£58**   ❶
GL7 5EE  (01285) 740000
*There are fewer reports than we would like on
this very contemporary country house five-year-
old, tipped by a number of reporters as "a lovely
hotel, with food to match".*
/ **Details:** www.barnsleyhouse.com; 9 pm, Sat & Sun

9.45 pm; children: 18+ after 7.30 pm.
**Accommodation:** 18 rooms, from £275.

**The Village Pub**          £42   ❸❸❸
GL7 5EF   (01285) 740421
"A tasty place to go for a relaxing bite!"; this
"impressively-situated" inn – associated with
nearby Barnsley House and serving a menu of
"robust" classics – pleases all who comment on
it. / **Details:** www.thevillagepub.co.uk; 9.30 pm, Sun
9 pm. **Accommodation:** 6 rooms, from £125.

BARRASFORD, NORTHUMBERLAND   8–2A

**Barrasford Arms**          £40   ⓣ
NE48 4AA   (01434) 681237
Limited, and rather up-and-down, commentary
this year on Tony Binks's remote inn; supporters
still tip it as a "reliably good" destination, though.
/ **Details:** www.barrasfordarms.co.uk; 9 pm; closed
Mon L & Sun D; no Amex; children: 18 + in bar after
9.30pm. **Accommodation:** 7 rooms, from £85.

BARTON-ON-SEA, HAMPSHIRE   2–4C

**Pebble Beach**          £49   ❷❷❷
Marine Drive  BH25 7DZ   (01425) 627777
"One of the best al fresco dining experiences in
the country", say fans, is to be had at this clifftop
venue overlooking the Solent, which not only
offers "great sea-views", but Pierre Chevillard's
"brilliant seafood" too; eat in the somewhat
"dated" interior though, and the whole
experience can seem "ho-hum".
/ **Details:** www.pebblebeach-uk.com; 9 pm, Fri & Sat
9.30 pm; booking advisable. **Accommodation:** 4
rooms, from £90.

BARWICK, SOMERSET   2–3B

**Little Barwick House**          £63   ❷❷❸
BA22 9TD   (01935) 423902
Tim and Emma Ford's "comfortable and
homely" restaurant-with-rooms, in a Georgian
dower house, almost invariably satisfies reporters
– service is "friendly" and "attentive", and fans
applaud the "immaculate" cooking too.
/ **Details:** www.littlebarwick.co.uk; take the A37 Yeovil
to Dorchester road, turn left at the brown sign for Little
Barwick House; Tue-Fri 9 pm, Sat 9.30 pm; closed Mon,
Tue L & Sun; children: 5+ . **Accommodation:** 6
rooms, from £69 pp.

BASLOW, DERBYSHIRE   5–2C

**Fischers at Baslow Hall**   £72   ❷❷❸
Calver Rd  DE45 1RR   (01246) 583259
"Beautiful food in a gorgeous setting" (and
"wonderful accommodation" too) again wins
rave reviews for Max and Susan Fischer's small
and "cosy" Peak District country house hotel; it's

a little "expensive", though, and critics can find
the atmosphere on the "stuffy" side.
/ **Details:** www.fischers-baslowhall.co.uk; on the A623;
Sun-Fri 8.30 pm, Sat 9 pm; no jeans or trainers;
children: 12+ at D, 8+ L . **Accommodation:** 11
rooms, from £155.

**Rowley's**          £41   ❸❸❸
Church Ln  DE45 1RY   (01246) 583880
"Smart cooking, in an informal setting" wins a
consistent thumbs-up for this "pleasantly
modernised pub/restaurant", run by the Fischers
of Baslow Hall.
/ **Details:** www.rowleysrestaurant.co.uk; 9 pm, Fri &
Sat 10 pm; closed Sun D; no Amex.

BATH, SOMERSET   2–2B

**Bath Priory Hotel**          £105   ❷❷④
Weston Rd  BA1 2XT   (01225) 331922
This "peaceful and elegant" country house dining
room is enthusiastically acclaimed for "the
highest of standards" all-round, including
"fabulous" cuisine under the direction of Michael
Caines from Gidleigh Park (same owners); prices,
though, can seem "desperately high", and some
reporters find the setting "rather dull".
/ **Details:** www.thebathpriory.co.uk; 9.30 pm; no jeans
or trainers; children: 8+ D; SRA-65%.
**Accommodation:** 27 rooms, from £210.

**Bistro La Barrique**          £39   ❷❷❸
31 Barton St  BA1 1HG   (01225) 463861
With its "brilliant list of over 50 wines by the
glass or pitcher", and its "interesting French
small plates", this "really good tapas-bistro, near
the Theatre Royal", can make a very handy
stand-by. / **Details:** www.bistrolabarrique.co.uk;
10 pm; closed Sun; no Amex.

**Casanis**          £50   ❸❷❸
4 Saville Row  BA1 2QP   (01225) 780055
"A real jewel!"; this "well-rounded, cute little
Gallic bistro" in an "out-of-the-way" location
inspires huge local support, thanks to its "fine
and satisfying" cooking, and its "attentive and
professional" service. / **Details:** www.casanis.co.uk;
10 pm; closed Mon & Sun; no Amex.

**The Circus**          £43   ❷❷❸
34 Brock St  BA1 2LN   (01225) 466020
"Tucked away near the eponymous address"
(and the Royal Crescent), this popular bistro
makes a "delightful" option – it has a "beautiful"
location, and is consistently praised for its
"imaginative" cuisine in "generous" portions.
/ **Details:** www.thecircuscafeandrestaurant.co.uk;
10 pm; closed Sun; children: 7+ at D.

**Colonna & Smalls** £ 12 🅣
6 Chapel Row BA1 1HN (07766) 808067
*Top tip for caffeine-fiends – a "light and airy"
café in the city-centre, offering "without doubt
the best coffee in the area" ("from a passionate
team"); also a collection of cakes which is "small,
but perfectly formed".*
/ *Details: www.colonnaandsmalls.co.uk; 5.30 pm, Sun
4 pm; no Amex; max. table size 6.*

**Demuths** £ 46 ❷❸④
2 North Parade Pas BA1 1NX
(01225) 446059
*"Still Bath's best veggie", this "imaginative" spot,
not far from the Abbey, offers a "seasonally-
changing" menu that almost invariably
impresses; it can seem "fairly pricey, though, for a
place with such basic décor".*
/ *Details: www.demuths.co.uk; 9.30 pm; booking:
max 10.*

**The Dower House**
**Royal Crescent Hotel** £ 90
16 Royal Cr BA1 2LS (01225) 823333
*This townhouse-hotel, formerly a member of he
now-defunct Von Essen group, was sold as our
survey for the year was concluding, so no rating
seems appropriate; dining standards during the
'interregnum' seem to have stood up remarkably
well, though – hopefully a promising sign for the
future.* / *Details: www.royalcrescent.co.uk; 9.30 pm,
Fri & Sat 10 pm; no jeans or trainers; booking: max 8.*
**Accommodation:** *45 rooms, from £199.*

**The Eastern Eye** £ 36 ❸❷❷
8a Quiet St BA1 2JS (01225) 422323
*A Georgian ballroom provides the "spectacular"
but "bizarre" setting for this "cramped" Indian
canteen – popular with reporters generally, and
especially recommended as a "great place for
groups".* / *Details: www.easterneye.co.uk; 11.30 pm.*

**The Garrick's Head** £ 46 ❸❸❸
7-8 St. John's Pl BA1 1ET (01225) 318368
*"A character pub, by the theatre, recently
transformed into a place to eat, but it still feels
like a pub" – its "really great" grub pleases all
who report on it, and there's "a nice range of
ales and ciders on tap" too.*
/ *Details: www.garricksheadpub.com; 9 pm.*

**Gascoyne Place** £ 39 🅣
1 Sawclose BA1 1EY (01225) 445854
*A Georgian gastropub, so to speak, tipped as a
"top choice for visitors"; its pre-theatre menu is
praised for offering some "unusually interesting
choices" too.* / *Details: www.gascoyneplace.co.uk;
9.30 pm, Fri-Sun 10 pm.*

**Hon Fusion** £ 30 ❷❷④
25 Claverton Buildings BA2 4LD
(01225) 446020
*There's a reason "the crowd often seems to be
mainly Chinese"; this small restaurant – "over
the river, behind Bath Spa station" – is "run by a
family from Hong Kong", and has quickly
become "by far and away the best of its type in
town".* / *Details: www.honfusion.com; 11 pm;
no Amex.*

**The Hudson Bar & Grill** £ 56 🅣
14 London St BA1 5BU (01225) 332323
*Above a trendy bar, a "super steakhouse, using
the finest meat cooked absolutely to perfection"
– prices, though, are well up with those being
charged in the metropolis!*
/ *Details: www.hudsonbars.co.uk; 10.30 pm; D only,
closed Sun.*

**Jamie's Italian** £ 43 ④❸④
10 Milsom Pl BA1 1BZ (01225) 432340
*"A whole lot better than most chains", say fans
of this outlet of Jamie O's Italian multiple, citing
its "helpful" service and kid-friendly formula; here
as elsewhere, however, "standards are dropping"
and the food seems ever more "standard".*
/ *Details: www.jamieoliver.com; 11 pm, Sun
10.30 pm.*

**Lime Lounge** £ 40 🅣
11 Margarets Buildings BA1 2LP
(01225) 421251
*A "cheap 'n' cheerful" bistro tipped as worth
seeking out – "it's a short walk from the centre,
in a pleasant alley close to the Royal Crescent".*
/ *Details: www.limeloungebath.co.uk; 9 pm, Fri-Sat
9.30 pm.*

**Marlborough Tavern** £ 45 🅣
35 Marlborough Buildings BA1 2LY
(01225) 423731
*"A great little pub not far from the Royal
Crescent"; "you need to book" – the food is
"good value", and service "spot-on".*
/ *Details: www.marlborough-tavern.com; 9.30 pm,
Fri & Sat 10 pm, Sun 9 pm; no Amex.*

**The Olive Tree**
**Queensberry Hotel** £ 61 ❷④❸
Russell St BA1 2QF (01225) 447928
*"Innovative" cuisine, with "superb" wine too, wins
very high praise from fans of this popular
basement dining room of a "lovely" and
"romantic" hotel; as ever, though, there's the odd
gripe that it's "slightly pricey" for what it is.*
/ *Details: www.thequeensberry.co.uk; 9.45 pm; closed
Mon L.* **Accommodation:** *29 rooms, from £125.*

### The Pump Room £46 ⓣ
Stall St BA1 1LZ (01225) 444477
*It's the unusually "beautiful" setting which makes this gorgeous, airy Georgian room a top tip for first-time visitors to this magnificent city – prices are high, and service can be "shoddy".*
/ **Details:** www.searcys.co.uk; L only; no booking, Sat & Sun.

### Rajpoot £37 ⓣ
4 Argyle St BA2 4BA (01225) 466833
*It's "a bit too fancy if you just want a quick curry", but this subterranean stalwart in a striking Georgian cellar is tipped for "the best Indian food in Bath… if you don't mind the prices". / **Details:** www.rajpoot.com; 11 pm.*

### Raphael £40 ⓣ
Upper Borough Walls BA1 1RN
(01225) 480042
*A "welcoming bistro", tipped for its "fresh" and "tasty" fare; some reporters find it "cosy" – others feel the "long and narrow space doesn't make for the best ambience".*
/ **Details:** www.raphaelrestaurant.co.uk; 10.15 pm.

### The Wheatsheaf £51 ❷❷❷
Combe Hay BA2 7EG (01225) 833504
*"A romantic hide-away, a few minutes outside the city-centre"; this "lovely" gastropub-with-rooms – in an "amazing" village setting, and with "stunning" gardens – may be "a bit out-of-the-way", but it's "well worth the detour" for food that's "of good quality and fairly-priced".*
/ **Details:** www.wheatsheafcombehay.co.uk; 9.30 pm; closed Mon & Sun D; no Amex. **Accommodation:** 4 rooms, from £120.

### Yak Yeti Yak £32 ❸❷❷
12 Pierrepont St BA1 1LA (01225) 442299
*A "fun" basement on the fringe of the city-centre which makes a "charming" and "different" spot for a "cheap 'n' cheerful" night out – "the authenticity is underlined by pictures of the staff outside their Nepalese homes".*
/ **Details:** www.yakyetiyak.co.uk.

### Yen Sushi £33 ❷❸④
11-12 Bartlett St BA1 2QZ
(01225) 333313
*"A little gem, infinitely superior to the chain sushi places" – a "friendly" conveyor-operation, it attracts only positive reports, not least as a destination "with children".*
/ **Details:** www.yensushi.co.uk; 10.30 pm.

### The Wellington Arms £48 ❷❷❶
Baughurst Rd RG26 5LP (0118) 982 0110
*"The most charming pub ever!" – Jason King & Simon Page's "hospitable" fixture has a big fan club for its "enticing and very well-executed dishes, using a lot of home-grown and local produce"; a new extension means it's "less cramped" and "easier to book nowadays… thank goodness!"*
/ **Details:** www.thewellingtonarms.com; 9.30 pm; closed Sun D; no Amex. **Accommodation:** 2 rooms, from £130.

### China Rose £38 ❷❸❸
16 South Pde DN10 6JH (01302) 710461
*"A Chinese with a bit of class", where "the food always impresses… even if it is always the same!" / **Details:** www.chinarose.co.uk; 10 pm, Fri & Sat 10.30 pm; D only.*

### The Dower House £35 ⓣ
Market Pl DN10 6JL (0130) 271 9696
*"You have failed to recognise this restaurant despite the fact it was awarded Best British Curry 2011!" – this "buzzing" subcontinental is tipped by a small fan club for its "stunning" food. / **Details:** www.dower-house.com.*

### The Cape Etc. £43 ❸❷❸
Station Rd HP9 1NN (01494) 681137
*"A perfect place for breakfast or lunch", this "excellent local eatery" attracts a hymn of praise for its "delicious" food and its "warm welcome"; the standard of dinner ("with a South African influence") can come as a "pleasant surprise" too. / **Details:** www.thecapeonline.com; 9.30 pm; closed Sun-Tue D; no Amex.*

### Crazy Bear £62 ④④❷
75 Wycombe End HP9 1LX
(01494) 673086
*"If they concentrated as much on the food as they do on the decor", this ultra-"glam" hang-out "would be a taste sensation", too often, however, "they don't", and this "very novel" venue (with Thai and British menus) is "massively let down by the food and attitude of the staff".*
/ **Details:** www.crazybeargroup.co.uk/beaconsfield; 10 pm; children: Bar, not after 6pm.
**Accommodation:** 17 rooms, from £156.

**Royal Saracens Head    £42** 🇹
6-8 London End  HP9 2JH   (01494) 674119
*At the heart of this super-cute commuter town,
this updated boozer provides a "buzzy" and
"very busy" destination, and a "real family
venue" to boot; "the food's not especially
memorable, but it's a fun place", and offers
"good value".
/ Details: www.theroyalsaracens.co.uk; 10 pm, Fri &
Sat 10.30 pm, Sun 9 pm.*

**The Royal Standard
of England    £39** 🇹
Brindle Ln  HP9 1XS   (01494) 673382
*As the name proclaims, a top tip for those in
search of an "historic" destination – the "oldest
pub in England" is a "great place to take
visitors"… in which context the food, if of no
great ambition, seems to hold up remarkably
well! / Details: www.rsoe.co.uk; 10.45 pm; no Amex.*

**Spice Merchant    £43** ❷❸④
33 London End  HP9 2HW   (01494) 675474
*Most reporters say this "contemporary" spot is a
"top-class" Indian, where standards "never
falter"; those who find the portions on the small
side, though, may find it a touch "over-priced".
/ Details: www.spicemerchantgroup.com; 11 pm, Sun
9.30 pm.*

**The Wild Garlic    £50** ④⑤④
4 The Sq  DT8 3AS   (01308) 861446
*Fans of Masterchef winner Mat Follas's
restaurant seem able to enjoy his "well-produced
and balanced" meals, in spite of the long pauses
that too often punctuate them – sceptics just
find that sometimes "appalling" service leads to
"disappointment" overall.
/ Details: www.thewildgarlic.co.uk; 9 pm; closed
Mon D, Tue D & Sun D; no Amex.
Accommodation: 1 room, at about £120.*

**Fish On The Green    £53** ❷❷❸
Church Ln  ME14 4EJ   (01622) 738 300
*"An oasis in the Maidstone desert"; this
"excellent-value" fish-specialist (which also offers
meat and veggie options) is of particular note for
its "fantastic" set lunch deal.
/ Details: www.fishonthegreen.com; 9.30 pm; closed
Mon & Sun D; no Amex.*

**The Terrace**

**Montagu Arms Hotel    £78** 🇹
SO42 7ZL   (01590) 612324
*In a smart New Forest inn – nowadays a 4-star
hotel – a dining room of some ambition, tipped
for "outstanding" food.
/ Details: www.montaguarmshotel.co.uk; 9.30 pm;
closed Mon & Tue L; no jeans or trainers; children: 12+
D. Accommodation: 22 rooms, from £148.*

**The Loft Restaurant**

**Ye Olde Bull's Head    £57** 🇹
Castle St  LL58 8AP   (01248) 810329
*Tipped as something of an "oasis" locally – the
"well-appointed" but "expensive" dining room of
an ancient coaching inn; also worthy of mention
– the relaxed modern brasserie at the rear of
the pub, which offers "very good value".
/ Details: www.bullsheadinn.co.uk; on the High Street;
9.30 pm; D only, closed Mon & Sun; no jeans; children:
7+ at D. Accommodation: 26 rooms, from £105.*

**Devonshire Arms    £41** 🇹
Devonshire Sq  DE4 2NR   (01629) 733259
*A top tip for those in search of "a great option
before, or after, visiting Chatsworth"; this
"charming" estate-inn is a "pleasant" venue,
offering "hearty" fare – "better enjoyed at the
bar than in the restaurant".
/ Details: www.devonshirebeeley.co.uk; 9.30 pm;
bookings for breakfast. Accommodation: 8 rooms,
from £120.*

**Cayenne    £45** ❷❷❸
7 Ascot Hs, Shaftesbury Sq  BT2 7DB
(028) 9033 1532
*"Better since Paul Rankin returned to the stoves
full-time" – this "darkly intimate" city-centre
operation "rarely disappoints"; lunchtime and
early-bird menus offer "great value" too.
/ Details: www.cayenne-restaurant.co.uk; 10 pm, Fri &
Sat 11 pm; closed Mon, Tue & Wed L.*

**Deanes    £60** 🇹
36-40 Howard St  BT1 6PF
(028) 9056 0000
*Michael Deane is a big name in the Province;
reporter feedback on his large city-centre
restaurant-cum-brasserie is relatively subdued,
but it is still sometimes tipped as a "good-all-
round-experience".*

/ **Details:** www.michaeldeane.co.uk; 10 pm; closed Sun.

**Ginger** £44 🇹
7-8 Hope St BT2 5EE (0871) 426 7885
Tipped by fans as "the best venue in Belfast", Simon McCance's self-proclaimedly 'bohemian' bistro, near the Europa Hotel, attracts particular praise for making good use of "first-class local produce". / **Details:** www.gingerbistro.com; 9.30 pm, Mon 9 pm, Fri & Sat 10 pm; closed Mon L & Sun; no Amex.

**James Street South** £50 ❷❸❸
21 James Street South BT2 7GA
(028) 9043 4310
"A fine-dining restaurant" in the city-centre that's really maintained its standards", and where "Niall McKenna's food "tastes as good as it looks". / **Details:** www.jamesstreetsouth.co.uk; 10.45 pm; closed Sun.

**The Merchant Hotel** £69 🇹
16 Skipper Street BT1 2DZ
(028) 9023 4888
"An experience like no other in Belfast" – these "sumptuous" former bank premises are tipped for their "stunning" and "opulent" surroundings; while the decor wows everyone, however, the food scores hits and misses.
/ **Details:** www.themerchanthotel.com; 9.45 pm, Sun 8.30 pm. **Accommodation:** 62 rooms, from £220.

**Mourne Seafood Bar** £39 ❶❷❸
34-36 Bank St BT1 1HL (028) 9024 8544
"Just how a seafood restaurant should be"; you may have to queue for entry to this "really wonderful" and "reasonably-priced" spot, but the wait "is always worthwhile"; there's a seaside branch in Dundrum.
/ **Details:** www.mourneseafood.com; Mon 5 pm, Tue & Wed 9.30 pm, Thu, Fri & Sat 10.30 pm, Sun 6 pm; closed Mon D & Sun D; no booking at L.

**Neill's Hill** £39
229 Upper Newtownards Rd BT4 3JF
(028) 9065 0079
Formerly called Alden's, this out-of-town restaurant was rebranded in early-2012; let's hope that the "consistently high standards", and "very good value" for which the former incarnation was tipped become even more apparent now!
/ **Details:** www.aldensrestaurant.com; 2m from Stormont Buildings; 10 pm, Fri & Sat 10.30 pm; closed Sun D.

**Il Pirata** £32 🇹
279-281 Upper Newtownards Rd BT4 3JF
no tel
A new Italian restaurant, tipped as a "superb addition to the Northern Ireland restaurant scene, combining top-class cooking, service and atmosphere with a suburban neighbourhood vibe"; "in this part of the world, options like 'small plates' are a bit of a novelty".
/ **Details:** www.facebook.com/ilPirataBelfast.

**Tedfords Restaurant** £48 🇹
5 Donegall Quay BT1 3EA (028) 9043 4000
Near the Waterfront Hall, a three-floor operation tipped for excellent cuisine, and "the best pre-theatre deal on the planet!"
/ **Details:** www.tedfordsrestaurant.com; 9.30 pm; closed Mon, Tue L, Sat L & Sun.

**Isle of Eriska** £62 ❷❷❸
PA37 1SD (01631) 720371
With its "much lighter and more imaginative cuisine" (under new chef Simon Mckenzie), this "isolated" but "lovely" and "romantic" country house hotel (on its own island) looks set to emerge as a real culinary destination.
/ **Details:** www.eriska-hotel.co.uk; 9 pm; D only; no jeans or trainers. **Accommodation:** 25 rooms, from £325.

**The Gatsby** £54 ❸❷❷
97 High St HP4 2DG (01442) 870403
"A stylish Art Deco restaurant which occupies the foyer of a 1930s picture palace"; the food ("fine") is sometimes seen as playing a supporting role, but this is still hailed as "the best place in town". / **Details:** www.thegatsby.net; 10.30 pm; booking: max 10.

**The Pipe & Glass Inn** £51 ❶❷❶
West End HU17 7PN (01430) 810246
"An exceptional pub that's well worth a detour"; James & Kate Mackenzie's "posh-rustic" operation remains one of Yorkshire's most popular destinations – with its "imaginative and seasonal cooking", it's "a real example of how to do the rural gastro thing properly".
/ **Details:** www.pipeandglass.co.uk; 9.30 pm; closed Mon & Sun D; no Amex.

**Whites** £48 🇹
12-12a North Bar Without HU17 7AB
(01482) 866121

"The proprietor likes to please his guests", says a fan of this "lovely local eatery", which offers "good local and seasonal dishes"; critics, though, can find standards a touch "variable".
/ *Details:* www.whitesrestaurant.co.uk; 9 pm; closed Mon & Sun; no Amex; Booking essential.
*Accommodation:* 4 rooms, from £85.

---

BEXHILL-ON-SEA, EAST SUSSEX        3–4C

**De La Warr Pavilion**        **£ 34**   🐵
Marina  TN40 IDP    (01424) 229119
"You go for the sea views!", but the food at this monument to Art Deco is "better than expected, given the location" – some of the dishes are "very good". / *Details:* www.dlwp.com; 2.30 pm, Sat & Sun 3 pm; L only; no booking.

---

BIDDENDEN, KENT        3–4C

**The Three Chimneys**        **£ 50**   ❸④❷
Hareplain Rd  TN27 8LW    (01580) 291472
"Always a favourite local hostelry" – this "wonderful" inn is "as reliable as ever" so far as most reporters are concerned; service, though, could perhaps do with a bit of work.
/ *Details:* www.thethreechimneys.co.uk; A262 between Biddenden and Sissinghurst; 9.30 pm; no Amex.

**The West House**        **£ 60**   ❶❸④
28 High St  TN27 8AH    (01580) 291341
"West End cooking at its best, but at decidedly un-West End prices" – almost all reporters affirm the "sublime" (and "witty") quality of the cuisine at this "stunner" of a restaurant, housed in an ancient weaver's cottage; there's also quite a consensus, though, that there's decidedly "no buzz". / *Details:* www.thewesthouserestaurant.co.uk; 8.45 pm; closed Mon, Sat L & Sun D; no Amex.

---

BIGBURY-ON-SEA, DEVON        1–4C

**Burgh Island Hotel**        **£ 79**   ❷❷❶
TQ7 4BG    (01548) 810514
"Nothing says 'I love you' like a stay here!" – with its Art Deco "grandeur" and its "wonderful" sea-views, this Agatha Christie-esque hotel is a real gem; under the new chef, the food is impressive too. / *Details:* www.burghisland.com; 8.30 pm; D only, ex Sun open L & D; no Amex; jacket & tie; children: 12+ at D. *Accommodation:* 25 rooms, from £390.

**The Oyster Shack**        **£ 52**   ❶❷❸
Millburn Orchard Farm, Stakes Hills  TQ7 4BE    (01548) 810876
A "groovy" (if "shabby") shack where the seafood is "mouthwateringly fresh" – a "fun" sort of destination, that pleases almost all who

comment on it; "nice approach along a coastal road" too. / *Details:* www.oystershack.co.uk; 9 pm.

---

BILDESTON, SUFFOLK        3–1C

**The Bildeston Crown**
**The Crown Hotel**        **£ 58**   ❸④④
High St  IP7 7EB    (01449) 740510
"The Crown would stand up well in London", say fans of this ambitious pub-cum-restaurant, where the food can be "superb"; it comes at "high prices" however, and "service doesn't always live up". / *Details:* www.thebildestoncrown.com; from the A14, take the B115 to Bildeston; 9.45 pm, Sun 9 pm.
*Accommodation:* 13 rooms, from £150.

---

BILLERICAY, ESSEX        3–2C

**The Magic Mushroom**        **£ 47**   ❷❷❸
Barleyland Rd  CM11 2UD    (01268) 289963
"An island of good cuisine amongst a sea of chips and burgers!" – Darren Bennet's "highly professional" operation remains well appreciated for its "super cooking", and from an "interesting menu" too.
/ *Details:* www.magicmushroomrestaurant.co.uk; next to "Barleylands Farm"; midnight; closed Mon & Sun D.

---

BIRCHANGER, ESSEX        3–2B

**The Three Willows**        **£ 39**   🐵
Birchanger Ln  CM23 5QR    (01279) 815913
"Very reliable for first-class fresh fish, simply cooked" – this unpretentious village inn makes a particularly handy tip for those looking for a deviation from the M11 (J8). / *Details:* one mile from Birchanger Green service station on M11; 9 pm; closed Sun D; no Amex; children: 14.

---

BIRMINGHAM, WEST MIDLANDS        5–4C

**Annexe**        **£ 38**   🐵
220 Corporation St  B4 6QB
(0121) 236 1171
A top tip for a city-centre 'night out' or a party, this is a bar/restaurant on quite a scale, where the food – if not necessarily the main point – can be "great", if you hit the right night; black and white movies, projected overhead, contribute to the atmosphere. / *Details:* www.annexe.co; 9.30 pm; closed Sun.

**Asha's**        **£ 38**   ❷❷❷
12-22 Newhall St  B3 3LX    (0121) 200 2767
"As close to eating in a fine restaurant in India proper as one can hope for"; this "lively, brasserie-style spot, in the heart of the city", is hailed for its "authentic, home-style fine curries with an original twist (and at lower prices than the equivalent 'gastronomic' Indians of the

Lasan

Opus

Simpsons

Purnells

*capital)". / **Details:** www.ashasuk.co.uk; 10.30 pm, Thu-Sun 11 pm; closed Sat L & Sun L.*

/ **Details:** www.jyotis.co.uk; 10 pm; closed Mon, Tue-Thu D only; no Amex.

**Bank** £52 🅣
4 Brindleyplace B1 2JB (0121) 633 4466
*Outpost of a brand long dead in London, this city-centre operation is still sometimes tipped as a venue for a "good business lunch", but it's "far too big to have any character or atmosphere". / **Details:** www.bankrestaurants.com; 10.45 pm, Sun 9.45 pm.*

**Carters** £54 ❷❷❷
2C Wake Green Rd B13 9EZ
(0121) 449 8885
*"Good to find such high-class cooking in a neighbourhood like Moseley" – this is, on all of the early reports, a "perfect lively local restaurant", and one where the cooking is both "innovative" and "consistent" too. / **Details:** www.cartersofmoseley.co.uk.*

**Cielo** £51 🅣
6 Oozells Sq B1 2JB (0121) 632 6882
*A useful Brindleyplace Italian, particularly tipped for its "pleasant" and "attentive" service; "good veggie selection" too. / **Details:** www.cielobirmingham.com; 11 pm, 10 pm Sun; Max booking: 20, Sat & Sun D.*

**Edmunds** £65
6 Central Sq B1 2JB (0121) 633 4944
*In the year which has seen a change of ownership, reports on this ambitious Brindleyplace all-rounder were rather up-and-down; given the difficulty of allocating them between the two régimes, we've postponed a rating till next year. / **Details:** www.edmundsrestaurant.co.uk; 10 pm; closed Mon, Sat L & Sun.*

**Hotel du Vin et Bistro** £51 ❹❸❹
25 Church St B3 2NR (0121) 200 0600
*"Predictable, but fine!" – one reporter manages to capture the almost invariably middle-of-the-road flavour of reports inspired by this city-centre outpost of the Gallic hotel/bistro concept. / **Details:** www.hotelduvin.co.uk; 10 pm, Fri & Sat 10.30 pm; booking: max 12. **Accommodation:** 66 rooms, from £160.*

**Jyoti** £23 ❷❷❹
105 Stratford Rd B28 8AS
(0121) 778 5550I
*"The setting is not pretty", but "the cooking more than makes up for it", at this "Formica-topped" city-centre Gujarati café – "we were amazed at the amount of food we received for the price, and you can BYO"!*

**Lasan** £74 ❶❷❸
3-4 Dakota Buildings, James St B3 1SD
(0121) 212 3664
*"Somewhere to rival Benares (Mayfair)... but in Birmingham!"; this "brilliant and unusual" venture achieves many, and consistent, plaudits for its "inspirational" take on Indian cuisine – "this has to be one of the best restaurants in the UK"; it has a café sibling in Hall Green. / **Details:** www.lasan.co.uk; 11 pm; closed Sat L; no trainers.*

**Loves**
**The Glasshouse** £60 ❶❷❸
B16 8FL (0121) 454 5151
*"Innovative and excellent food, and pleasant service and ambience too" – chef/patron Steve Love and his team demonstrate "excellent attention to detail" at this waterside city-centre venture; surprisingly, it still generates relatively few reports. / **Details:** www.loves-restaurant.co.uk; 9 pm, Fri-Sat 9.30 pm; closed Mon, Tue L, Wed L, Thu L & Sun.*

**Opus Restaurant** £49 ❹❸❸
54 Cornwall St B3 2DE (0121) 200 2323
*"A good location" helps make this city-centre spot an extremely popular business destination – perhaps that's why "the bills seem to be getting bigger as the portions seem to get smaller!" / **Details:** www.opusrestaurant.co.uk; 9.30 pm; closed Sat L & Sun; SRA-71%.*

**Purnells** £71 ❶❷❷
55 Cornwall St B3 2DH (0121) 212 9799
*"Inspired", "exquisite", "stunning"; Glynn Purnell's "understated" and "welcoming" (if slightly "stark") city-centre dining room isn't just Brum's top spot nowadays – his "original" and "complex" food puts it firmly in the UK's premier culinary league. / **Details:** www.purnellsrestaurant.com; 9.15 pm; closed Mon, Sat L & Sun; children: 6+.*

**Saffron** £35 ❷❷❸
126 Colmore Row B3 3AP
(0121) 212 0599
*A smart modern Indian, "handy for the business district", which "marries the flavours of India with a French plating style"; it wins praise from most (if not quite all) reporters for food that's not just "technically accomplished", but "beautiful and flavoursome" too. / **Details:** www.saffronbirmingham.co.uk.*

**San Carlo**     **£44**   ④❸❸
4 Temple St   B2 5BN   (0121) 633 0251
*"Improved" in recent times, this "buzzy" city-centre Italian pleases most reporters, especially those who praise its "beautiful" fish dishes; it's "too crowded", though, and can seem "pricey, for what it is". / **Details:** www.sancarlo.co.uk; 11 pm.*

**Simpsons**     **£79**   ❶❶❷
20 Highfield Rd   B15 3DU   (0121) 454 3434
*Andreas Antona's "very atmospheric" Georgian villa, in leafy Edgbaston, is Brum's best all-rounder, and hailed in reports for providing "an experience of sheer, unadulterated quality", not least chef Luke Tipping's "luxurious" cuisine; particularly on the wine front, though, "it could be a bit less pricey".
/ **Details:** www.simpsonsrestaurant.co.uk; 9 pm, Fri & Sat 9.30 pm; closed Sun D. **Accommodation:** 4 rooms, from £160.*

**Turners**     **£81**   ❸④④
69 High St   B17 9NS   (0121) 426 4440
*"A diamond in the rough", say fans of this ambitious Harbourne dining room, hailing Richard Turner's "absolutely brilliant" cuisine; this high-street location is "not great", though, contributing to a feeling in some quarters that it's "a pricey place for what it is".
/ **Details:** www.turnersrestaurantbirmingham.co.uk; 9.30 pm; closed Mon & Sun; no Amex.*

**Baan Thitiya**     **£36**   ❷❷❷
102 London Rd   CM23 3DS
(01279) 658575
*"Top-quality ingredients are beautifully presented, and great value too", at this "friendly", "efficient" and "eager-to-please" Thai restaurant, in a former pub; only possible qualification? — "it can get a bit noisy".
/ **Details:** www.baan-thitiya.com; 11 pm.*

**Mallory Court**     **£80**   ❸❷❷
Harbury Ln   CV33 9QB   (01926) 330214
*This Lutyens-designed country house hotel remains well-reputed for its "superb food, service and ambience", and is "ideal for a romantic meal"; for a small minority of reporters, however, "inconsistent" standards can lead to the odd "disappointment". / **Details:** www.mallory.co.uk; 2m S of Leamington Spa, off B4087; 8.30 pm; closed Sat L; no trainers; SRA-53%. **Accommodation:** 31 rooms, from £149.*

**Kinloch House**     **£66**   ❷❶❸
PH10 6SG   (01250) 884237
*Few reports on this remote Georgian country house hotel; all feedback, though, continues to acclaim its "very professional" all-round standards, and to recommend it as a place for "big occasions". / **Details:** www.kinlochhouse.com; past the Cottage Hospital, turn L, procede 3m along A923, (signposted Dunkeld Road); 8.30 pm; jacket required. **Accommodation:** 18 rooms, from £230.*

**The Curlew**     **£41**   ❷❷❸
Junction Rd   TN32 5UY   (01580) 861394
*"Always a treat!"; this former pub now seems to be growing into the Michelin star it was – rather prematurely – awarded a couple of years ago, and practically all reports glow with praise for its "inventive" cuisine, and its "thoughtful, well-researched" wine list.
/ **Details:** www.thecurlewrestaurant.co.uk; 9.30 pm, Sun 9 pm; closed Mon.*

**Froggies at
The Timber Batts**     **£51**   ❶
School Ln   TN25 5JQ   (01233) 750237
*"Joel Gros continues to inspire with his classic Gallic fare", at this "authentic" operation, housed in a good old-fashioned (15th-century) English inn. / **Details:** www.thetimberbatts.co.uk; 9 pm; closed Mon & Sun D; booking essential.*

**Lord Clyde**     **£43**   ❷❷❸
Kerridge   SK10 5AH   (01625) 562123
*"A little-known gem of a place", where the chef-patron "is producing some great dishes" – all reports concur that the cooking at this nicely-located inn is "very skillful".
/ **Details:** www.thelordclyde.co.uk; 9 pm; closed Mon & Sun D.*

**Plough at Bolnhurst**     **£42**   ❷❷❷
MK44 2EX   (01234) 376274
*"An excellent pub-restaurant that manages to provide not only great food but also a pubby atmosphere" – Martin Lee's "smart and attractive gastropub in pleasant countryside" is "all-round excellent every time!"
/ **Details:** www.bolnhurst.com; 9.30 pm; closed Mon & Sun D; no Amex.*

**Burlington**
**The Devonshire Arms**   **£91**   ④❷❷
BD23 6AJ   (01756) 718 111
*"Steve Smith's cooking goes from strength to strength", says a fan of the Duke of Devonshire's grand and "romantically-located" rural hotel; critics, however, feel the food is rather "expensive" for what it is, although the attractions of the "biblical" wine list are not in doubt. / **Details:** www.thedevonshirearms.co.uk; 9.30 pm, Sat & Sun 10 pm; closed Mon; jacket at D; children: 7. **Accommodation:** 40 rooms, from £250.*

**The Devonshire Brasserie**
**The Devonshire Arms**   **£50**   ⭕
BD23 6AJ   (01756) 710710
*If the main restaurant seems a little pricey, the "lively" adjoining brasserie is sometimes tipped as an alternative; "it offers OK value, although gourmet it is not". / **Details:** www.devonshirehotels.co.uk; on A59, 5m NE of Skipton; 9 pm, Fri & Sat 9.30 pm. **Accommodation:** 40 rooms, from £200.*

**The Lion Inn**   **£38**   ❸❸❸
Main Rd CM3 3JA   (01245) 394900
*"What everyone wants in a gastropub – good, fresh fare, thoughtfully served, without any pretensions"; a "good place for families", it is "exceptionally popular", and can be "very noisy". / **Details:** www.lioninnhotel.co.uk; 9 pm, Sun 8 pm; no Amex. **Accommodation:** 15 rooms, from £105.*

**Chez Fred**   **£26**   ❷❸⑤
10 Seamoor Rd BH4 9AN   (01202) 761023
*Fred Capel's "upmarket" chippy has been a popular local fixture for over 30 years, and is "always busy" and "crowded"; practically all accounts attest to its "solid and consistent" charms, including "excellent" grub. / **Details:** www.chezfred.co.uk; 9.45 pm, 9 Sun; closed Sun L; no Amex; no booking.*

**Edge**   **£55**   ⭕
2 Studland Rd BH4 8JA   (01202) 757 007
*Still not many reports, but fans tip this top-floor restaurant as "the best-kept secret in town", and praise its "superb" sea-views, "funky decor" and "slick" management; commentary on the actual food, however, is notable by its absence. / **Details:** www.edgerestaurant.co.uk; 9.30 pm.*

**Ocean Palace**   **£33**   ⭕
8 Priory Rd BH2 5DG   (01202) 559127
*Near the pier, a "busy old-style Chinese", offering "good food but little ambience". / **Details:** www.oceanpalace.co.uk; 11 pm.*

**WestBeach**   **£49**   ❸④❷
Pier Approach BH2 5AA   (01202) 587785
*Thanks to its "wonderful location on the beach" (with "superb views"), this "fab fish place" is often tipped as "the best restaurant in Bournemouth"; the harsh would allege "that's not saying very much", but all reports affirm its "good quality". / **Details:** www.west-beach.co.uk; 10 pm.*

**Horse & Groom**   **£40**   ❷❷❸
GL56 9AQ   (01386) 700413
*"Welcoming" staff help set an upbeat tone at Will and Tom Greenstock's "genuine" Cotswold inn, where the "simple, good seasonal cooking – mostly locally sourced" – has won a large local fan club. / **Details:** www.horseandgroom.info; 9 pm, Fri & Sat 9.30 pm; closed Sun D; no Amex.*

**Miller Howe**   **£68**   ❷❷❸
Rayrigg Rd LA23 1EY   (01539) 442536
*An "enchanting" setting and the "beautiful dining room with view of the lake" have long earned renown for this "classic" Lakeland country house hotel – the scenery has eclipsed the food in recent times, but all reports this year hail it as "superb". / **Details:** www.millerhowe.com; on A592 between Windermere & Bowness; 8.45 pm. **Accommodation:** 15 rooms, from £160.*

**Akbar's**   **£27**   ⭕
1276 Leeds Rd BD3 8LF   (01274) 773311
*Not a huge amount of feedback on this Indian stalwart that's spawned quite a Northern empire; fans tip it for "good food, promptly served, and service that's better than average". / **Details:** www.akbars.co.uk; midnight, Sun 11.30 pm; D only; L.*

**Karachi**   **£25**   ❶❸④
15-17 Neal St BD5 0BX   (01274) 732015
*"I was introduced to the Karachi when a curry still cost 2/6 – the cost has gone up, but the quality is just the same!"; this Formica-tabled veteran (the city's oldest Indian) still delivers "fantastic" curries (in particular 'the Rick Stein')*

at knock-down prices. / **Details:** 1 am, 2 am Fri & Sat; no credit cards.

**Mumtaz** £27 ❷❷④
Great Horton Rd  BD7 3HS
(01274) 571861
"A tremendous curry house"; "despite its enormous size", this "friendly" and "buzzing" "institution" is "always a pleasant and relaxing place to eat", and its dishes are often "exceptionally good". / **Details:** www.mumtaz.com; midnight.

**Prashad** £28 ❷❷❸
86 Horton Grange Rd  BD7 2DW
(01274) 575893
Fans claim it's "the best vegetarian restaurant in England!", and this "special" and "different" curry house is praised by all of the many reporters who comment on it for its "fresh" and "inventive" cuisine, and its "terrific value" too.
/ **Details:** www.prashad.co.uk; 10.30 pm; closed Mon; no Amex.

**Zouk** £33 🅣
1312 Leeds Rd  BD3 8LF  (01274) 258025
"Ignore the ambience"; this "café-style venue" is tipped for its "wonderfully tasty" subcontinental fare ("especially the fish starters").
/ **Details:** www.zoukteabar.co.uk; midnight; no Amex; no shorts.

**Nonsolovino** £53 🅣
417 Chatsworth Rd  S40 3AD
(01246) 276760
A "fine selection of good Italian wines" is the stand-out attraction at this town-centre wine bar, which is attached to an Italian wine merchants; it is also tipped for its food.
/ **Details:** www.nonsolovino.co.uk; 9.30 pm; closed Mon.

**The White Horse** £44 ④❸❸
Main Rd  PE31 8BY  (01485) 210262
"Stunningly-located with views over the salt-marshes", this popular restaurant offers an "inventive" menu; culinary standards are a bit up-and-down, though, making this a destination most enjoyed "on the terrace on a warm summer lunchtime".
/ **Details:** www.whitehorsebrancaster.co.uk; 9 pm; no Amex. **Accommodation:** 15 rooms, from £94.

**Caldesi in Campagna** £62 ❶❶❸
Old Mill Ln  SL6 2BG  (01628) 788500
"Always a delight"; Giancarlo Caldesi's grand rustic four-year-old offers some "marvellous" Italian food and "kind" service too; "this may not be the best restaurant in Bray, but it's quite possibly the best value".
/ **Details:** www.caldesi.com; 9.30 pm; closed Mon & Sun D.

**Crown Inn** £49 ❷❸❷
High St  SL6 2AH  (01628) 621936
"Much simpler than other Heston offerings in Bray, but none the worse for that" – this "genuine"-feeling pub gives little hint of the great man's involvement... other than its all-round professional standards.
/ **Details:** www.crownatbray.com; 9.30 pm, Fri & Sat 10 pm; booking advised at weekends.

**The Fat Duck** £221 ❶❷④
High St  SL6 2AQ  (01628) 580333
"So amazing, it defies words" – Heston Blumenthal's "mind-blowing" "theatre-on-a-plate" offers most visitors to his world-famous (if "surprisingly small") HQ a "transcendental" experience; "the only thing more incredible than the food is the bill" however... for which might you expect to see the great man a bit more often? / **Details:** www.thefatduck.co.uk; 9 pm; closed Mon & Sun.

**The Hind's Head** £57 ❷❷❸
High St  SL6 2AB  (01628) 626151
Right by the Fat Duck, Heston B's ownership of this "cosy" and "unpretentious" 15th-century inn has helped make it one of the best-known in the country; "Scotch eggs to die for" and the famous triple-cooked chips are highlights of "this cheaper way to enjoy his culinary skills"; main problem? – "too many tables".
/ **Details:** www.hindsheadbray.com; 9.30 pm; closed Sun D.

**Riverside Brasserie** £57 🅣
Monkey Island Ln, Bray Marina  SL6 2EB
(01628) 780553
"Pre-dinner drinks on the patio, watching the sun sink over the Thames" help make a trip to this hard-to-find outfit, in Bray Marina, a "memorable" experience – it's primarily tipped as a summer destination.
/ **Details:** www.riversidebrasserie.co.uk; 9.30 pm.

**Waterside Inn** £182 ❶❷❶
Ferry Rd  SL6 2AT  (01628) 620691
"Practically perfect"; the Roux family's "sunshine-

filled" dining room, with views on to a "sublime" Thames-side location, may be "old-school" but its performance is "world-class" – for full-blooded "traditional" Gallic hospitality and romance, you won't find better (well, not this side of the Channel anyway…)
/ **Details:** www.waterside-inn.co.uk; off A308 between Windsor & Maidenhead; 10 pm; closed Mon & Tue; no jeans or trainers; booking: max 10.
**Accommodation:** 11 rooms, from £220.

| BREARTON, NORTH YORKSHIRE | 8–4B |
|---|---|

**The Malt Shovel** £46 **T**
HG3 3BX (01423) 862929
Is it because "Yorkshire folk find it expensive"? – surprisingly little survey commentary on this pub in a very pretty village, which fans tip as "excellent all-round".
/ **Details:** www.themaltshovelbrearton.co.uk; off A61, 6m N of Harrogate; 9.30 pm; closed Mon, Tue & Sun D; no Amex.

| BRECON, POWYS | 2–1A |
|---|---|

**The Felin Fach Griffin** £45 ❷❷❸
Felin Fach LD3 0UB (01874) 620111
"A delightful, informal and welcoming place" – with its "sophisticated" cooking, this "good-value" gastropub-with-rooms, "wonderfully-located" at the foot of the Brecon Beacons, remains one of Wales's best-loved destinations.
/ **Details:** www.eatdrinksleep.ltd.uk; 20 mins NW of Abergavenny on A470; 9 pm, Fri & Sat 9.30 pm; no Amex. **Accommodation:** 7 rooms, from £115.

| BRENTWOOD, ESSEX | 3–2B |
|---|---|

**Alec's** £51 ❷❷❷
Navestock Side CM14 5SD
(01277) 375 696
This former pub has undergone "a complete metamorphosis", and is now an "impressive and barn-like" (150-seat) space that's "always packed and noisy", thanks to its "excellent" fish, and "the best steaks" too.
/ **Details:** www.alecsrestaurant.co.uk; 10 pm, Sun 4.30 pm; closed Mon, Tue L, Wed L & Sun D; no Amex; children: 12+.

| BRIDPORT, DORSET | 2–4B |
|---|---|

**Hive Beach Cafe** £38 ❷❹❸
Beach Rd DT6 4RF (01308) 897070
"A West Bay crab, caught that morning was huge and great value!" – typical of the "fresh, well-executed seafood" that makes this "beautifully-located" seaside "shack" such a "wonderful" destination… "as long as it's not too busy or crowded".

/ **Details:** www.hivebeachcafe.co.uk; no bookings.
**Accommodation:** 2 rooms, from £95.

**Riverside** £51 ❸❸❹
West Bay DT6 4EZ (01308) 422011
For "a London-quality meal" served "right by the harbour", Arthur Watson's popular destination has been a local feature for over 50 years now, offering fish that's "beautifully cooked, simple and delicious"; it's "quite pricey", though, and one or two reporters fear it's beginning to "rest on its laurels".
/ **Details:** www.thefishrestaurant-westbay.co.uk; 9 pm; closed Mon & Sun D; no Amex.

| BRIGHTON, EAST SUSSEX | 3–4B |
|---|---|

**Arch 139** £41
139 King's Road Arches BN1 2FN
(01273) 821218
The former Due South – a local hotspot which has 'wobbled' in recent times – was relaunched under unchanged ownership in mid-2012; it is now the beachside equivalent of Riddle & Finns, in the Lanes – the same menu and same no-booking policy apply. / **Details:** www.arch139.com; 9.45 pm.

**Basketmakers Arms** £34 ❸❸❷
12 Gloucester Rd BN1 4AD
(01273) 689006
"Brighton's best old-fashioned pub food"; no wonder this "gem" of North Laine boozer, gets "very busy and crowded" – "go early!".
/ **Details:** www.basketmakersarms.co.uk; 8.30 pm; no booking.

**Bill's at the Depot** £36 ❹❸❸
100 North Rd, The Depot BN1 1YE
(01273) 692894
"Not quite hitting the heights of past days now there's a corporate hand on the tiller" – this "noisy" and "popular" North Laine diner can still be a "fun" destination, though, especially for its "brilliant" brunch; beware queues.
/ **Details:** www.bills-website.co.uk; 10 pm; no Amex.

**Casa Don Carlos** £31 ❸❷❸
5 Union St BN1 1HA (01273) 327177
"Always cramped and heaving, but feels like the real deal" – this "great tapas restaurant, in the heart of the Lanes" is a "friendly" spot, still "loved by tourists and locals alike".
/ **Details:** 11 pm, Thu 9 pm, Fri-Sun 10 pm; closed Thu L.

**The Chilli Pickle** £41 ❷❸❹
17 Jubilee St BN1 1GE (01273) 900383
"By far Brighton's best Indian" – this "inventive" spot has won a vast following with the

Gingerman

Chilli Pickle

JACKPO

English's

"unmatched flavours and sheer inventiveness" of
its cuisine; the odd let-down is not unknown,
though, and the "rather chain-like" new interior
strikes some long-term fans as "sterile".
/ **Details:** www.thechillipickle.com; 10.30pm, Sun
10.15pm; closed Tue.

**The Coal Shed**            **£50**   ❸❸④
8 Boyces St  BN1 1AN   (01273) 322998
"Brighton's attempt at emulating London's
booming steakhouse scene" generally gets the
thumbs-up for its "fabulous" dishes ("if at a
price"); "don't forget your earplugs", though.
/ **Details:** www.coalshed-restaurant.co.uk; 10 pm.

**Donatello**            **£30**   🅣
1-3 Brighton Pl  BN1 1HJ   (01273) 775477
For somewhere "fast, friendly, and as cheap as
chips?", this "buzzing" Lanes Italian is a top local
tip… "too many large groups" notwithstanding.
/ **Details:** www.donatello.co.uk; 11.30 pm.

**The Restaurant at Drakes**
**Drakes Hotel**            **£59**   ④❷④
44 Marine Pde  BN2 1PE   (01273) 696934
"The food goes from strength to strength", say
fans of this "well above-average" fine dining
"oasis", beneath a Kemptown boutique hotel; its
small basement setting "lacks ambience",
however, and one or two critics were generally
unimpressed this year.
/ **Details:** www.therestaurantatdrakes.co.uk; 9.45 pm.
**Accommodation:** 20 rooms, from £105.

**English's**            **£50**   ④④④
29-31 East St  BN1 1HL   (01273) 327980
In its charming setting, in the heart of the Lanes,
this "crammed-in" fish-and-seafood veteran (of
over 150 years' standing) again inspires mixed
reports; prices are the main sticking point –
"feels like twice what you'd pay elsewhere"!
/ **Details:** www.englishs.co.uk; 10 pm, Sun 9.30 pm.

**Fishy Fishy**            **£45**   ❸❷❸
36 East St  BN1 1HL   (01273) 723750
"Staff remain unflustered despite an amazing
turnover of tables", at this "cosy" city-centre fish
bistro; "attractively-located" in a Lanes
townhouse, it offers a "really lovely comfort-food"
formula. / **Details:** www.fishyfishy.co.uk; 9.30 pm,
Fri & Sat 10 pm.

**Food for Friends**            **£40**   ❸④❸
17-18 Prince Albert St  BN1 1HF
(01273) 202310
"We didn't actually realise it was a veggie
restaurant… but we enjoyed it anyway!"; the
year following a revamp of this Lanes institution
has seen rather up-and-down feedback, but the

optimistic view is that it has ended up "much
improved". / **Details:** www.foodforfriends.com;
10 pm, Fri & Sat 10.30 pm; no booking, Sat L & Sun L.

**Gars**            **£35**   🅣
19 Prince Albert St  BN1 1HF
(01273) 321321
"Great Sunday dim sum" is a top tip at this
Lanes fixture – "Chinese isn't well-represented in
Brighton, but fab Gars just about makes up for
it!" / **Details:** www.gars.co.uk; 11 pm.

**The Ginger Dog**            **£44**   ❷❷❷
12 College Pl  BN2 1HN   (01273) 620 990
Fans claim it's "the best outlet of the 'Ginger'
group", and this "fabulous little gastropub", on a
Kemptown corner, is a "stylish" but "relaxed"
venue, where the menu offers "interesting
choices and excellent value".
/ **Details:** www.gingermanrestaurants.com; off Eastern
Road near Brighton College; 10 pm.

**The Ginger Pig**            **£46**   ❷❷❸
3 Hove St  BN3 2TR   (01273) 736123
"Some of the best food in town" ("seasonal", and
often with an "esoteric" twist) has won a huge
following for this Hove gastropub –
unsurprisingly, it's often pretty "busy", and gets
quite "noisy" too.
/ **Details:** www.gingermanrestaurant.com; 10 pm, Sun
9pm; no trainers.

**Gingerman**            **£47**   ❶❷❸
21a Norfolk Sq  BN1 2PD   (01273) 326688
Ben McKellar's "wonderful small restaurant", on
the Hove/Brighton border, is the original member
of the leading local group; despite its "cramped"
interior, it inspires a lot of praise for its "serious,
but unfussy" cuisine.
/ **Details:** www.gingermanrestaurants.com; 9.45 pm;
closed Mon.

**Hotel du Vin et Bistro**            **£51**   ④④❸
Ship St  BN1 1AD   (01273) 718588
"Nowhere else is quite like this in Brighton", says
one of the many fans of this "lovely" outpost of
the Gallic hotel/bistro chain, themed around fine
wine; especially on the service front, though,
reports are deeply mixed, and critics attack an
"expensive" destination offering "very ordinary"
food. / **Details:** www.hotelduvin.com; 9.45 pm;
booking: max 10. **Accommodation:** 49 rooms,
from £210.

**Indian Summer**            **£42**   ❷❷❸
69 East St  BN1 1HQ   (01273) 711001
Feedback hasn't been 100% consistent of late,
but most reporters still say that the "subtle" and
"creative" cuisine of this Lanes fixture "redefines

Indian food"; "only problem is, it spoils the experience of going anywhere else!"
/ *Details:* www.indian-summer.org.uk; 10.30 pm, Sun 10 pm; closed Mon L.

**Iydea**   £14   🌐
17 Kensington Gdns  BN1 4AL
(01273)  667 992
In the Lanes, a "fast", "friendly" and "great-value" veggie café, tipped for its "innovative" and "tasty" daily specials. / *Details:* www.iydea.co.uk; 5.30 pm; no Amex or Maestro.

**Jamie's Italian**   £43   ④④④
11 Black Lion St  BN1 1ND
(01273) 915480
Reports on this "big and popular" Lanes outpost of the TV chef's empire are very mixed – fans vaunt a "bright" and "bustling" establishment with "wonderful" food and "great" staff... but critics can just see a "pricey", "pretentious" and "disappointing" place, where "everything is over-sold". / *Details:* www.jamiesitalian.com; 11 pm, Sun 10.30 pm.

**The Regency**   £30   ❸❸④
131 Kings Rd  BN1 2HH   (01273) 325014
A perennial top choice for family visits – a "busy" and "bustling" chippy, overlooking the sea, offering a "wide-ranging" menu; even the least enthusiastic report notes that it's "definitely better than the competition!"
/ *Details:* www.theregencyrestaurant.co.uk; 10 pm.
*Accommodation:* 30 rooms, from £50.

**Riddle & Finns**   £47   ❷❷❷
12a Meeting House Ln  BN1 1HB
(01273) 323008
"A rare find!"; this "superbly informal" Lanes fish parlour – with its "charming" style and "really top" seafood – has become Brighton's most commented-on destination; "it would be better if you could book", though, and "the frenetic style, and shared tables are not for everyone".
/ *Details:* www.riddleandfinns.co.uk; 10 pm, Fri & Sat 11 pm; no reservations.

**Sam's Of Brighton**   £45   🌐
1 Paston Pl  BN2 1HA   (01273) 676222
Well-known locally, a Kemptown bistro (with a twin at Sevendials) that's a particular brunch favourite; in other respects though, it's seen as "a reliable local, without hitting any highs".
/ *Details:* www.samsofbrighton.co.uk; 10 pm; closed Mon & Sun D.

**Terre à Terre**   £50   ❷❸④
71 East St  BN1 1HQ   (01273) 729051
"Still the best, and most ambitious, vegetarian

cooking in the UK" – still an oft-made claim for this long-celebrated Lanes phenomenon (est. 1991); some diners, however, feel "overwhelmed by the sheer menu-choice", and ratings have suffered as the occasional meal of late has seemed "stodgy" or "unexciting".
/ *Details:* www.terreaterre.co.uk; 10.30 pm; booking: max 8 at weekends.

**Warung Tujuh**   £35   ❷❷❸
7 Pool Valley  BN1 1NJ   (01273) 720 784
"A wonderful discovery in the very heart of Brighton" – this "excellent" Indonesian is praised by all who report on it for its "terrific" food, and at "exceptional-value" prices too.
/ *Details:* www.warungtujuh.com; 11 pm.

BRISTOL, CITY OF BRISTOL   2–2B

**A Cappella**   £27   🌐
184c, Wells Rd, Lower Knowle  BS4 2AL
(0117) 9713377
"An extremely friendly cafe serving freshly-prepared food all day and delicious pizzas by night"; it is tipped not least for the al fresco dining – "an added bonus on sunny evenings".
/ *Details:* www.acappellas.co.uk.

**The Albion**   £46   ❸④❸
Boyces Ave  BS8 4AA   (0117) 973 3522
"Still always buzzing seven days a week" – this "comfy and welcoming" gastropub, "tucked-away in a Clifton cul-de-sac", remains "a very consistent performer", offering "reliable" cooking in a "homely" atmosphere.
/ *Details:* www.thealbionclifton.co.uk; 10 pm; closed Mon L & Sun D.

**Bell's Diner**   £53   ❷❷❸
1 York Rd  BS6 5QB   (0117) 924 0357
"On a slightly downtrodden-looking street" in Boho Montpelier, Chris Wicks's "really special" neighbourhood fixture is quite a "wow", thanks to its "interesting and unusual flavour combinations", presented "without pretension"; arguably it's "Bristol's best", but the fan club is almost exclusively a local one.
/ *Details:* www.bellsdiner.co.uk; 9.30 pm, Fri & Sat 10 pm; closed Mon, Sat L & Sun.

**Berwick Lodge**   £61   🌐
Berwick Drive  BS10 7TD   (0117) 9581590
Never quite achieving the volume of feedback you'd hope for from a dining room presided over by Chris Wicks (of Bell's Diner fame), this country house hotel is nonetheless tipped for "well-produced" fare, and its "enthusiastic, and knowledgeable" wine service.

/ **Details:** www.berwicklodge.co.uk; no Amex.
**Accommodation:** 10 rooms, from £90.

**Bordeaux Quay**            **£48**    ④④❸
Canons Way   BS1 5UH    (0117) 943 1200
As usual, rather up-and-down feedback on this
large eco-conscious brasserie, whose "lovely
dock-views" are best from the "more formal"
upstairs dining room; the middle course view is
that it's "a great place to go with friends", even if
"the cooking lacks any real excitement".
/ **Details:** www.bordeaux-quay.co.uk; 10.30 pm; closed
Mon, Tue-Sat D only, closed Sun D; SRA-77%.

**Casamia**            **£68**    ❷❸❸
38 High St   BS9 3DZ    (0117) 959 2884
"Exquisite", "wonderful", "really clever"… – the
praise for the cooking at the Sanchez-Inglasias
family's "incredibly inventive" Westbury on Trym
spot goes on and on; "some other local
restaurants which offer much less of an
experience charge far more!"
/ **Details:** www.casamiarestaurant.co.uk; midnight;
closed Mon, Tue L, Wed L, Thu L, Fri L & Sun; no Amex.

**The Cowshed**            **£48**    ⓣ
46 Whiteladies Rd   BS8 2NH
(0117) 973 3550
"A great steakhouse, at reasonable prices", this
Clifton spot is tipped as a "carnivore's heaven",
particularly for the "excellent-value set lunch".
/ **Details:** www.thecowshedbristol.com; 9.45 pm, Fri &
Sat 10.15 pm, Sun 9.30 pm.

**Dynasty**            **£34**    ❷❸❸
16a St. Thomas St   BS1 6JJ    (0117) 925 0888
"Invariably excellent dim sum" – the best bet at
this decade-old Chinese restaurant, which is "still
one of the very best".
/ **Details:** www.dynasty-bristol.co.uk; 11 pm, 10 pm.

**Fishers**            **£41**    ⓣ
35 Princess Victoria St   BS8 4BX
(0117) 974 7044
In Clifton, a top tip for "fresh fish, simply cooked,
to a consistently good standard"; "it's always
busy, though competitors keep opening up
nearby". / **Details:** www.fishers-restaurant.com;
10.30 pm, Sun 10 pm.

**Flinty Red**            **£41**    ❷❷④
34 Cotham HIll   BS6 6LA    (0117) 923 8755
"Terrific" small plates – "great flavours
presented with confidence" – win a hymn of
praise to this "small and unpretentious"
bistro/wine bar, in Cotham; it's owned by a
nearby merchant, and the "first-class" wines
include a "great selection by the glass".

/ **Details:** www.flintyred.co.uk; 10 pm; closed Mon L &
Sun; booking essential.

**Greens' Dining Room**            **£42**
25 Zetland Rd   BS6 7AH    (0117) 924 6437
"Don't be put off by the rather downbeat 'caff'
look" – reporters are unanimous in their praise
for this "friendly" and "reasonably-priced"
Redlands bistro, with its "imaginative" cooking;
STOP PRESS – as of late October 2012 it's
changed chef and owner, hence we've removed
the ratings! / **Details:** www.greensdiningroom.com;
10 pm; closed Mon & Sun; no Amex.

**Hotel du Vin et Bistro**            **£51**    ❸❸❷
Sugar Hs, Narrow Lewins Mead   BS1 2NU
(0117) 925 5577
It may feel a bit "formulaic", but this "busy" city-
centre outpost of the Gallic hotel 'n' bistro chain
occupies a "stylish" converted warehouse, and
pleases most reporters with its "tasty" and
"nicely-presented" food and, of course, its
"suitably fantastic" wine list.
/ **Details:** www.hotelduvin.com; 9.45 pm; booking:
max 10. **Accommodation:** 40 rooms, from £145

**Lido**            **£46**    ❷④❶
Oakfield Pl   BS8 2BJ    (0117) 933 9533
"An enchanting location" ("scrutinise the
swimmers as you eat!") creates a "magical"
atmosphere at this "unique" Victorian lido, in
Clifton; it serves North African food (somewhat
like London's Moro), which is "reliable, and
sometimes truly excellent".
/ **Details:** www.lidobristol.com; 10 pm; closed Sun D;
no Amex.

**Maitreya Social**            **£38**    ⓣ
89 St Marks Rd   BS5 6HY    (0117) 951 0100
"Experimental cooking and staff who are so
eager to please" still win praise for this basic
veggie café (previously Café Maitreya); even
some ongoing supporters, though, feel it's "not as
good" since it changed hands.
/ **Details:** www.maitreyasocial.co.uk; 9.45pm; closed
Mon & Sun L; no Amex.

**Muset**            **£46**    ❷❸④
16 Clifton Rd   BS8 1AS    (0117) 973 2920
This Clifton offshoot of Ronnies (Thornbury) is
acclaimed by all reporters as a "top-class
addition to the Bristol culinary scene"; "for a
small place", though, even fans can find it
"expensive", or a tad "pretentious".
/ **Details:** www.themuset.com; 10.15 pm; closed
weekday L.

**Primrose Café**            **£45**    ❷❷❸
1 Clifton Arcade, 6 Boyces Ave   BS8 4AA
(0117) 946 6577

The Albion

Maitreya Social

Berwick Lodge

riverstation

*"Marvellous by day, and with top-quality food in the evenings"* – this *"remarkable"* café does a great brunch and a *"lovely afternoon tea and cakes"* too; by night, it serves cuisine that's *"original and fresh"* – fish is *"particularly good"*. / **Details:** www.primrosecafe.co.uk; 10 pm; Sun D; no booking at L.

**Prosecco**  **£38**  ❸④④
25 The Mall  BS8 4JG   (0117) 973 4499
In Clifton, a small family-owned restaurant, hailed by most reporters for its *"friendly"* charm, and its *"very genuine"* Italian cooking; as last year though, the odd off-night is also reported. / **Details:** www.proseccoclifton.com; 11 pm; closed Mon & Sun, Tue-Thu L; no Amex.

**riverstation**  **£41**  ❸❷❷
The Grove  BS1 4RB   (0117) 914 4434
A stylishly-converted river-police station, offering great *"views over the docks"* (particularly from the first-floor restaurant); it's a *"friendly"* place, with *"pretty good"* cooking (and *"excellent cocktails in the downstairs bar"*). / **Details:** www.riverstation.co.uk; 10.30 pm, Fri & Sat 11 pm; closed Sun D; no Amex.

**Rockfish**  **£53**  ❷❷❸
128-130 Whiteladies Road  BS8 2RS (0117) 9737384
*"Mitch Tonks's posh chippy, overlooking the Dart"* – a *"light and airy"* venue, it offers *"very well-prepared and cooked fish"*, *"helpful"* service and a *"good wine selection"* too. / **Details:** www.rockfishgrill.co.uk; 10 pm, Fri & Sat 10.30 pm; closed Mon & Sun.

**The Thali Café**  **£28**  ❸❸❸
12 York Rd  BS6 5QE   (0117) 942 6687
*"Very good overall, whether eating-in or using their excellent tiffin-tin takeaway"*; this Montpelier Indian (also in Clifton) is a slightly *"different"* sort of operation, offering a *"short, well-realised menu"* of *"basic but really tasty dishes"*. / **Details:** www.thethalicafe.co.uk; 10.30 pm; closed weekday L; no Amex.

**Poopdeck**  **£46**  ❷❸❸
14 The Quay  TQ5 8AW   (01803) 858681
*"A tiny and lovely 'oil-cloth' tablecloths cafe, up a flight of stairs overlooking the harbour"* – it's tipped for *"beautifully-cooked fish"*, and its *"fun"* style. / **Details:** www.poopdeckrestaurant.com.

**Druidstone Hotel**  **£44**  ❶
SA62 3NE   (01437) 781221
With its *"amazing"* cliff-top setting, *"beautiful"* gardens and ever-*"quirky"* vibe (*"back in 1973, the waitress used to wear wellingtons!"*), this family-friendly hotel has always been something of a 'destination' – after a variable patch, it's tipped for *"improved"* food of late too. / **Details:** www.druidstone.co.uk; from B4341 at Broad Haven turn right, then left after 1.5m; 9.30 pm. **Accommodation:** 11 rooms, from £75.

**Buckland Manor**  **£76**  ❷❸❷
WR12 7LY   (01386) 852626
A *"stunningly beautiful"* country house, in a *"delightful"* Cotswold location; given the consistency of reports on the *"very good"* food, we've maintained a rating even though it changed hands (from Von Essen to Gidleigh Park proprietor Andrew Brownsword) during the reporting year. / **Details:** www.bucklandmanor.co.uk; 2m SW of Broadway on B4632; 9 pm; jacket & tie at D; booking: max 8; children: 12+. **Accommodation:** 13 rooms, from £295.

**Russell's**  **£47**  ❸❸❸
20 High St  WR12 7DT   (01386) 853555
Management changes notwithstanding, this *"busy"* but *"relaxed"* restaurant-with-rooms, elegantly-housed in the heart of a picturebook town, remains a popular destination, not least for its *"good lunchtime menu"*. / **Details:** www.russellsofbroadway.co.uk; 9.30 pm; closed Sun D. **Accommodation:** 7 rooms, from £98.

**The Pig**  **£52**  ④④❸
Beaulieu Rd  SO42 7QL   (01590) 622354
For its many fans, this is a *"super boutique hotel located deep in the New Forest"*, which offers *"top-notch"* locally-sourced dishes in a *"delightfully-furnished conservatory"*; critics sense *"hype"*, though, and are scathing about *"slapdash"* presentation and *"inefficient"* service. / **Details:** www.thepighotel.co.uk/; 9.30 pm. **Accommodation:** 26 rooms, from £125.

**The Grumpy Mole**  **£42**  ❶
RH3 7JS   (01737) 845101
A roadside inn that trades as an informal restaurant nowadays – it's consistently tipped for its *"enjoyable"* food, and its *"friendly"* service.

/ **Details:** www.thegrumpymole.co.uk; 9.30 pm;
no Amex.

---

BROMESWELL, SUFFOLK          3–1D

**British Larder**          **£49**  ❷❸❸
Oxford Rd IP12 2PU   (01394) 460 310
"A converted inn, where a South African couple
cook clean-tasting, fresh, locally-sourced classic
foods with a twist" – an "unexpected pleasure"
that pleases almost all of the many who
comment on it (although, for a minority, it can
seem a little "hyped").
/ **Details:** www.britishlardersuffolk.co.uk; 9 pm, Fri-Sat
9.30 pm; no Amex.

---

BROMLEY, KENT          3–3B

**Tamasha**          **£45**  ❸❷❷
131 Widmore Rd  BR1 3AX
(020) 8460 3240
"Delicious Indian grub in a wonderful colonial
ambience" again inspires high praise for this
"suburban jewel". / **Details:** www.tamasha.co.uk;
10.30 pm; no shorts. **Accommodation:** 7 rooms,
from £75.

---

BROUGHTON, NORTH YORKSHIRE   8–4B

**Bull at Broughton**          **£40**  ❷❷❸
BD23 3AE   (01756) 792065
The Yorkshire outpost of the Northcote-inspired
Ribble Valley Inns group is acclaimed by all who
report on it for its "capable" food (with much
local sourcing, of which the group was a
pioneer); it's "well-priced" too.
/ **Details:** www.thebullatbroughton.com; 8.30 pm,
Fri & Sat 9 pm, Sun 8 pm.

---

BRUNDALL, NORFOLK          6–4D

**Lavender House**          **£62**  ❷❷❸
39 The St  NR13 5AA   (01603) 712215
"Back on top form now that proprietor Richard
Hughes is back behind the stoves", this "always
ambitious" village-restaurant – in a thatched
building of "character" – offers food many
reporters think is "fantastic".
/ **Details:** www.thelavenderhouse.co.uk; 9.30 pm;
D only, closed Sun & Mon; no Amex.

---

BRUTON, SOMERSET          2–3B

**At The Chapel**          **£44**  ❸❷❷
28 High St  BA10 0AE   (01749) 814070
"A delightful refurbishment of an old chapel into
a bright and buzzy café, bakery, and wine store"
– a "surprising" venue, whose "Wallpaper
magazine" style "feels more 'big city' than its
chocolate-box village location would suggest".

/ **Details:** www.atthechapel.co.uk; 9.30 pm; closed
Sun D. **Accommodation:** 5 rooms, from £100.

---

BUCKFASTLEIGH, DEVON          1–3D

**Riverford Field Kitchen**     **£40**  ❶❷❸
Wash Barn, Buckfast Leigh  TQ11 0JU
(01803) 762074
"Eating Riverford's stunningly tasty organic
vegetables sitting amidst the fields in which they
are grown is a unique experience", and the
"unfussy but inventive" food at this "surprisingly
swanky" communal-table farm canteen has
made it a smash hit; "puddings are pretty special
too". / **Details:** www.riverford.co.uk; 8 pm; closed
Mon D & Sun D; no Amex.

---

BUCKHORN WESTON, DORSET          2–3B

**The Stapleton Arms**       **£40**  ❶
Church Hill  SP8 5HS   (01963) 370396
A trendified rural inn tipped for its "well-
decorated" Georgian interior, and its "excellent
pub grub".
/ **Details:** www.thestapletonarms.com; 10 pm.
**Accommodation:** 4 rooms, from £90.

---

BUCKLAND MARSH, OXFORDSHIRE   2–2C

**The Trout Inn**          **£47**  ❶
Tadpole Bridge  SN7 8RF   (01367) 870382
A Thames-side inn, tipped for its "olde-worlde
charm" in winter, and its nice garden for the
summer too; it doesn't attract as much feedback
as we'd like, but fans say the food is "beautifully
prepared and presented", and the wines are
"eclectic" too. / **Details:** www.trout-inn.co.uk;
11 pm; closed Sun D; no Mastercard.
**Accommodation:** 6 rooms, from £120.

---

BUNBURY, CHESHIRE          5–3B

**The Dysart Arms**          **£39**  ❷❷❷
Bowes Gate Rd  CW6 9PH
(01829) 260183
Perhaps the best outpost of the locally-prominent
Brunning & Price gastropub chain, universally
recommended for its "consistently good pub
food", and in a "delightful" village too.
/ **Details:** www.dysartarms-bunbury.co.uk; 9.30 pm,
Sun 9 pm.

---

BUNNY, NOTTINGHAMSHIRE          5–3D

**Rancliffe Arms**          **£40**  ❶
139 Loughborough Rd  NG11 6QT
(0115) 98447276
Why tip this pretty old country inn? – its carvery,
"using only local produce", is "outstanding".
/ **Details:** www.rancliffearms.co.uk; 9 pm.

| BURFORD, OXFORDSHIRE | 2–2C |
|---|---|

**The Bull at Burford** £48 ❷❷❷
105 High St OX18 4RG (01993) 822220
"Great food in an historic hotel!"; le patron used
to work at Le Gavroche, and it shows in the
"excellent" cuisine at this "friendly" town-centre
spot. / **Details:** www.bullatburford.co.uk; 9 pm;
no Amex. **Accommodation:** 13 rooms, from £75.

**The Swan Inn** £43 ❹❸❶
Swinbrook OX18 4DY (01993) 823339
Tipped as "a top place to take foreign visitors",
this "picturebook pub on the banks of the
Windrush" may offer food that's on the "plain"
side, but few reporters would dispute that a visit
here is a "very enjoyable" experience.
/ **Details:** www.theswanswinbrook.co.uk; 9 pm, Fri &
Sat 9.30 pm. **Accommodation:** 6 rooms,
from £120.

| BURNHAM MARKET, NORFOLK | 6–3B |
|---|---|

**Hoste Arms** £50
The Green PE31 8HD (01328) 738777
This famous inn – known for its "fun" and
"lively" style – has always been a "lovely place to
stay", and for the most part a good place to eat
too; new owners took over from the founding
family as the survey for the year was concluding,
however, hence we've removed its rating for the
time being. / **Details:** www.hostearms.co.uk; 6m W
of Wells; 9.15 pm; no Amex. **Accommodation:** 52
rooms, from £112.

| BURNHAM ON CROUCH, ESSEX | 3–2C |
|---|---|

**Contented Sole** £41 ❸❸❷
80 High St CM0 8AA (01621) 786900
"An isolated but charming restaurant", "set in a
lovely building in a picturesque riverside village"
– reports are few but say it "deserves a wider
clientele", thanks not least to its "excellent" fish
cuisine. / **Details:** www.contentedsole.co.uk; 10 pm;
closed Tue & Sun D.

| BURY ST EDMUNDS, SUFFOLK | 3–1C |
|---|---|

**Maison Bleue** £48 ❷❷❷
30-31 Churchgate St IP33 1RG
(01284) 760623
"A full-on-French experience" but "without
sneers!"; this "unfussy" and "charming" fish and
seafood restaurant (part of the Crépy family's
empire) is "one of the best places to eat in East
Anglia" – a "quiet" and "genuine" location, where
the food is "beautifully presented".
/ **Details:** www.maisonbleue.co.uk; 9 pm, Sat 9 pm;
closed Mon & Sun; no Amex.

**Pea Porridge** £41 ❶❷❸
28-29 Cannon St IP33 1JR (01284) 700200
"Tucked-away, but worth seeking out" – Justin
Sharp's "squashed but fun" and "romantic"
three-year-old wins extremely high praise, both
for its "lovely" staff and for its "different" and
"imaginative" selection of "gutsy" bistro dishes.
/ **Details:** www.peaporridge.co.uk; 10 pm; closed
Mon & Sun; no Amex.

**Valley Connection** £33 ❷❷❸
42 Churchgate St IP33 1RG
(01284) 753161
"Good food, good value, and a good location
overlooking the square too" – if you're looking for
a curry, this "pleasant" spot is the top tip
hereabouts. / **Details:** www.valley-connection.com;
11.30 pm.

| BUSHEY HEATH, HERTFORDSHIRE | 3–2A |
|---|---|

**The Alpine** £46 ❸❸❸
135 High Rd WD23 1JA (020) 8950 2024
Some "genuinely imaginative" touches make this
relatively "reasonably-priced" Italian stalwart of
more than strictly local interest; "book for
downstairs, where there's much more
atmosphere"… but beware "packed-in"
Saturday nights.
/ **Details:** www.thealpinerestaurant.co.uk; 10.30 pm;
closed Mon.

| BUSHEY, HERTFORDSHIRE | 3–2A |
|---|---|

**St James** £44 ❸❷❸
30 High St WD23 3HL (020) 8950 2480
"A star in the culinary desert of metroland!" –
this very "welcoming" spot is "an absolute
stalwart", with a large, and very contented,
following among local reporters.
/ **Details:** www.stjamesrestaurant.co.uk; opp St James
Church; 9.30 pm; closed Sun D; booking essential.

| CAMBER, EAST SUSSEX | 3–4C |
|---|---|

**The Beach Bistro**
**Gallivant Hotel** £44 ❷❷❸
New Lydd Rd TN31 7RB (01797) 225057
This New England-style hotel, by Camber Beach,
is a "friendly" destination, well suited to those
with kids in tow; "fresh fish is a feature here, and
they treat it well".
/ **Details:** www.thegallivanthotel.com; 9 pm, Fri-Sat
9.30 pm.

| CAMBRIDGE, CAMBRIDGESHIRE | 3–1B |
|---|---|

**Alimentum** £64 ❷❸❹
152-154 Hills Rd CB2 8PB (01223) 413000
A "must-visit destination in Cambridge and East
Anglia"; Mark Poynton's minimalist five-year-old

offers "fresh modern cuisine", "without flim-flam
or trickery", of truly "outstanding" quality; shame,
though, about the "terrible" city-fringe location,
"cold" ambience and "high prices".
/ **Details:** www.restaurantalimentum.co.uk; 10 pm;
closed Sun D; booking essential.

**Bill's**                    **£40**    **⊤**
34-35 Green St  CB2 3JX  (01223) 329638
Outpost of what's fast becoming a nationwide
chain, a newcomer tipped for food that's "really
good, by Cambridge standards"; it's ideal for "a
relaxed coffee and a sandwich", but the more
substantial evening offer also has its fans.
/ **Details:** www.bills-website.co.uk; 11 pm, Sun
10.30 pm.

**The Cambridge**
**Chop House**            **£46**    **❸❸❸**
1 Kings Pde  CB2 1SJ  (01223) 359506
Well located opposite King's College, this highly
popular, mainly subterranean spot offers "simple
but tasty", "traditional" British fare to a generally
"solid" standard.
/ **Details:** www.cambridgechophouse.co.uk; 10.30 pm,
Sat 11 pm, Sun 9.30 pm.

**Cotto**                    **£63**    **❶❷④**
183 East Rd  CB1 1BG  (01223) 302010
"Many tempting choices" confront those who
seek out this "spectacularly good" restaurant,
and the service is "helpful and caring" too; only
real downsides? - "it deserves a better location"
(you enter through a café), and evening opening
is limited. / **Details:** www.cottocambridge.co.uk;
9.15pm; D only, Wed-Sat; children: 5+ in the evenings.

**d'Arry's**                 **£45**    **⊤**
2-4 King St  CB1 1LN  (01223) 505015
A rather up-and-down year for reports on this
gastropub behind Christ's College; it's tipped to
get back on top form, though, following the
recent return of the original chef!
/ **Details:** www.darrys.co.uk; 10 pm; no Amex; need
8+ to book.

**Dojo**                     **£30**    **⊤**
1-2 Millers Yd, Mill Ln  CB2 1RQ
(01223) 363471
"Not haute cuisine, but incredibly tasty and
satisfying" - this "efficient" pan-Asian is a "buzzy
and lively student hang-out, where plates are
piled high with cheap 'n' cheerful noodles and
broths". / **Details:** www.dojonoodlebar.co.uk; 11 pm;
no Amex; no booking.

**Fitzbillies**              **£29**    **❸❸❸**
52 Trumpington St  CB2 1RG
(01223) 352500

"A much-beloved institution lives on" - Tim
Hayward's resurrected cake shop is proving "a
welcome addition to the lacklustre Cambridge
scene"; it still does "the great sticky buns of
yesteryear", but is now also "a good destination
for a light lunch" (or for dinner, Fri & Sat).
/ **Details:** www.fitzbillies.com; 8pm, Fri & Sat
9.45 pm; closed Sun D.

**Hotel du Vin et Bistro**   **£50**   ④⑤④
15-19 Trumpington St  CB2 1QA
(01223) 227330
"Why can't they get this right?"; this potentially
extremely "atmospheric" dining room is - even
by the mixed standards of this bistro/hotel chain
- a poor performer; "indifferent and
disorganised service" in particular is often a let-
down. / **Details:** www.hotelduvin.com; 9.45 pm, Fri &
Sat 10.30 pm. **Accommodation:** 41 rooms,
from £180.

**Jamie's Italian**          **£43**   ④④④
The Old Library, Wheeler St  CB2 3QJ
(01223) 654094
Many, but mixed, reports on the TV's chef's
"beautifully-housed" chain-outlet - fans say it's a
"good family venue" with a nice "buzz", but
critics are more inclined to find it a "pricey"
place, where neither food nor service measures
up. / **Details:** www.jamieoliver.com; 11 pm, Sun
10.30 pm.

**Loch Fyne**               **£43**   ④④④
37 Trumpington St  CB2 1QY
(01223) 362433
This conveniently-located but "cramped" branch
of the national fish-chain remains one of the city-
centre's most popular destinations; even fans,
though, can sometimes find it rather "dull"!
/ **Details:** www.lochfyne-restaurants.com; 10 pm, Sat
10.30 pm.

**Midsummer House**         **£108**  **❶❷❸**
Midsummer Common  CB4 1HA
(01223) 369299
Daniel Clifford's picturesquely-sited Cam-side
property has grown in renown over the years,
and his "daring and individual" cuisine -
delivered in a tasting-menu format - nowadays
ranks it amongst the UK's top-10 culinary
destinations; a minority, though, can still find the
approach a touch "pretentious".
/ **Details:** www.midsummerhouse.co.uk; 9.30 pm;
closed Mon, Tue L & Sun.

**Oak Bistro**              **£44**   ④❸④
6 Lensfield Rd  CB2 1EG  (01223) 323361
This "reliable" bistro fills a gap in the "badly-
served" city-centre dining scene, and attracts
numerous upbeat reports; that said, the food is

*"not outstanding".*
/ **Details:** www.theoakbistro.co.uk; 10 pm; closed Sun.

**Rainbow Café**          £31   Ⓣ
9a King's Pde  CB2 1SJ   (01223) 321551
*"Great for a pre-theatre meal", this cellar-café,
near King's College, is strongly tipped for its
"interesting variety of veggie and vegan fare" –
"always plentiful", and with "truly wonderful"
puds a highlight.* / **Details:** www.rainbowcafe.co.uk;
9 pm; closed Mon & Sun D; no Amex; no booking.

**Sea Tree**          £31   Ⓣ
13 The Broadway  CB1 3AH
(01223) 414349
*"Going from strength to strength", a three-year-
old chippy, off Mill Road, tipped for its "lovely
fresh fish", and "friendly" service too.*
/ **Details:** www.theseatree.co.uk; 9 pm sun; closed
Thu L, Fri L & Sat L.

**St John's Chop House**   £50   Ⓣ
21-24 Northampton St  CB3 0AD
(01223) 353 110
*Sometimes tipped as "far superior to sibling, the
Cambridge Chophouse", this no-nonsense
establishment serves hearty traditional fare most
reports say is "good value".*
/ **Details:** www.stjohnschophouse.co.uk; 10.30 pm, Sat
11 pm, Sun 9.30 pm.

**Restaurant 22**          £50   ④❸④
22 Chesterton Rd  CB4 3AX
(01223) 351880
*"It really does feel like eating in someone's front
room", at this "intimate" villa, "well away from
the touristy bits of Cambridge"; for fans, it
remains "the best place in town in terms of
value", but there were also a couple of
"disappointing" reports this year.*
/ **Details:** www.restaurant22.co.uk; 9.30 pm; closed
Tue-Sat L ; children: 12+.

CANTERBURY, KENT          3–3D

**Apeksha**          £32   ❷❷❸
24 St Peters St  CT1 2BQ   (01227) 780079
*"Lovely staff, and the best curry around"; near
Westgate Tower, this "imaginative" Indian is a
real all-round crowd-pleaser; "the dishes seem
lighter than usual, and veggies are well catered
for too".* / **Details:** www.apeksha.co.uk; 11.30 pm.

**Café des Amis**          £38   ❸❸❸
95 St Dunstan's St  CT2 8AD
(01227) 464390
*"Always reliable and good value" – this long-
established Mexican, by the Westgate, is a "jolly"
sort of place, where the food is "tasty" and*

*"freshly-cooked"; it attracts a good number of
reports, invariably positive.*
/ **Details:** www.cafedez.com; 10 pm, Fri & Sat
10.30 pm, Sun 9.30 pm; booking: max 6 at D Fri-Sat.

**Cafe Mauresque**          £37   ❷❷❷
8 Butchery Ln  CT1 2JR   (01227) 464300
*"By a long way, the best place of its kind in
town" – this loungey and "intimate" hang-out,
just off the main drag, offers some "divine"
Moroccan small plates, and "an interesting and
eclectic selection of Spanish wines" to go with
'em.* / **Details:** www.cafemauresque.com; 10 pm,
Fri & Sat 10.30 pm.

**Deeson's**          £44   ❷❷❷
25-26 Sun St  CT1 2HX   (01227) 767854
*"An independent restaurant with excellent food
and service, located right next to the cathedral";
all reports agreed that "with its imaginative
cooking, it delivers time after time".*
/ **Details:** www.deesonsrestaurant.co.uk.

**Goods Shed**          £44   ❷❸❷
Station Road West  CT2 8AN
(01227) 459153
*"Hearty" dishes come in "huge portions" at this
"wonderfully casual" venue – an ex-railway shed,
where you eat overlooking the "brilliant array of
produce" sold below at the (permanent)
Farmers' Market, near Canterbury West; it's
perhaps most obviously a brunch or lunch
destination.* / **Details:** www.thegoodsshed.net;
9.30 pm; closed Mon & Sun D.

**Michael Caines**
**ABode Canterbury**   £71   ⑤④④
High St  CT1 2RX   (01227) 766266
*"Strange menus sometimes", "really dreadful
service", "why did I bother?" – year in, year out,
the criticisms of this city-centre dining room
(overseen from afar by the famous Gidleigh Park
chef) just keep on coming; the lunchtime grazing
menus, though, do offer "exceptional value".*
/ **Details:** www.michaelcaines.com; 10 pm; closed
Sun D. **Accommodation:** 72 rooms, from £105.

CARDIFF, CARDIFF          2–2A

**Casanova**          £39   ❷❸④
13 Quay St  CF10 1EA   (029) 2034 4044
*A "tiny dining room, near the city-centre",
sometimes described as "the best Italian
restaurant in South Wales" (and with "real flair
and imagination" too).*
/ **Details:** www.casanovacardiff.com; 10 pm; closed
Sun.

FSA

**Happy Gathering** £32 ❷❸❸
233 Cowbridge Road East CF11 9AL
(029) 2039 7531
*"The best Chinese near Cardiff!"; this old-school fixture – located, appropriately enough, in Canton – has been a fixture of the city for 25 years now; it is most recommended "for groups" or "with kids".*
*/ Details: www.happygatheringcardiff.co.uk; 10.30 pm, Sun 9 pm.*

**Mint and Mustard** £41 ❷❷④
134 Whitchurch Rd CF14 3LZ
(02920) 620333
*"Certainly the best curry in Cardiff", this Gabalfa spot offers a take on Indian cuisine that's "completely different from others hereabouts"; and the results are "unusually good" too.*
*/ Details: www.mintandmustard.com; 11 pm; D only; no shorts.*

**The Potted Pig** £44 ④❸❸
27 High St CF10 1PU (029) 2022 4817
*An "interesting" city-centre newcomer, hailed as a "fantastic addition", in large part thanks to its very "interesting setting in a former bank vault"; the food is "fine, but stretches no boundaries".*
*/ Details: www.thepottedpig.com; 9 pm; closed Mon & Sun D.*

**Vegetarian Food Studio** £18 ❶❶④
109 Penarth Rd CF11 6JT (029) 2023 8222
*"A small family-run Indian place" whose Gujarati thalis (a whole meal for about £7!) deliver up "amazing vegetarian food at bargain prices", with "friendly and personal" service too; BYO cuts costs even further (£1 corkage).*
*/ Details: www.vegetarianfoodstudio.co.uk; 9.30 pm; closed Mon; no Amex.*

**Woods Brasserie** £44 ❸❷❸
Pilotage Building, Stuart St CF10 5BW
(029) 2049 2400
*For some reporters, this "attractive, glass-fronted restaurant" in Cardiff Bay is an "above-average" performer, and "probably the best all-round place in Cardiff, now Le Gallois has gone".*
*/ Details: www.woods-brasserie.com; 10 pm; closed Sun D.*

CARLISLE, CUMBRIA 7–2D

**Alexandros** £36 🅣
68 Warwick Rd CA1 1DR (01228) 592227
*"A real gem in a restaurant-wasteland"; this family-run Greek establishment is tipped for its "reliably delicious" dishes "from an owner who really cares". / Details: www.thegreek.co.uk; 9.30 pm; closed Mon L & Sun.*

CARTMEL FELL, CUMBRIA 7–4D

**The Masons Arms** £43 🅣
Strawberry Bank LA11 6NW
(01539) 568486
*A fell-side pub, tipped for its "wholesome yet inventive dishes, splendid beers, great warm fires and friendly atmosphere"; summer visitors benefit from a large al fresco area too.*
*/ Details: www.strawberrybank.com; W from Bowland Bridge, off A5074; 9 pm. Accommodation: 7 rooms, from £75.*

CARTMEL, CUMBRIA 7–4D

**L'Enclume** £93 ❶❸④
Cavendish St LA11 6PZ (01539) 536362
*"Out-of-this-world amazing" cuisine – featuring "visually stunning" tasting menus with an increasingly Cumbrian slant – have made Simon Rogan's "theatrical" former smithy one of the UK's top foodie shrines; its "stark" setting can seem "cold" or "stiff" however, and it's "priced for southern in-comers".*
*/ Details: www.lenclume.co.uk; J36 from M6, down A590 towards Cartmel; 9 pm; closed Mon L & Tue L; children: 10+. Accommodation: 12 rooms, from £99.*

**Rogan & Co** £42 ❶❶❷
Devonshire Sq LA11 6QD (01539) 535917
*"It may be sacrilege to say it, but the warmer, more informal, atmosphere in Simon Rogan's bistro made this a more enjoyable dinner than our night at L'Enclume!"; "the value for money is better here", confirms another reporter, "and in many cases the food is as good!"*
*/ Details: www.roganandcompany.co.uk; 9 pm; closed Mon & Tue; no Amex.*

CASTLE COMBE, WILTSHIRE 2–2B

**Bybrook Restaurant**
**Manor House Hotel** £86 ❶❷④
Manor House Hotel and Golf Course SN14 7HR (01249) 782206
*Chef Richard Davies's food is "consistently excellent", and there's a "serious" wine list too at this "lovely" country house hotel; the weakest link is the dining room – "large, and lacking atmosphere". / Details: www.exclusivehotels.co.uk; 9.30 pm; closed Mon L; no jeans or trainers; children: 11+. Accommodation: 48 rooms, from £260.*

CAVENDISH, SUFFOLK 3–1C

**The George** £46 🅣
The Green CO1 8BA (01787) 280248
*"Above-average" and "remarkably consistent" too – a 16th century gastropub-with-rooms tipped*

for its "tasty" and "well-presented" cuisine.
/ **Details:** www.thecavendishgeorge.co.uk; 9.30 pm;
closed Sun D. **Accommodation:** 5 rooms, from £60.

CHADDESLEY CORBETT, WORCESTERSHIRE
5–4B

**Brockencote Hall**       **£58**   ❷❷❷
DY10 4PY   (01562) 777876
So far, the "very modern" refit of this formerly
family-owned country house hotel has had no
negative impact on its "superbly presented" food
or its "super-friendly" service, or its "romantic"
ambience – if anything, it seems to have
improved since moving into corporate ownership!
/ **Details:** www.brockencotehall.com; on A448, outside
village; 9 pm; no trainers. **Accommodation:** 21
rooms, from £120.

CHAGFORD, DEVON                          1–3C

**Gidleigh Park**          **£130**  ❶❶❷
TQ13 8HH   (01647) 432367
It's "worth the treacherous drive" to reach this
"magical" (if sometimes slightly "hushed")
country house hotel on the fringe of Dartmoor –
England's top foodie destination in this year's
survey; chef Michael Caines's is "obsessively
brilliant", and the cellar is magnificent too – "the
superlatives never cease".
/ **Details:** www.gidleigh.com; from village, right at
Lloyds TSB, take right fork to end of lane; 9.30 pm;
no jeans or trainers; children: 8+ at L + D.
**Accommodation:** 24 rooms, from £325.

**22 Mill Street**         **£61**   ❶
22 Mill St  TQ13 8AW   (01647) 432244
Don't want to fork out for Gidleigh Park just
down the lane? this "small" dining room
continues to be tipped for its "very good food
indeed" (although the chef, Ashley Wright, left to
go to Fowey in late-2012).
/ **Details:** www.22millst.com; 9.30 pm; closed Mon &
Sun; no trainers; children: 12+. **Accommodation:** 2
rooms, from £99.

CHANDLER'S CROSS, HERTFORDSHIRE3–2A

**Colette's**
**The Grove**              **£86**   ④④④
WD17 3NL   (01923) 296015
The fine-dining room of this "impressive" hotel is
"stunning", but even fans may feel "they're not
making the most of it" – the food often seems
"interesting and beautifully presented", but critics
think it "showy" and "overpriced", and they say
the room "lacks energy".
/ **Details:** www.thegrove.co.uk; 9.30 pm; D only, closed
Mon & Sun; children: 16+. **Accommodation:** 240
rooms, from £290.

**FSA**

**The Glasshouse**
**The Grove**              **£49**   ❸❸④
WD3 4TG   (01923) 296015
Somewhat ambivalent opinions on the buffet-
restaurant at this 'groovy-grand' country house
hotel – a few of the reports suggest quality has
"declined" over recent years, but most reporters
still think sampling from the huge spread an
"enjoyable experience overall".
/ **Details:** www.thegrove.co.uk; 9.30 pm, Sat 10 pm.
**Accommodation:** 227 rooms, from £310.

CHELTENHAM, GLOUCESTERSHIRE   2–1C

**Le Champignon Sauvage**  **£62**   ❶❷
24-28 Suffolk Rd  GL50 2AQ
(01242) 573449
David Everitt-Mathias's "exemplary" cuisine –
"with many lesser-used ingredients" used in
"unexpected combinations" – again wins
adulation for this 25-year-old venture, as does
wife Helen's "lovely" service and the "brilliant,
un-greedily priced wine list"; too early, though, to
rate the impact of a recent refurb on the
ambience.
/ **Details:** www.lechampignonsauvage.co.uk; 9 pm;
closed Mon & Sun.

**The Curry Corner**       **£44**   ❷❷❷
133 Fairview Rd  GL52 2EX
(01242) 528449
"Like no other 'Indian'", say fans of this long-
established Bangladeshi "gem" – the worst
anyone says about the cooking is that it's
"consistently good", and some reporters say it's
"superb". / **Details:** www.thecurrycorner.com;
11 pm; closed Mon & Fri L.

**The Daffodil**           **£47**   ❸❸❷
18-20 Suffolk Pde  GL50 2AE
(01242) 700055
The setting itself is always going to top the bill at
this "beautifully-converted", "dramatic" and
"romantic" Art Deco cinema; rising survey
ratings, however, tend to support those who feel
"the food has got a lot better in the last couple
of years". / **Details:** www.thedaffodil.com; 10 pm,
Sat 10.30 pm; closed Sun.

**Lumière**                **£65**   ❶❷❸
Clarence Pde  GL50 3PA  (01242) 222200
With its "superb" and "inventive" cuisine, and its
"well-tailored" wine matches, Jon Howe & Helen
Aubrey's three-year-old restaurant "has settled
down as a reliably first-class destination" – this
year it even out-ranked the legendary
Champignon Sauvage as the town's best
restaurant! / **Details:** www.lumiere.cc; 9 pm; closed
Mon & Sun, Tue L; children: 8+ D.

**The Royal Well Tavern**  £44  T
5 Royal Well Pl  GL50 3DN
(01242) 221212
*Not much feedback of late on this city-centre gastropub; fans, though, still proclaim it a "real gem". / **Details:** www.theroyalwelltavern.com; 10 pm, Sat 10.30 pm.*

**La Brasserie**
**Chester Grosvenor**  £55  ❸❷❷
Eastgate  CH1 1LT  (01244) 324024
*"A great take on a classic Parisian brasserie" – this very "traditionally comfortable and smart" rendezvous, right by the iconic Eastgate clock, is a "good, dependable all-rounder", where the food is sometimes "excellent" (and always "pricey"). / **Details:** www.chestergrosvenor.com; 10 pm, Sun 9 pm. **Accommodation:** 80 rooms, from £230.*

**1539**  £53  ❸❷❶
The Racecourse  CH1 2LY  (01244) 304 611
*Sweeping views of the racecourse add a sense of occasion to this "super" modern restaurant nestling by the city wall; it's perhaps not a place of culinary pilgrimage, but standards of food and wine are "solid" at worst. / **Details:** www.restaurant1539.co.uk; 10 pm; closed Sun D.*

**Joseph Benjamin**  £42  ❷❷❸
140 Northgate St  CH1 2HT
(01244) 344295
*Just within the city walls, "a restaurant and deli priding itself on fresh, locally-sourced ingredients" – all reports praise its consistently "delicious" cooking. / **Details:** www.josephbenjamin.co.uk; 9.30 pm; closed Mon, Tue D, Wed D & Sun D.*

**MPW Steakhouse**
**Doubletree by Hilton**  £56  ④④❸
Warrington Rd, Hoole  CH2 3PD
(01244) 408800
*Marco Pierre White branding is often reason enough to avoid a restaurant, and so it appears from the few, highly inconsistent reports on this new hotel-conservatory-steakhouse, just outside the city. / **Details:** www.mpwsteakhousechester.co.uk; 10 pm, Fri & Sat 10.30 pm; closed Sun. **Accommodation:** 140 rooms, from £50.*

**Michael Caines**
**ABode Hotels**  £71  ❷❸❷
Grosvener Rd  CH1 2DJ  (01244) 347000
*It's not just the "wonderful views of the castle and the River Dee" which make the top-floor dining room of this landmark modern hotel a*

"wonderful" destination – all reports rate the food as "top-class" too.
*/ **Details:** www.michaelcaines.com; 9 pm, Sat 10 pm; closed Sun; no jeans or trainers.* **Accommodation:** 85 rooms, from £.

**Moules A Go Go**  £38  T
39 Watergate Row  CH1 2LE
(01244) 348818
*Tipped particularly as a lunchtime destination, this large bistro offers "the menu the name suggests, and it enjoys "a fabulous location in the city's unique medieval 'rows'". / **Details:** www.moulesagogo.co.uk; 10 pm, Sun 9 pm.*

**Simon Radley**
**The Chester Grosvenor**  £97  ❷❷❷
Eastgate  CH1 1LT  (01244) 324024
*"A fantastic experience every time"; this formal fine-dining room in this swish city-centre hotel, owned by the Duke of Westminster, is an unusually grand affair (with, for example, a 1000+ bins wine list); it doesn't inspire a huge volume of feedback, but all attests to its impressive consistency and excellence. / **Details:** www.chestergrosvenor.com; 9 pm; D only, closed Mon & Sun; no trainers; children: 12+. **Accommodation:** 80 rooms, from £180.*

**Sticky Walnut**  £41  ❸❷❸
11 Charles St  CH2 3AZ  (01244) 400400
*Tucked-away in the suburb of Hoole, a "small and romantic" restaurant noted for an "innovative" menu (with "many dishes containing walnuts"); critics may decry this as a "pseudo-chic" outfit, but most reporters seem to like it. / **Details:** www.stickywalnut.com; 10 pm, Sun 3 pm; closed Mon & Sun D.*

**Nonna's**  £45  ❷❸④
131 Chatsworth Rd  S40 2AH
(01246) 380035
*"At last, Chesterfield has a place it can be proud of"; this "ultra-modern spin-off from the Sheffield original" has made quite a local name with its good Italian food and "efficient" service; "amid those hard surfaces", though, "noise levels just build and build". / **Details:** 11 pm; closed Mon.*

**Castleman Hotel**  £41  T
DT11 8DB  (01258) 830096
*Tipped as something of a "best-kept secret" – this manor house hotel certainly doesn't gather a huge following among reporters, but those fond of traditional style say the food here is*

*"fantastic". / **Details:** www.castlemanhotel.co.uk; 1m off the A354, signposted; 9 pm; D only, ex Wed & Sun open L & D; no Amex. **Accommodation:** 8 rooms, from £80.*

## CHICHESTER, WEST SUSSEX          3–4A

### Comme Ça          £37     ❸❷❸
67 Broyle Rd  PO19 6BD    (01243) 788724
*"A touch of France, near the Festival Theatre" – Michel Navet's long-established Gallic fixture (est. 1985) is "an untiring favourite" for most reporters; even fans can find its performance "predictable" though, and the odd detractor finds it "time-warped" and "uninspiring".*
*/ **Details:** www.commeca.co.uk; 9.30 pm, Fri & Sat 10.30 pm; closed Mon, Tue L & Sun D.*

### Field & Fork
**Pallant House Gallery**     £42    ❷❸❸
9 North Pallant  PO19 1TJ   (01243) 770 827
*"The best gallery-dining I know!" – this "impressive" venue attracts mountains of praise for its "interesting and well-executed" fare ("with produce from the owners' allotment"); the interior's "functional" but there's a lovely sunny courtyard for fine days.*
*/ **Details:** www.fieldandfork.co.uk; 8.45 pm; closed Mon, Tue D, Wed D & Sun D.*

### The Kennels          £61     ❸❷❶
Goodwood Hs  PO18 0PX   (01243) 755000
*"Overpriced, but then that setting does have to be paid for!" – this "stylish but relaxed" restaurant, gloriously located in the Goodwood Estate, inspires uniformly positive reports... except when it comes to the bill.*
*/ **Details:** www.goodwood.co.uk/thekennels.*

### Lemongrass          £38     ⓣ
5-6 Saint Pancras  PO19 7SJ
(01243) 533280
*Not far from the town-centre, a smart establishment fans insist would "rival any good Thai restaurant in London"; it offers "all the old favourites, and some novelties too".*
*/ **Details:** www.lemongrasssussex.co.uk; 10.45 pm; no Amex.*

## CHILGROVE, WEST SUSSEX          3–4A

### The Fish House          £60     ⓣ
High St  PO18 9HX   (01243) 519444
*"A great fish restaurant, in the middle of the countryside" – all reports on this former pub, on the edge of the South Downs, remain very positive, but we've reduced it to a 'tip' simply because the volume of feedback this year was rather limited. / **Details:** www.thefishhouse.co.uk;*

*9.30 pm, Fri & Sat 10 pm, Sun 9 pm; no Amex.*
***Accommodation:** 15 rooms, from £150.*

## CHINNOR, OXFORDSHIRE          2–2D

### The Sir Charles Napier     £55    ❷❷❷
Spriggs Alley  OX39 4BX   (01494) 483011
*"Fantastic food, on top of the Chilterns"; Julie Griffiths's "hospitable" (if "hard to find") inn has long been particularly known as a classy but "informal" escape for Londoners, offering "sophisticated" cooking that's "expertly produced", if a little pricey.*
*/ **Details:** www.sircharlesnapier.co.uk; Tue-Fri 9.30 pm, Sat 10 pm; closed Mon & Sun D.*

## CHIPPING CAMPDEN, GLOUCESTERSHIRE 2–1C

### The Ebrington Arms          £44    ❷❸❷
GL55 6NH   (01386) 593 223
*"So nice to see a small family-run pub delivering high standards of innovative food" – this "beautifully-located" inn is praised by almost all reporters for its "consistently good" and "innovative" cuisine.*
*/ **Details:** www.theebringtonarms.co.uk; 9 pm.*

## CHIPPING NORTON, OXFORDSHIRE  2–1C

### Wild Thyme          £46    ❶❶❷
10 New St  OX7 5LJ   (01608) 645060
*"A diamond among the dross"; this small (and rather "cramped") family-run restaurant-with-rooms is, as all reports confirm, somewhere "you can order anything on the menu, and be delighted"; "booking essential at weekends".*
*/ **Details:** www.wildthymerestaurant.co.uk; 9 pm; closed Mon L & Sun. **Accommodation:** 3 rooms, from £75.*

## CHIPSTEAD, KENT          3–3B

### The George & Dragon          £41    ❸❷❸
39 High St  TN13 2RW   (01732) 779 019
*"Great use of local produce" and "attentive" service too make this "lovely" inn popular with most reporters who comment on it, even if it can seem to be on the "expensive" side.*
*/ **Details:** www.georgeanddragonchipstead.com; 9.30 pm, Sun 8.30 pm; no Amex.*

## CHRISTCHURCH, DORSET          2–4C

### The Jetty          £54     ❷❷❶
95 Mudeford  BH23 3NT   (01202) 400950
*"A fantastic location overlooking Christchurch Harbour" isn't the only attraction of this "sophisticated and glamorous spot, on the water's edge"; staff show "great attention to detail" and Alex Aitken's "light and fresh"*

cooking – particularly of "wonderful, fresh fish" – is "superb". / **Details:** www.thejetty.co.uk; 9.45 pm, Sun 9 pm; SRA-71%.

CIRENCESTER, GLOUCESTERSHIRE          2–2C

**Made By Bob**          £41          ❷④④
The Cornhall 26 Market Pl  GL7 2NY
(01285) 641818
"A bistro that's breathed life into the heart of Cirencester"; "in a wealthy town, where you often struggle to find a decent place to eat", this handily-located spot has made quite a splash. / **Details:** www.foodmadebybob.com; 9.30; closed Mon D, Tue D, Wed D, Sat D & Sun D.

CLACHAN, ARGYLL AND BUTE          9–3B

**Loch Fyne Oyster Bar**          £49          ❷❷❸
PA26 8BL   (01499) 600236
The famous lochside original of the eponymous chain is no longer part of the group it spawned; it remains "hugely popular" ("even though it is so out-of-the-way") and – the odd gripe notwithstanding – still tipped on most accounts for its "superb" seafood.
/ **Details:** www.loch-fyne.com; 10m E of Inveraray on A83; 8 pm.

CLAVERING, ESSEX          3–2B

**The Cricketers**          £44          ❸❸❸
Wicken Rd  CB11 4QT   (01799) 550442
"Jamie Oliver's folks continue to do a good job!"; his parents' "crowded but reliable" inn, by the village green, consistently dishes up "wholesome" food that's "definitely a cut above the norm" – seems they can still teach Junior a thing or two! / **Details:** www.thecricketers.co.uk; on B1038 between Newport & Buntingford; 9.30 pm; no Amex. **Accommodation:** 14 rooms, from £95.

CLIFTON, CUMBRIA          8–3A

**George & Dragon**          £45          ❷❸❷
CA10 2ER   (01768) 865381
It's not just the location, "within easy reach of Penrith and the M6", that wins a big following among reporters for this "solid" gastropub – it serves "delicious very-locally-sourced food, from the owner's estate" (including "delicious steaks") in a "jolly" atmosphere.
/ **Details:** www.georgeanddragonclifton.co.uk; on the A6 in the village of Clifton; 9 pm. **Accommodation:** 12 rooms, from £92.

CLIMPING, WEST SUSSEX          3–4A

**Bailiffscourt Hotel**          £71          ❿
BN17 5RW   (01903) 723511
"A fantastic hotel, and the restaurant

complements it really well" – this 1920s/medieval country house (in "lovely grounds") is tipped for the deft use it makes of "lots of really good fresh, local produce". / **Details:** www.hshotels.co.uk; 9.30 pm; booking: max 8; children: 7+. **Accommodation:** 39 rooms, from £205.

CLIPSHAM, RUTLAND          6–4A

**The Olive Branch**          £47          ❷❷❸
Main St  LE15 7SH   (01780) 410355
"It's not quite as exciting as it once was", but this "lovely" gastroboozer – in a "beautiful village setting" off the A1 – remains a formidable "all-rounder"; Sean Hope's "intensely flavoured" cooking and "excellent wine" are served in a "lovely" (if "cramped") setting.
/ **Details:** www.theolivebranchpub.com; 2m E from A1 on B664; 9.30 pm, Sun 9 pm; no Amex; SRA-71%. **Accommodation:** 6 rooms, from £135.

CLITHEROE, LANCASHIRE          5–1B

**Inn at Whitewell**          £44          ❷❸❷
Forest of Bowland  BB7 3AT
(01200) 448222
This "secluded gem" – a "fantastic coaching inn, in the beautiful Trough of Bowland", with "lovely" views – remains a major destination thanks to its "outstanding locally-sourced food", and its "inventive" wine list; it can seem too pricey, however, and "the bar is cosier than the restaurant". / **Details:** www.innatwhitewell.com; 9.30 pm; bar open L & D, restaurant D only; no Amex. **Accommodation:** 23 rooms, from £113.

CLYTHA, MONMOUTHSHIRE          2–1A

**Clytha Arms**          £48          ❿
NP7 9BW   (01873) 840206
Two decades in the ownership of the Canning family, this "quirky" rural inn is a top tip in these parts for those is search of "wholesome and interesting" cuisine; service, though, can be "painfully slow". / **Details:** www.clytha-arms.com; on Old Abergavenny to Raglan road; 9.30 pm; closed Mon L & Sun D. **Accommodation:** 4 rooms, from £80.

COBHAM, SURREY          3–3A

**La Capanna**          £58          ❿
48 High St  KT11 3EF   (01932) 862121
This long-established restaurant – with its "historic" setting in a "picturesque" 16th-century building, complete with minstrels' gallery – is tipped as your classic "special-occasion" destination; the food (Italian) plays something of

*a supporting role. / Details: www.lacapanna.co.uk; 11 pm.*

---

COCKERMOUTH, CUMBRIA          7–3C

**Kirkstile Inn**          £39  ❸❷❶
Loweswater  CA13 0RU  (01900) 85219
*"Good, honest, unpretentious pub food in a gorgeous location"* – all reports agree that a meal at this *"beautifully-located"* coaching inn is *"just what you need after a walk in the fells".*
/ *Details: www.kirkstile.com; 9 pm; no Amex.*
*Accommodation: 10 rooms, from £46.50.*

---

COLERNE, WILTSHIRE          2–2B

**Lucknam Park**          £105  ❷❶❷
SN14 8AZ  (01225) 742777
*It's the all-round standards of the dining experience at this Palladian country house hotel which particularly wow reporters; that's not, however, to detract from the quality of Hywel Jones's cooking – the least positive description says it was "very good"!*
/ *Details: www.lucknampark.co.uk; 6m NE of Bath; 10 pm; closed Mon, Tue–Sat D only, closed Sun D; jacket and/or tie; children: 5+ D & Sun L.*
*Accommodation: 42 rooms, from £330.*

**Lucknam Park (Brass.)**    £56  ❶
SN14 8AZ  (01225) 742777
*Don't overlook the number two dining room of this privately-owned country house hotel – it's tipped as "even better than the main restaurant" by some reporters, and its garden location is a "winner" too.*
/ *Details: www.lucknampark.co.uk; 6m NE of Bath.*

---

COLNE, LANCASHIRE          5–1B

**Banny's Restaurant**       £28  ❷❶❸
1 Vivary Way  BB8 9NW  (01282) 856220
*"An upmarket fish 'n' chip emporium" that "does what it says on the tin"* – *"perfectly cooked" fish, "proper-size" chips and good "honest" service are provided in "pleasant", "modern" surroundings. / Details: www.bannys.co.uk; 9 pm; no Amex.*

---

CONGLETON, CHESHIRE          5–2B

**Pecks**          £54  ❸❷❸
Newcastle Rd  CW12 4SB  (01260) 275161
*"Quite sophisticated in style, but informal and friendly", this local institution has made its name with no-choice one-sitting dinners, of which "amazing" puddings are a highlight; "top-value" set lunches too. / Details: www.pecksrest.co.uk; off A34; 8 pm; closed Mon & Sun D; booking essential.*

---

COOKHAM, BERKSHIRE          3–3A

**Bel & The Dragon**        £50  ❷❸❷
High St  SL9 9SQ  (01628) 521263
*By the Stanley Spencer Museum, a "slick"-looking gastroboozer (part of a small chain), commended for its food in all reports, and well-designed to please "both couples and families"; "get a table at the edge", advises one regular – "the big ones in the middle don't have nearly as much atmosphere".*
/ *Details: www.belandthedragon-cookham.co.uk; 10 pm, Sun 9.30 pm; no Amex.*

**Cookham Tandoori**        £38  ❶
SL6 9SL  (01628) 522584
*"An alternative to the much-lauded Maliks", this prettily-housed subcontinental is tipped for offering "well-cooked" dishes in a "pleasant" environment.*
/ *Details: www.spicemerchantgroup.com; 11 pm; no Amex.*

**Maliks**          £40  ❶❷❸
High St  SL6 9SF  (01628) 520085
*"You'd probably have to go to India to get a better curry!" – this "rural" (Berkshire-style!) converted pub offers "awesome" cooking, and the service is "fantastic" too; "not cheap, but at least you get what you pay for..."*
/ *Details: www.maliks.co.uk; from the M4, Junction 7 for A4 for Maidenhead; 11.30 pm, Sun 10.30 pm.*

**Luke's Dining Room
Sanctum on The Green**      £51  ④⑤④
The Old Cricket Common  SL6 9NZ
(01628) 482638
*This chic little restaurant-with-rooms inspires a fair number of reports; the food is often "good", but some reporters find their visits totally spoilt by "pretentious" and "unhelpful" service.*
/ *Details: www.lukesdiningroom.co.uk; 9.30 pm; closed Mon & Sun D; booking: max 6 on Sat.*
*Accommodation: 9 rooms, from £120.*

**The White Oak**          £40  ❷❷❸
The Pound  SL6 9QE  (01628) 523043
*"The new chef is doing great things", say fans of the "good", occasionally "sublime", cooking at this "welcoming" gastropub, which is now firmly "back on track". / Details: www.thewhiteoak.co.uk; 9.30 pm; closed Sun D.*

---

COPSTER GREEN, LANCASHIRE      5–1B

**Yu And You**          £43  ❸❷❸
500 Longsight Rd  BB1 9EU
(01254) 247111
*Some reports say you get "the best Chinese food in the North", at this "not cheap, but always*

good-value" Ribble Valley spot; after its Ramsay
TV success, though, even fans may sense an
element of "hype". / **Details:** www.yuandyou.com;
off the A59 7 miles towards Clitheroe; 11 pm, Fri & Sat
2 am; D only, closed Mon.

---

CORSE LAWN, GLOUCESTERSHIRE          2–1B

**Corse Lawn Hotel**          **£51**   ❸❷❸
GL19 4LZ   (01452) 780771
"Consistent quality" and "a warm welcome" still
makes the Hine family's "delightful, if isolated"
restaurant-with-rooms, in a Queen Anne house, a
"charming" destination – quite an achievement
for a team that's been in place for 35 years!
/ **Details:** www.corselawn.com; 5m SW of Tewkesbury
on B4211; 9.30 pm. **Accommodation:** 18 rooms,
from £160.

---

CORTON DENHAM, SOMERSET          2–3B

**The Queen's Arms**          **£40**   ❸❸❷
DT9 4LR   (01963) 220317
"A favourite hide-away where my mobile ceases
to work…" – this "smart but barely-furnished
inn" makes a "great place to stay"; reports on
the food run the whole gamut from "superb" to
"confused", but most are upbeat.
/ **Details:** www.thequeensarms.com; 10 pm, Sun
9.30 pm. **Accommodation:** 5 rooms, from £110.

---

COWLEY, GLOUCESTERSHIRE          2–1C

**Cowley Manor**          **£51**   🅣
GL53 9NL   (01242) 870900
This chichi country house hotel – "they could just
put on a Sunday afternoon coach back to
Notting Hill!" – inspired relatively few survey
comments; the dining room, however, is tipped as
a "stunning" destination, with "spectacular"
views, and "top-quality" cuisine.
/ **Details:** www.cowleymanor.com; 10 pm, Fri & Sat
11 pm. **Accommodation:** 30 rooms, from £245.

---

CRANBROOK, KENT          3–4C

**Apicius**          **£56**   ❶❷❸
23 Stone St TN17 3HF   (01580) 714666
"A great find in a pretty village"; Faith Hawkins
& Timothy Johnson's "calm", if somewhat
"brightly-lit", spot may be obscurely located, but
its "superlative" cuisine is some of the best in the
South East; especially at weekends, it's "very
popular". / **Details:** www.restaurant-apicius.co.uk;
9 pm; closed Mon, Tue, Sat L & Sun D; no Amex;
children: 8+.

---

CRAYKE, NORTH YORKSHIRE          5–1D

**Durham Ox**          **£39**   ❸❷❷
Westway  YO61 4TE   (01347) 821506
"A great and welcoming village pub in the
prettiest of villages", whose "good, solid pub
food" helps make a trip "a very enjoyable
occasion". / **Details:** www.thedurhamox.com;
9.30 pm, Sun 8.30 pm. **Accommodation:** 5 rooms,
from £100.

---

CREIGIAU, CARDIFF          2–2A

**Caesars Arms**          **£46**   ❷❷❸
Cardiff Rd  CF15 9NN   (029) 2089 0486
"Choose your own fish or meat, to be cooked in
front of you"; that's the long-running formula of
this "friendly" and "bustling" rural inn – "a busy
place on the outskirts of Cardiff".
/ **Details:** www.caesarsarms.co.uk; beyond Creigiau,
past the golf club; 10 pm; closed Sun D.

---

CRICKHOWELL, POWYS          2–1A

**The Bear**          **£39**   ④④❸
High St  NP8 1BW   (01873) 810408
This impressive old coaching inn still charms
most reporters, both in its "classic" bar and in its
"lovely stone-walled dining room"; Welsh
hospitality, however, seems in short supply, and
the odd "lacklustre" day on the food front is not
unknown. / **Details:** www.bearhotel.co.uk; 9.30 pm;
D only, ex Sun open L only, closed Mon; children: 10+.
**Accommodation:** 36 rooms, from £95.

---

CROSTHWAITE, CUMBRIA          7–4D

**The Punch Bowl**          **£43**   ❷❸❷
LA8 8HR   (01539) 568237
"Tucked away in a quiet corner of the south
Lakes", this "rustic" gastropub weaves its spell
over almost all who comment on it; the food "if
standard, is always enticing and precise" (and the
accommodation is also highly praised).
/ **Details:** www.the-punchbowl.co.uk; off A5074
towards Bowness, turn right after Lyth Hotel; 9.30 pm.
**Accommodation:** 9 rooms, from £120.

---

CROYDON, SURREY          3–3B

**Albert's Table**          **£44**   ❷④④
49c South End  CR0 1BF   (020) 8680 2010
"A real surprise in drab south Croydon" – Joby
Wells's "friendly" restaurant has gathered an
impressive fan club among reporters, thanks to
food that's usually "well up to West End
standards"; the set lunch, in particular, offers
"brilliant value". / **Details:** www.albertstable.co.uk;
10.30 pm; closed Mon & Sun D; no Amex.

**Fish & Grill**  £44  🅣
48-50 South End  CR0 1DP
(020) 8774 4060
"A useful stand-by in an area not well endowed with good restaurants"; Malcolm Johns's bistro is a handy tip if you find yourself in these parts, though even fans can find it a touch "pricey" for what it is. / **Details:** www.fishandgrill.co.uk; 11.30 pm.

**McDermotts Fish & Chips** £24  ❶❶❷
5-7 The Forestdale Shopping Centre
Featherbed Ln  CR0 9AS  (020) 8651 1440
"Fish cooked to perfection!"; Tony McDermott's upscale fish 'n' chip restaurant, in Forestdale, is "not only affordable, but family-friendly too". / **Details:** www.mcdermottsfishandchips.co.uk; 9.30 pm, Sat 9 pm; closed Mon & Sun.

CRUDWELL, WILTSHIRE  2–2C

**The Potting Shed**  £44  ❹❸❸
The St  SN16 9EW  (01666) 577833
A "lovely" Cotswolds pub in a "beautiful" location, serving food that's often "wonderful"; it "suffers from over-popularity", though, and some reporters fear it's "resting on its laurels" too. / **Details:** www.thepottingshedpub.com; 9.30 pm, Sun 9 pm; no Amex. **Accommodation:** 12 rooms, from £95.

CUCKFIELD, WEST SUSSEX  3–4B

**Ockenden Manor**  £76  ❸❸❸
Ockenden Ln  RH17 5LD  (01444) 416111
"A high-quality gastronomic experience but without becoming precious" – this country house hotel still, on most reports, serves up some of the best food in Sussex; a couple of meals this year, though, were "very disappointing" – hopefully just a blip! / **Details:** www.hshotels.co.uk; 9 pm; no jeans or trainers. **Accommodation:** 28 rooms, from £183.

CUPAR, FIFE  9–3D

**The Peat Inn**  £61  ❶❷❷
KY15 5LH  (01334) 840206
"Superb as always!"; the Smeddle family's famous country inn is praised in practically all reports for its "great attention to detail", its sourcing of "the finest local ingredients", and its "well-drilled" service – "a wonderful dining experience". / **Details:** www.thepeatinn.co.uk; at junction of B940 & B941, SW of St Andrews; 9 pm; closed Mon & Sun. **Accommodation:** 8 rooms, from £180.

DALRY, NORTH AYRSHIRE  9–4B

**Braidwoods**  £64  ❶❶❷
Drumastle Mill Cottage  KA24 4LN
(01294) 833544
"Undoubtedly one of Scotland's very finest restaurants" – Keith & Nicola Braidwood's "wonderful" converted croft attracts the highest praise for its "always-imaginative menus and wonderful wines, in a cosy and peaceful setting". / **Details:** www.braidwoods.co.uk; 9 pm; closed Mon, Tue L & Sun D; children: 12+ at D.

DANEHILL, EAST SUSSEX  3–4B

**Coach And Horses**  £54  ❷❸❸
School Ln  RH17 7JF  (01825) 740369
"Almost as many dogs as human patrons" advertise the "real-pub" credentials of this rural boozer, but it is also praised for its "delicious", "restaurant-quality" food, and its "super" selection of beers and wines. / **Details:** www.coachandhorses.co; off A275; 9 pm, Fri-Sat 9.30 pm, Sun 3 pm; closed Sun D.

DARTMOUTH, DEVON  1–4D

**The Angel**
**Angelique Hotel**  £48  ❹❺❺
2 South Embankment  TQ6 9BH
(01803) 839425
The one-time Carved Angel is a site with a great history behind it, and its operator, Alan Murchison, is undoubtedly a 'pro'; reports on this seaside restaurant-with-rooms, however, suggest that this is an operation where he still "hasn't got a grip". / **Details:** www.angeliquedartmouth.co.uk; 9 pm, Fri-Sat 9.30 pm; closed Mon, Tue L & Sun D. **Accommodation:** 7 rooms, from £95.

**The Seahorse**  £62  ❶❸❸
5 South Embankment  TQ6 9BH
(01803) 835147
"Utterly divine" fresh fare – "they use the best and freshest seafood on the daily market" – is "done to perfection" at Mitch Tonks's "understated but special" dining room, near the river. / **Details:** www.seahorserestaurant.co.uk; 10 pm; closed Mon, Tue L & Sun D.

DEDHAM, ESSEX  3–2C

**Milsoms**  £45  ❹❸❷
Stratford Rd  CO7 6HW  (01206) 322795
For Constable Country trippers, the Milsom family's "reasonably-priced" all-day brasserie offers an "acceptable" standard of cuisine, in a "grand" old building. / **Details:** www.milsomhotels.com; 9.30 pm, Fri & Sat

10 pm; no booking. **Accommodation:** 15 rooms, from £120.

**The Sun Inn** £40 ④④❸
High St CO7 6DF (01206) 323351
For its many supporters, this "lovely" Constable Country destination is "a great local pub, with interesting Italian-style food and a very good wine list"; even fans, though, can find standards – particularly of service – "a bit hit-and-miss".
/ **Details:** www.thesuninndedham.com; Fri & Sat 10 pm, 9.30 pm. **Accommodation:** 7 rooms, from £80.

**Le Talbooth** £66 ❸②❶
Gun Hill CO7 6HP (01206) 323150
In a pretty Constable Country house, by a river, this famous destination is just the sort of "classic", "high-class" restaurant you imagine Poirot might have visited on a day off; it has just celebrated its diamond jubilee, and (just like HM) is celebrating a vintage year.
/ **Details:** www.milsomhotels.com; 5m N of Colchester on A12, take B1029; 9 pm; closed Sun D; no jeans or trainers.

DENHAM, BUCKINGHAMSHIRE     3–3A

**Swan Inn** £42 ❷❷❷
Village Rd UB9 5BH (01895) 832085
"A fun gastropub, in a quaint setting, offering good wholesome food", and at "reasonable prices" too; it inspires reports with a model degree of consistency, so no wonder it can be "hard to get a table".
/ **Details:** www.swaninndenham.co.uk; 9.30 pm, Fri & Sat 10 pm.

DERBY, DERBYSHIRE     5–3C

**Anoki** £42 ❸❷❸
First Floor, 129 London Rd DE1 2QN (01332) 292888
Surprisingly "spectacular", this former Art Deco cinema, in the city-centre, offers "the best Indian food in the area", and an "excellent range" too; "go early – it can get noisy later on".
/ **Details:** www.anoki.co.uk; 11.30 pm; D only, closed Sun.

**Darleys** £53 ❸②❷
Darley Abbey Mill DE22 1DZ (01332) 364987
"A really good all-round experience"; this "slick" and "well-priced" operation pleases almost all who comment on it – well-rated food, "lovely" views over the Derwent, and "friendly" service too. / **Details:** www.darleys.com; 9 pm; closed Sun D; no Amex.

**Ebi Sushi** £37 ❶②④
Abbey St DE22 3SJ (01332) 265656
"Very small and in an unprepossessing part of town", it may be, but – as "the preponderance of Japanese diners" makes clear – this oriental café provides an "authentic" standard of sushi and other fare "unmatched" in the Midlands; why here? – "Toyota's just down the road".
/ **Details:** 10.30 pm; D only, closed Mon & Sun; no Amex.

DINTON, BUCKINGHAMSHIRE     2–3C

**La Chouette** £55 ❷❸❸
Westlington Grn HP17 8UW (01296) 747422
Brace yourself for le patron's "unique brand of rudeness", but the quality of Freddie-the-Belgian's "spot-on" cuisine makes most reporters forgiving; "when you know him, you realise he only means 10% of what he says…" / **Details:** off A418 between Aylesbury & Thame; 9 pm; closed Sat L & Sun; no Amex.

DODDISCOMBSLEIGH, DEVON     1–3D

**The NoBody Inn** £40 ④❸❷
EX6 7PS (01647) 252394
An ancient and "very welcoming" inn (with garden), with quite a name as a tourist stop-off; the cooking, however, is much less of an attraction than the "fascinating wine list, put together with passion", and the "excellent cheese list, with lots of UK varieties".
/ **Details:** www.nobodyinn.co.uk; off A38 at Haldon Hill (signed Dunchidrock); 9 pm, Fri & Sat 9.30 pm; no Amex. **Accommodation:** 5 rooms, from £60.

DORCHESTER, DORSET     2–4B

**Sienna** £63 ❶②④
36 High West St DT1 1UP (01305) 250022
"An unbelievable labour of love"; this decade-old restaurant offers a "wonderful" (and "affordable") tasting menu that some reporters hail as the "best food in Dorset"; main problem? – "the dining room is just too small for a relaxing dinner". / **Details:** www.siennarestaurant.co.uk; 9 pm; closed Mon, Tue L & Sun; no Amex; children: 12+.

DORKING, SURREY     3–3A

**Little Dudley House** £50 ❶
77 South St RH2 2JU (01306) 885550
"Eat in the modern conservatory, or the olde-worlde dining room", when you visit this 18th-century venue; fans tip it as "one of the best restaurants in this part of Surrey", but its ratings are undercut by quite a few decidedly "average"

*reports. / **Details:** www.littledudleyhouse.co.uk;
9.30 pm, Fri & Sat 10 pm; closed Sun.*

**Restaurant Two To Four**   **£47**   ❸❷❸
2-4 West St RH4 1BL   (01306) 889923
*"Good-quality food, friendly service, sensible
prices" – the formula may not sound earth-
shattering, but it pleases all who comment on
this "nice little spot", occupying a three-floor,
timbered building. / **Details:** www.2to4.co.uk;
10 pm; closed Mon & Sun.*

**Tanroagan**   **£54**   ❷❸❸
9 Ridgeway St IM1 1EW   (01624) 612 355
*The Isle of Man's top restaurant address is
"always busy", thanks to its "amiable" (if
sometimes overstretched) service, and the
"lovely, fresh fish and seafood, cooked really
well"; tables, though, are "a bit too close together
for complete comfort".
/ **Details:** www.tanroagan.co.uk; 9.30 pm; closed
Sat L & Sun; no Amex.*

**The Old Inn**   **£58**   ❶❷❸
EX6 6QR   (01647) 281 276
*"Fans of Duncan Walker's time at 22 Mill Street
(Chagford) will find not much changed in his new
operation" – all reports acclaim the all-round
high standards of this "cosy" and "intimate"
restaurant-with-rooms.
/ **Details:** www.old-inn.co.uk; 9 pm; closed Sun-Tue,
Wed L, Thu L; no Amex; children: 14.
**Accommodation:** 3 rooms, from £90.*

**The Rocks**   **£38**   🅣
Marine Rd EH42 1AR   (01368) 862287
*An aptly-named waterside inn, tipped for the
"fresh seafood" you'd hope for, as well as some
"fantastic" meat dishes; "friendly" service too.
/ **Details:** www.herocksdunbar.co.uk; 9 pm; no Amex.
**Accommodation:** 11 rooms, from £75.*

**The Three Chimneys**   **£85**   ❶❷❶
Colbost IV55 8ZT   (01470) 511258
*"Such love and respect for the food!" – Eddie
and Shirley Spear's "very remote" and
"stunningly-located" former crofter's cottage, by
Loch Dunvegan, is "worth the long drive", thanks
not least to its "amazing" cooking, majoring in
seafood; there's the odd call, though, for "plainer"
dishes and "a more informal" style.
/ **Details:** www.threechimneys.co.uk; 5m from
Dunvegan Castle on B884 to Glendale; 9.45 pm; closed*

*Sun L; children: 8+. **Accommodation:** 6 rooms,
from £295.*

**Bistro 21**   **£48**   ❸❷❷
Aykley Heads Hs DH1 5TS
(0191) 384 4354
*Just outside the city-centre, an outpost of Terry
Laybourne's empire (based in distant Newcastle),
long known as one of Durham's better eateries;
its "friendly and efficient" staff serve up food
that's "consistently good and well-presented".
/ **Details:** www.bistrotwentyone.co.uk; 10 pm; closed
Sun.*

**Finbarr's**   **£46**   🅣
Flass Vale DH1 4BG   (0191) 370 9999
*It "may be rather out-of-the-way", but this 2010
opening is enjoying a "growing reputation" for its
"very accomplished" cuisine, and "attentive
service" too. / **Details:** www.finbarrsrestaurant.co.uk;
9.30 pm, Sun 9 pm.*

**Gourmet Spot**
**Farnley Tower Hotel**   **£56**   ❷❸⑤
The Avenue DH1 4DX   (0191) 384 6655
*It's not the location ("off-centre"), the wine list
("pedestrian") or the dining room ("too small")
which makes this basement restaurant stand
out… but cuisine that's "of good quality", and
"not afraid of experimentation".
/ **Details:** www.gourmet-spot.co.uk; 9.30 pm; D only,
closed Mon & Sun. **Accommodation:** 13 rooms,
from £80.*

**Oldfields**   **£45**   ④④④
18 Claypath DH1 1RH   (0191) 370 9595
*"Support for local food producers" is a hallmark
of this "conveniently central" all-day brasserie,
and most reporters rate its food highly; even
some fans admit to "occasional disappointment"
however, and others find standards "below
expectations".
/ **Details:** www.oldfieldsrealfood.co.uk; 10 pm, Sun
9 pm.*

**Jolly Sportsman**   **£47**   ❸❸❷
Chapel Ln BN7 3BA   (01273) 890400
*"Very reliable and enjoyable" – Bruce Wass's
"well-located" inn enjoys "a scenic setting by the
South Downs", and is consistently praised for its
"top-class" food, and "long and affordable wine
list" (plus an "unbelievable range of whiskies").
/ **Details:** www.thejollysportsman.com; NW of Lewes;
9.15 pm, Sat 10 pm; no Amex.*

| EAST GRINSTEAD, WEST SUSSEX | 3–4B |
| --- | --- |

**Gravetye Manor**     **£75**   ④④❶
Vowels Ln  RH19 4LJ  (01342) 810567
*Still something of a feeling of 'work in progress',
at this (potentially) "magical" Elizabethan manor
house, which has emerged from receivership in
recent times – reporters clearly want the
management to succeed, but the feeling lingers
that standards are not yet up to the prices.
/ Details: www.gravetyemanor.co.uk; 2m outside
Turner's Hill; 9.30 pm, Sun 9 pm; booking: max 8;
children: 7+.* **Accommodation:** *17 rooms,
from £200.*

| EAST HENDRED, OXFORDSHIRE | 2–2D |
| --- | --- |

**The Eyston Arms**     **£48**   ❶
High St  OX12 8JY  (01235) 833320
*"An out-of-the-way place that's worth a bit of a
drive" – this "pleasant, buzzy pub", near the
Ridgeway, impresses reporters with food that's
"always good". / Details: www.eystons.co.uk; 9 pm;
closed Sun D.*

| EAST LAVANT, WEST SUSSEX | 2–4D |
| --- | --- |

**The Royal Oak**     **£49**   ❸❷❸
Pook Ln  PO18 0AX  (01243) 527 434
*"Château Latour anyone?"; the global wine list at
this "great country pub" is "quite outstanding" –
the food rather plays second fiddle, but it never
seems to disappoint.
/ Details: www.royaloakeastlavant.co.uk; 9 pm, Sat
9.30 pm; no shorts.* **Accommodation:** *8 rooms,
from £110.*

| EAST LOOE, CORNWALL | 1–4C |
| --- | --- |

**Trawlers**     **£44**   ❷❷❷
On The Quay  PL13 1AH  (01503) 263593
*"First-class ingredients, careful cooking, friendly
and professional service and an attractive setting
right on the harbour" – no wonder this seaside
fish restaurant is "highly recommended" by all
who comment on it.
/ Details: www.trawlersrestaurant.co.uk; 9.30 pm.*

| EAST WITTON, NORTH YORKSHIRE | 8–4B |
| --- | --- |

**Blue Lion**     **£48**   ❶
DL8 4SN  (01969) 624273
*This "well-loved" Dales inn is, say fans, a "really
special" destination, and strongly tipped for its
"imaginative", game-led cuisine; even the odd
supporter, though, may note that it's "not
cheap". / Details: www.thebluelion.co.uk; between
Masham & Leyburn on A6108; 9.15 pm; no Amex.*
**Accommodation:** *15 rooms, from £94.*

| EASTBOURNE, EAST SUSSEX | 3–4B |
| --- | --- |

**The Mirabelle**
**The Grand Hotel**     **£63**   ❸❷❸
King Edwards Pde  BN21 4EQ
(01323) 412345
*"Improved", of late – the top dining room at this
unusually grand seaside hotel strikes
traditionalists as "impressive in every way".
/ Details: www.grandeastbourne.com; 9.45 pm; closed
Mon & Sun; jacket or tie required at D.*
**Accommodation:** *152 rooms, from £199.*

| EASTON GRAY, WILTSHIRE | 2–2C |
| --- | --- |

**Dining Room**
**Whatley Manor**     **£98**   ❶❶④
SN16 0RB  (01666) 822888
*"Imaginative" and "beautiful" – Martin Bruge's
food distinguishes this "luxurious" country house
hotel as an establishment "of the highest
quality"; so, indeed, does every other aspect of
the operation… except, perhaps, the
atmosphere of the dining room itself, which can
feel "staid". / Details: www.whatleymanor.com; 8
miles from J17 on the M4, follow A429 towards
Cirencester to Malmesbury on the B4040; 9.30 pm;
D only, closed Mon-Tue; no jeans or trainers; children:
12+.* **Accommodation:** *23 rooms, from £305.*

| EDINBURGH, CITY OF EDINBURGH | 9–4C |
| --- | --- |

**Angels With Bagpipes**     **£49**   ④④❸
343 High St, Royal Mile  EH1 1PW
(0131) 220 1111
*"Surprisingly interesting Scottish grub in a great
location" – fans much approve this atmospheric
Royal Mile outpost of the Valvona & Crolla
empire; for critics, though, there's "a massive
imbalance between the prices and what's on the
plate". / Details: www.angelswithbagpipes.co.uk;
9.45 pm.*

**Bell's Diner**     **£28**   ❶
7 St Stephen St  EH3 5EN  (0131) 225 8116
*For a "legendary" burger, this "totally relaxed"
Stockbridge "institution" is quite possibly the top
tip in town. / Details: 10 pm; closed weekday L &
Sun L; no Amex.*

**Café Fish**     **£46**   ❷❸❸
15 North West Circus Pl  EH3 6SX
(0131) 225 4431
*On the fringe of the New Town, former bank
premises provide the "light" and "airy" setting for
a restaurant whose "superb" seafood is
complimented by all who comment on it.
/ Details: www.cafefish.net; 9.30 pm, Sun 8.30 pm.*

# FSA

**Café Marlayne**  £41  ❷❸❸
1 Thistle St  EH2 1EN  (0131) 226 2230
*"A popular local brasserie, delivering simple, well-cooked food at reasonable prices" – all reports on this New Town bistro are to pretty much the same effect; ditto mentions of its sibling at 13 Antigua Street, just off Leith Walk.*
*/ Details: www.cafemarlayne.com; 10 pm; no Amex.*

**The Café Royal Bar**  £42  ⓣ
19 West Register St  EH2 2AA
(0131) 556 1884
*The 150-year-old setting could make this New Town veteran one of Edinburgh's most striking institutions – all reporters acclaim its atmosphere; its seafood menu, though, scores hits and misses. / Details: www.caferoyal.org.uk; 9.30 pm; children: 5.*

**Le Café St-Honoré**  £46  ❷❷❸
34 NW Thistle Street Ln  EH2 1EA
(0131) 226 2211
*"Snuck down a wee lane", in the New Town, this "old-fashioned" bistro offers a "touch of Paris", and is – say fans – very "under-rated"; the setting, though, is all rather "squashed-in".*
*/ Details: www.cafesthonore.com; 10 pm; SRA-66%.*

**Calistoga Central**  £42  ⓣ
70 Rose St  EH2 3DX  (0131) 2251233
*Central but oddly hidden-away, this New Town bistro is tipped for its "interesting" and "well-presented" cuisine, with a Californian twist, and its "excellent wines at modest mark-ups" too.*
*/ Details: www.calistoga.co.uk; 10 pm; closed Sun.*

**The Castle Terrace**  £68  ❶❶❷
33/35 Castle Ter  EH1 2EL  (0131) 229 1222
*"A perfect meal every time!"; Tom Kitchin's "relaxed" spin-off, near the Castle, generates a "lovely buzz" and (nearly) all reporters are swept away by the "top-class" modern Scottish cuisine; the lunch menu, in particular, is "a steal".*
*/ Details: www.castleterracerestaurant.com; 10 pm; closed Mon & Sun.*

**Centotre**  £48  ⓣ
103 George St  EH2 3ES  (0131) 225 1550
*A fashionable Italian in a grand former bank, sometimes tipped for its "lively" atmosphere, and its use of "quality" ingredients; it can seem "overpriced", though, and standards are too variable to make it a 'safe' recommendation.*
*/ Details: www.centotre.com; 10 pm, Fri & Sat 11 pm, Sun 8 pm.*

**David Bann**  £38  ❸④④
56-58 St Marys St  EH1 1SX
(0131) 556 5888
*It's sometimes "inconsistent" nowadays, but this contemporary café, in the Old Town, is "still a good bet for veggies and carnivores alike" – hit lucky, and you can get some "fascinating" dishes, and "it's easy to forget there's no meat on the menu!" / Details: www.davidbann.com; 10 pm, Fri & Sat 10.30 pm.*

**Divino Enoteca**  £45  ❷❷❷
5 Merchant St  EH1 2QD  (0131) 225 1770
*In a cellar just off the Royal Mile, this recent offshoot of the locally popular Vittoria empire is beginning to make a name for its "authentic" Italian food, and "even better wine".*
*/ Details: www.vittoriagroup.co.uk; midnight, Fri & Sat 1 am; closed Sun.*

**Dusit**  £44  ❷❸④
49a Thistle St  EH2 1DY  (0131) 220 6846
*"A brilliant, classy Thai", offering a "great and varied selection of dishes" in "huge" portions; service is "attentive" too – indeed, it can be "too speedy" for some tastes – and the setting is "cramped" and "noisy". / Details: www.dusit.co.uk; 11 pm.*

**L'Escargot Bleu**  £39  ❷❷❸
56 Broughton St  EH1 3SA  (0131) 557 1600
*"You could be in Paris!" – "good food" and "good value" are the themes of all feedback on this "genuinely French" bistro; it has a sibling at the other end of the New Town, L'Escargot Blanc.*
*/ Details: www.lescargotblanc.co.uk; 10 pm, Fri & Sat 10.30 pm; closed Sun; no Amex.*

**Favorita**  £39  ❷❷❸
325 Leith Walk  EH6 8JA  (0131) 554 2430
*"A bustling Italian with authentic food, eager staff and reasonable prices" – offering "the best pizza in town" this "family-favourite" is "rapidly becoming quite a local institution".*
*/ Details: www.la-favorita.com; 11 pm; no Amex.*

**First Coast**  £33  ⓣ
97-101 Dalry Rd  EH11 2AB
(0131) 313 4404
*Near Haymarket Station, a "casual" restaurant "of character", tipped for its "good" and "tasty" dishes; service impresses too, though "it can slow down at busy times".*
*/ Details: www.first-coast.co.uk; 10.30 pm; closed Sun.*

**Fishers Bistro**  £42  ❶❷❸
1 The Shore  EH6 6QW  (0131) 554 5666
*"In an old and attractive part of the Leith waterfront", this "popular" fish restaurant has long been known for its "excellent value" – a "warm", "friendly" and "bustling" sort of place,*

Angels with Bagpipes

Grainstore

Ondine

*"well worth finding".*
/ **Details:** *www.fishersbistros.co.uk; 10.30 pm.*

**Fishers in the City** £44 ❸❸❸
58 Thistle St EH2 1EN (0131) 225 5109
*"Cramped" but "pleasant", this New Town fish
bistro is universally hailed by reporters as an
"easy choice" – "perhaps a touch predictable,
but never disappointing".*
/ **Details:** *www.fishersbistros.co.uk; 10.30 pm.*

**Forth Floor**
**Harvey Nichols** £48 ❸❸❷
30-34 St Andrew Sq EH2 2AD
(0131) 524 8350
*"Splendid views of the city" and "food to match"
– general themes of reports on this elevated
department store dining room; another is the
fact that it is rather "overpriced".*
/ **Details:** *www.harveynichols.com; 10 pm; closed
Mon D & Sun D; SRA-65%.*

**Gardener's Cottage** £40 ❶
Royal Ter EH7 5DX (0131) 558 1221
*This intriguingly-located newcomer (near where
the A1 comes in to town) looks very much as its
name suggests; it opened too late to attract
survey commentary, but its unpretentious
charms have won extraordinary levels of press
attention.* / **Details:** *10 pm; closed Tue & Wed.*

**La Garrigue** £46 ❸❸❸
31 Jeffrey St EH1 1DH (0131) 557 3032
*A "very Gallic" bastion of the Old Town, offering
"bistro-style" cuisine, and a strong wine list, both
focussed on south-west France; results are often
"excellent", but can be "variable" too.*
/ **Details:** *www.lagarrigue.co.uk; 9.30 pm.*

**Grain Store** £58 ❷❹❶
30 Victoria St EH1 2JW (0131) 225 7635
*Carlo Coxon's "lovely" New Town warehouse –
complete with lots of "intimate nooks and
crannies" – is a "romantic" all-rounder offering
good food; service, though, can be a touch
"variable".*
/ **Details:** *www.grainstore-restaurant.co.uk; 10 pm.*

**Henderson's** £32 ❸❹❸
94 Hanover St EH2 1DR (0131) 225 2131
*For fans, "no visit to Edinburgh is complete"
without a trip to this characterful veteran, in a
New Town basement – it "never fails to please
with the good and interesting veggie scoff it's
now been serving for half a century!"*
/ **Details:** *www.hendersonsofedinburgh.co.uk; 10 pm;
closed Sun D; no Amex.*

**The Honours** £52 ❷❷❸
58a, North Castle St EH2 3LU
(0131) 220 2513
*Martin Wishart's "swankily-located" New Town
newcomer has made a "first-rate" initial
impression, thanks to sophisticated brasserie
cuisine from chef Paul Tambourini that's
"absolutely top-drawer" and "efficient" service
too; the atmosphere, though, can seem a little
"business-orientated".*
/ **Details:** *www.thehonours.co.uk; 10 pm; closed
Mon & Sun.*

**Indian Cavalry Club** £44 ❷❹❹
22 Coates Cr EH3 7AF (0131) 220 0138
*Since it moved premises a couple of years ago,
this New Town Indian has inspired much
numerical survey feedback, but not much actual
commentary; food ratings indicate high
satisfaction – service and ambience are more
middle-of-the-road.*
/ **Details:** *www.indiancavalryclub.co.uk; 10.45 pm.*

**The Kitchin** £84 ❶❶❷
78 Commercial Quay EH6 6LX
(0131) 555 1755
*"A very special place" – Tom Kitchin is often
seen in the kitchen of his "friendly" Leith
flagship, and it shows in the "perfect execution"
of "brilliant and passionate" cuisine that "takes
full advantage of the great product available on
his doorstep"; it's well "worth the wait for a
table".* / **Details:** *www.thekitchin.com; 10 pm; closed
Mon & Sun.*

**Mithas** £47 ❷❸❷
7 Dock Pl EH6 6LU (0131) 554 0008
*From the people behind Khushi's, a "luxurious"
Leith newcomer already sometimes hailed as
"Edinburgh's best subcontinental", thanks not
least to its "very fresh" dishes "like you've never
tasted before"; booze? – BYO or, rather oddly, go
to buy it in the in-house bar.*
/ **Details:** *www.mithas.co.uk; 10 pm; closed Mon;
children: 8.*

**Mother India's Cafe** £32 ❷❹❸
3-5 Infirmary St EH1 1LT (0131) 524 9801
*"Always full, and always spot-on" – thanks to its
"buzzing" style and its "perfectly sized mini
portions of gorgeously fresh and light curries",
this "chic and unusual" Indian "tapas bar", in the
Old Town, is almost as highly rated as the
Weegie original.*
/ **Details:** *www.motherindiaglasgow.co.uk; Sun 10 pm,
10.30 pm, Fri & Sat 11 pm; no Amex.*

**Mussel Inn**     **£40**    ❸❸④
61-65 Rose St EH2 2NH   (0131) 225 5979
*"Never not busy!"; "it may not be an attractive room", but "good food and good value" ensure a pretty much constant crush at this "friendly" New Town mussel-parlour.*
*/ **Details:** www.mussel-inn.com; 10 pm.*

**Number One**
**Balmoral Hotel**     **£90**    ❶❶❸
1 Princes St EH2 2EQ   (0131) 557 6727
*"Jeff Bland's star is still shining!", say fans of this "comfortable" and "stylish" chamber – long one of Edingburgh's top culinary destinations – beneath the grandest hotel in town; "it should feel overwhelmingly posh, but the straightforward and unpretentious staff make you feel completely at home".*
*/ **Details:** www.thebalmoralhotel.com; 10 pm; D only; no jeans or trainers; booking essential.*
**Accommodation:** *188 rooms, from £360.*

**Ondine**     **£55**    ❷❸❸
2 George IV Bridge EH1 1AD
(0131) 226 1888
*"Beautifully fresh seafood", in particular, has carved a very big name for Roy Brett's "swanky" and "vibrant" – if rather "blandly decorated" – three-year-old, oddly-located in an office block, just off the Royal Mile.*
*/ **Details:** www.ondinerestaurant.co.uk; 10 pm; booking: max 8.*

**The Outsider**     **£44**    ❸❷❷
15-16 George IV Bridge EH1 1EE
(0131) 226 3131
*"Unusual menus and a fun location too!" – this "laid back" Castle-view bistro may have no great culinary aspirations, but it rarely disappoints, and some reporters rate it their "top destination for a fun night out". / **Details:** 11 pm; no Amex; booking: max 12.*

**Le Petit Paris**     **£40**    ❸❸❸
38-40 Grassmarket EH1 2JU
(0131) 226 2442
*"Cramped but welcoming", this "excellent" bistro lives up to its name; "top-value set lunches" a highlight. / **Details:** www.petitparis-restaurant.co.uk; 11 pm; children: - .*

**Plumed Horse**     **£69**    ❷❷❷
50-54 Henderson St EH6 6DE
(0131) 554 5556
*A "very relaxed" Leith pub-conversion, praised for its "delicate and succulent" cuisine; particularly given the high profile it enjoys in other guidebooks, though, it inspires mystifyingly little survey commentary.*

*/ **Details:** www.plumedhorse.co.uk; 9 pm; closed Mon & Sun; children: 5+.*

**The Pompadour**
**by Galvin**     **£80**
The Caldeonian, Princes St EH1 2AB
(0131) 222 8777
*London's celebrated Galvin brothers come to town, with the late-2012 re-launch of this magnificent hotel dining room, which has the potential to become the major destination; they also operate a cheaper brasserie (formula price £45). / **Details:** www.galvinrestaurants.com; 10 pm; closed Mon & Sun.*

**Restaurant Martin**
**Wishart**     **£92**    ❶❷❸
54 The Shore EH6 6RA   (0131) 553 3557
*"Phenomenal", "sophisticated" and "intensely-flavoured" cuisine, and "attentive but unobtrusive service" have established Martin Wishart's "refined" Leith flagship as Edinburgh's foremost culinary destination; "it's a perfect place for business", but most reporters find the ambience "relaxed" too. / **Details:** www.martin-wishart.co.uk; 9.30 pm; closed Mon & Sun; no trainers.*

**Rhubarb**
**Prestonfield Hotel**     **£74**    ❸④❶
Priestfield Rd EH16 5UT   (0131) 225 1333
*"OTT", "positively Gothic", a "candlelit delight"… – the dining room of this country house on the fringe of the city makes a "fantastic" destination for romance; at its best, the food is "excellent" too, but it can also be "unremarkable", and service veers from "attentive" to "overbearing".*
*/ **Details:** www.prestonfield.com; 10 pm, Fri & Sat 11 pm; children: 12+ at D, none after 7pm.*
**Accommodation:** *23 rooms, from £295.*

**The Shore**     **£42**    ❷❷❷
3-4 The Shore EH6 6QW   (0131) 553 5080
*"A very busy and buzzy Leith fish-restaurant"; by night, live folk music adds interest, and fans find it "a seriously sexy place to eat and drink!"*
*/ **Details:** www.fishersbistros.co.uk; 10.30 pm.*

**The Stockbridge**     **£50**    ❶
54 St Stephen's St EH3 5AL
(0131) 226 6766
*Intimate in scale, and darkly decorated, this "romantic" restaurant serves "fabulous French dishes with a Scottish influence", as well as some "interesting" and "fairly-priced" wines.*
*/ **Details:** www.thestockbridgerestaurant.co.uk; 9.30 pm; closed Mon, Tue-Fri D only, Sat & Sun open L & D; children: 18+ after 8 pm.*

**Sweet Melindas** **£42** ❷❷❸
11 Roseneath St EH9 1JH (0131) 229 7953
A "small neighbourhood fish restaurant which maintains its high standards" – all reports concur that this Marchmont spot is a "real find".
/ **Details:** www.sweetmelindas.co.uk; 10 pm; closed Mon L & Sun; children: Not allowed .

**The Tower**
**Museum of Scotland** **£57** ⑤④④
Chambers St EH1 1JF (0131) 225 3003
"Really disappointing" – too often the verdict on this "up-itself" room-with-a-Castle-view; even one of the (few) reporters who found it "very good all-round" says he "wouldn't go back, because of the eye-watering prices"!
/ **Details:** www.tower-restaurant.com; 11 pm.

**21212** **£92** ❷❷❷
3 Royal Ter EH7 5AB (0845) 222 1212
"An astonishing tour de force of surprises" helps make Paul Kitching's Calton townhouse a "brilliant" destination for most reporters; as in his Manchester days, however, this style is a touch "polarising" – a minority of reporters finds his food "too fussy"(or even "messy and confused").
/ **Details:** www.21212restaurant.co.uk; 9.30 pm; closed Mon & Sun; children: 5 +.
**Accommodation:** 4 rooms, from £250.

**Valvona & Crolla** **£37** ⑤⑤④
19 Elm Row EH7 4AA (0131) 556 6066
"Don't understand the hype!" – what a shame this once-excellent Italian café, attached to the famous deli and wine-importer, continues to "slide", seeming "ever more to be trading on tourists"; the food is "not even slightly exciting", and "overpriced" too.
/ **Details:** www.valvonacrolla.com; 11.30 pm, Sun 6 pm.

**Wedgwood** **£56** ❷❷❸
267 Canongate EH8 8BQ (0131) 558 8737
"A top-notch restaurant worth going back to"; Paul Wedgwood's "small establishment in the Old Town" almost invariably impresses with its "well-crafted" cuisine; lunchtime is a particular "bargain".
/ **Details:** www.wedgwoodtherestaurant.co.uk; 10 pm.

**The Witchery**
**by the Castle** **£61** ❸❷❶
Castlehill, The Royal Mile EH1 2NF
(0131) 225 5613
"A Gothic extravaganza on the Royal Mile"; this fantastically "characterful" destination is not just of note for its "stunning" (ultra-"romantic") setting, but also for its "magnificent" wine list; fans say the food is "inventive and satisfying"

too, though arguably it tastes best "on someone else's expense account".
/ **Details:** www.thewitchery.com; 11.30 pm.
**Accommodation:** 8 rooms, from £325.

**The Oak Room**
**Great Fosters Hotel** **£79** ❸❸❶
Stroude Rd TW20 9UR (01784) 433822
"Spectacular gardens" add much to the dining experience at this "stunning" and "historic" Elizabethan mansion; fans say "the cooking is fantastic compared to other country house hotels", but not everyone is wowed.
/ **Details:** www.greatfosters.co.uk; 9.15 pm; closed Sat L; no jeans or trainers; booking: max 12.
**Accommodation:** 44 rooms, from £155.

**The Butcher's Arms** **£55** ❶❷❷
Lime St GL19 4NX (01452) 840 381
James and Elizabeth Winter's "lovely" rural inn "still looks and feels like a pub", but the food is – on all accounts – nothing short of "superb"; note that service hours are limited, and that children under 10 are not admitted.
/ **Details:** www.thebutchersarms.net.

**Sangster's** **£59** ❶
51 High St KY9 1BZ (01333) 331001
Pity we don't get more reports on the Sangster family's intimate village-restaurant; it's still tipped, though, for "fantastic food of the highest quality", and "excellent" service too.
/ **Details:** www.sangsters.co.uk; 8.30 pm; no Amex; no jeans or shorts; children: 12+ at D.

**La Cachette** **£41** ❶
31 Huddersfield Rd HX5 9AH
(01422) 378833
"Always reliable" – a consistent theme of reports on Jonathan Nichol's "straightforward" Gallic restaurant and wine bar.
/ **Details:** www.lacachette-elland.com; 9.30 pm, Fri & Sat 10 pm; closed Sun; no Amex.

**The Bay Horse** **£44** ❶
Bay Horse Ln LA2 0HR (01524) 791204
Well-known locally, a rural inn tipped for its "well-presented" and "consistently enjoyable" cuisine. / **Details:** www.bayhorseinn.com; 9 pm; closed Mon & Sun D; no Amex.

---

ELSLACK, NORTH YORKSHIRE          5–1B

**The Tempest Arms**          £41   ❷❷❷
BD23 3AY   (01282) 842 450
*"Always very busy, and always a treat!" – this "quietly-located" but "brilliant" boozer is an addiction for many reporters, thanks to its "genuine, locally sourced grub" (served in "hearty" portions), and its "excellent range of real ales". / Details: www.tempestarms.co.uk; 9 pm, Fri & Sat 9.30 pm, Sun 7.30 pm.*
*Accommodation: 21 rooms, from £89.95.*

---

ELY, CAMBRIDGESHIRE          3–1B

**The Boathouse**          £41   ④④❸
5-5A, Annesdale CB7 4BN   (01353) 664388
*With its "excellent location by the river" ("lovely views"), this "down-to-earth" venue is, say fans, "a delight"; reports on food and service are rather up-and-down, but supporters claim "improvement, since the recent refurbishment". / Details: www.cambscuisine.com/theboathouse; 9 pm, Fri-Sat 9.30 pm.*

**Old Fire Engine House**          £42   ❸❸❸
25 St Mary's St CB7 4ER   (01353) 662582
*"Homely, relatively simple food" and "welcoming" service have maintained the appeal of this "idiosyncratic" institution, by the cathedral – "part restaurant, part art gallery" – for over 40 years; "it's the still the only place I know which offers seconds!" / Details: www.theoldfireenginehouse.co.uk; 9 pm; closed Sun D; no Amex.*

---

EMSWORTH, HAMPSHIRE          2–4D

**Fat Olives**          £46   ❶❶❸
30 South St PO10 7EH   (01243) 377914
*"Consistently brilliant" and "elegantly presented" dishes, with "unfaltering" service, have won a disproportionately large fan club for the Murphys' "delightful" fixture, "in an old fisherman's house, in a street down to the harbour"; "it's small, so book ahead". / Details: www.fatolives.co.uk; 9.15 pm; closed Mon & Sun; no Amex; children: 8+ D & L, unless Sat L.*

**36 on the Quay**          £77   ❸④④
47 South St PO10 7EG   (01243) 375592
*Ramon Farthing is a "pleasant and talented" chef, say (generally silver-haired) fans of this harbour-view dining room, and they find his cooking "memorable" too; the interior "has its quirks", though, and a disgruntled minority complain of "disappointing" cooking and "slow" service. / Details: www.36onthequay.co.uk; off A27 between Portsmouth & Chichester; 9 pm; closed Mon &*

*Sun; no Amex. Accommodation: 5 (plus cottage) rooms, from £100.*

---

EPSOM, SURREY          3–3B

**Le Raj**          £32   ❷④④
211 Fir Tree Rd KT17 3LB   (01737) 371371
*"Excellent" food, "attractively presented", has won a strong local reputation for this suburban curry house which, on almost all accounts, remains well worth seeking out. / Details: www.lerajrestaurant.co.uk; 11 pm; no jeans or trainers.*

---

ESHER, SURREY          3–3A

**Good Earth**          £49   ❷❸❸
14-18 High St KT10 9RT   (01372) 462489
*"Expensive, but the food is superb" – this "refined" Chinese restaurant has been in business for over three decades, and its "professional" approach and all-round attention to detail remain impressive. / Details: www.goodearthgroup.co.uk; 11.15 pm, Sun 10.45 pm; booking: max 12, Fri & Sat.*

---

EVERSHOT, DORSET          2–4B

**Summer Lodge**          £76   ❸④④
DT2 0JR   (01935) 482000
*This "traditional" ("read chintzy") country house hotel in Hardy Country is a "luxurious" destination, best known for its "simply stunning wine list"; most reports say a meal here is plain "wonderful", but service can be "slow", and the odd reporter finds the whole experience "over-rated". / Details: www.summerlodgehotel.co.uk; 12m NW of Dorchester on A37; 9.30 pm; no jeans or trainers; SRA-77%. Accommodation: 24 rooms, from £231.*

---

EVESHAM, WORCESTERSHIRE          2–1C

**Evesham Hotel**          £47   ④❷❸
Coopers Ln WR11 1DA   (01386) 765566
*John Jenkinson is as charmingly "bonkers" a host as you could ever hope to find, but it's his huge and bizarrely compiled wine list (from which the vintages of La Belle France are rigorously excluded) that really puts his hotel dining room on the culinary map – the eclectic food is "no more than OK". / Details: www.eveshamhotel.com; 9.30 pm; Max 16. Accommodation: 40 rooms, from £123.*

---

EXETER, DEVON          1–3D

**The Hour Glass Inn**          £35   ❷❶❷
21 Melbourne St. EX2 4AU
(01392) 258722
*"Off the beaten track, but really worth the*

*effort"; this "lovely and authentic old-style pub"
offers "a delightful modern take on French and
British cuisines", and the landlord is "unfailingly
welcoming" too; "book a table in the restaurant",
or you may have to eat in the "jostling" bar.*

**Michael Caines**
**Royal Clarence Hotel**       **£69**  ❸④④
Cathedral Yd EX1 1HD   (01392) 223 638
*"The food now rivals Gidleigh Park" (Chagford),
claims one of the fans of this "buzzy", tightly-
packed dining room, overlooking the cathedral;
it's rather more "unpredictable", though, and
service in particular can be "hit-and-miss".*
/ **Details:** www.michaelcaines.com; 9.45 pm; closed
Sun; booking essential. **Accommodation:** 53 rooms,
from £79.

**Simply Allium**       **£35**
1 London St GL7 4AH   (01285) 712200
*The Graham family's well-reputed village-
restaurant relaunches in late-2012 in a new
'Simply' guise – expect a mix of 'bistro, brasserie
and British classics'.*
/ **Details:** www.alliumfood.co.uk/restaurant.html;
9 pm; closed Mon, Tue L, Sun D; booking: max 10.

**Indaba On The Beach**       **£45**  ❶
Swanpool TR11 5BG   (01326) 311886
*Overlooking Swanpool Beach, a bright,
contemporary-style restaurant where the
attraction is "beautifully cooked fresh fish and
seafood".* / **Details:** www.indabafish.co.uk.

**Rick Stein's Fish & Chips**       **£36**  ❸④④
Discovery Quay TR11 3XA
(01841) 532700
*"Sample the Stein experience, without breaking
the bank", at the TV-chef's chippy, plus upstairs
seafood bar, by the National Maritime Museum;
fans – some of whom "approached it
sceptically" – think results "truly excellent", but
there are also critics for whom the food "lacks
flair".* / **Details:** www.rickstein.com; 9 pm; no Amex;
no booking.

**Wheelhouse**       **£36**  ❷❷❷
Upton Slip TR11 3DQ   (01326) 318050
*"Quite simply the best fresh seafood" – there
are few reports on this tucked-away, side-street
"gem", but those who've discovered it couldn't
rate it more highly.* / **Details:** 9 pm; D only, closed
Sun-Tue; no credit cards.

**Inn at Farnborough**       **£44**  ❶
OX17 1DZ   (01295) 690615
*A self-explanatory joint – a 200-year old stone
inn – which is tipped for its essentially traditional
cuisine which nonetheless incorporates some
"novel ideas".*
/ **Details:** www.innatfarnborough.co.uk; 9.30 pm.

**The Museum Inn**       **£46**  ❸❸④
DT11 8DE   (01725) 516261
*This "friendly" inn, which has always had a bit of
a name for its food, changed hands during the
survey year; the chef remains, however, and a
post-transfer reporter tips the cooking as "even
better" under the new régime.*
/ **Details:** www.museuminn.co.uk; off the A354;
9.30 pm, 9 pm Sun; no Amex. **Accommodation:** 8
rooms, from £110.

**Read's**       **£79**  ❷④❸
Macknade Manor, Canterbury Rd ME13 8XE
(01795) 535344
*"A gem of a location" (a Queen Anne house)
adds to the appeal of the Pitchfords' long-running
(est. 1977) local destination – "always an
occasion", say fans, thanks to its "high
standards" (with "lunch particularly good value");
it can also seem "dated", though, and takes
some flak for service "on auto-pilot".*
/ **Details:** www.reads.com; 9.30 pm; closed Mon &
Sun. **Accommodation:** 6 rooms, from £165.

**The Oyster & Otter**       **£40**  ❷❷❷
Livesey Branch Rd BB2 5DQ
(01254) 203 200
*"An excellent, reasonably-priced fish restaurant";
the owners are a family of fish-merchants, and
their expertise shines through in all aspects of
this "polished" operation.*
/ **Details:** www.oysterandotter.co.uk; 9 pm, Fri & Sat
10 pm, Sun 9 pm.

**General Tarleton**       **£47**  ❷❷❷
Boroughbridge Rd HG5 0PZ
(01423) 340284
*Better than ever after a recent internal re-jig, this
"comfortable" inn, with its "super" food and
"efficient" service, attracts only positive reports –
a pretty handy place to know about anywhere,
but especially just off the A1!*

/ **Details:** www.generaltarleton.co.uk; 2m from A1, J48 towards Knaresborough; 9.15 pm.
**Accommodation:** 14 rooms, from £129.

---

FITTLEWORTH, WEST SUSSEX     3–4A

**The Swan Inn**     £45   ⓣ
Lower St RH20 1EN   (01798) 865429
*"A classic old coaching inn", stylishly refurbished in recent times, and tipped as a notably "friendly" and "welcoming" all-rounder.*
/ **Details:** www.swaninnhotel.co.uk.

---

FLAUNDEN, HERTFORDSHIRE     3–2A

**The Bricklayers Arms**     £50   ❷❷❸
Hogpits Bottom HP3 0PH   (01442) 833322
*"In the middle of nowhere, but evidently a highly successful operation" – this "outstanding" (and "quite expensive") pub "maintains high standards" of "consistently good food", and notably "pleasant" service too.*
/ **Details:** www.bricklayersarms.com; J18 off the M25, past Chorleywood; 9.30 pm, Sun 8.30 pm.

---

FLETCHING, EAST SUSSEX     3–4B

**The Griffin Inn**     £45   ❸❷❷
TN22 3SS   (01825) 722890
*On most accounts, this "incredible fine-dining pub" remains "the all-round-perfect place for Sunday lunch in winter, or for a summer BBQ"; there is also a small minority, though, for whom it's "living on past glories".*
/ **Details:** www.thegriffininn.co.uk; off A272; 9.30 pm, Sun 2.30 pm. **Accommodation:** 13 rooms, from £85.

---

FOLKESTONE, KENT     3–4D

**Rocksalt**     £44   ❷❸❶
4-5 Fishmarket CT19 6AA   (01303) 212 070
*"A brilliant addition to the Kent coast"; ex-Ramsay lieutenant Mark Sargeant's "funky" newcomer doesn't just offer "stunning" views, a "hip bar" and "good looking" interior – his "confident" cooking of "locally-sourced seasonal dishes" is often "divine" too (even if "the London prices can shock the locals!").*
/ **Details:** www.rocksaltfolkestone.co.uk; 10 pm; closed Sun D. **Accommodation:** 4 rooms, from £75.

---

FONTHILL GIFFORD, WILTSHIRE     2–3C

**Beckford Arms**     £44   ❷❸❸
SP3 6PX   (01747) 870 385
*"Everything a classy gastropub should be"; it's run by an ex-Babington House team (and attracts "the sort of punters you'd expect").*

/ **Details:** www.thebeckfordarms.co.uk; 9.30 pm, Sun 9 pm. **Accommodation:** 8 rooms, from £75.

---

FOREST GREEN, SURREY     3–3A

**The Parrot Inn**     £41   ❸❸❷
RH5 5RZ   (01306) 621339
*In a "great location" in the Surrey Hills, the Gotto family's "very reliable" pub uses a lot of top-quality meat from the owners' farm – the results are "tasty", and "a cut above your usual pub fare".* / **Details:** www.theparrot.co.uk; 10 pm; closed Sun D; no Amex.

---

FOREST ROW, WEST SUSSEX     3–4B

**Roochi**     £30   ⓣ
9 Hartfield Rd RH18 5DN   (01342) 825 251
*"Very popular" nowadays, a (surprisingly) grand but "friendly" contemporary Indian, tipped for "great baltis", in particular.*
/ **Details:** www.roochi.co.uk.

---

FORT WILLIAM, HIGHLAND     9–3B

**Crannog**     £48   ⓣ
Town Pier PH33 6DB   (01397) 705589
*Few reports (and no 'raves') on this long-established restaurant on the pier; fans, though, still acclaim its "fantastically fresh seafood".*
/ **Details:** www.crannog.net; 9.30 pm; no Amex.

---

FOWEY, CORNWALL     1–4B

**The Q Restaurant**

**The Old Quay House**     £53   ⓣ
28 Fore St PL23 1AQ   (01726) 833302
*With a "fabulous" setting, with "wonderful views over the estuary", this well-reputed hotel looks set to strengthen its culinary reputation, after the recent arrival of Ashley Wright from 22 Mill Street (Chagford).*
/ **Details:** www.theoldquayhouse.com; 9 pm; closed Tue L; children: 8+ at D. **Accommodation:** 11 rooms, from £140.

**Sam's**     £42   ❹❸❷
20 Fore St PL23 1AQ   (01726) 832273
*"Arrive early" ("about 6!"), if you want a high-season table at this "quirky" but "ever-popular" seaside bistro; it's the "busy" but "relaxed" atmosphere, though, that's the main draw – the food is "robust, rather than memorable".*
/ **Details:** www.samsfowey.co.uk; 9.30 pm; no Amex; no booking.

| FRESSINGFIELD, SUFFOLK | 3–1D |
|---|---|

**The Fox & Goose**  £46  ❸❷❷
Church Rd  IP21 5PB  (01379) 586247
*"Super and imaginative food, served in a gorgeous setting" makes this large inn a "lovely" destination for most reporters; the occasional "disappointingly ordinary" meal has been recorded of late, though – hopefully not the beginning of a trend!*
/ **Details:** *www.foxandgoose.net; off A143; 8.45 pm, Fri & Sat 9 pm, Sun 8.15 pm; closed Mon; no Amex; children: 9+ for D.*

| FRILSHAM, BERKSHIRE | 2–2D |
|---|---|

**The Pot Kiln**  £48  ❷❷❸
RG18 0XX  (01635) 201366
*"Stunningly good game" is the "mainstay of the menu" at this "lovely pub, in the middle of nowhere", although "veggies are well-catered for" too. / **Details:** www.potkiln.org; between J12 and J13 of the M4; 9 pm, Sun 8.30 pm; closed Tue.*

| FRITHSDEN, HERTFORDSHIRE | 3–2A |
|---|---|

**The Alford Arms**  £45  ❷❷❷
HP1 3DD  (01442) 864480
*"A lovely gastropub in a peaceful, rural setting", with "a deserved reputation for excellent British cooking", and a "genuinely friendly" style – it continues to attract a broad fan club.*
/ **Details:** *www.alfordarmsfrithsden.co.uk; near Ashridge College and vineyard; 9.30 pm, Fri & Sat 10 pm; booking: max 12.*

| FROXFIELD, WILTSHIRE | 2–2C |
|---|---|

**The Palm**  £36  ❸❷❸
Bath Rd  SN8 3HT  (01672) 871 818
*"The bling is fabulous!", at this grand Indian, just off the M4, which is recommended by fans for its "delicious" cooking; the occasional reporter this year, however, was not quite sure quality was up to the prices. / **Details:** www.thepalmindian.com.*

| GATESHEAD, TYNE AND WEAR | 8–2B |
|---|---|

**Raval**  £42  ❷❷④
Church St, Gateshead Quays  NE8 2AT
(0191) 4771700
*"A real odd-ball, given where it's located", this "inventive" Indian is praised by all reporters for its "delicious regional food"; even its greatest fans, though, may query "how they get by charging such high prices".*
/ **Details:** *www.ravalrestaurant.com; 11 pm; D only, closed Sun; no shorts.*

| GERRARDS CROSS, BUCKINGHAMSHIRE 3–3A | |
|---|---|

**Apple Tree**  £45  ❶
Oxford Rd  SL9 7AH  (01753) 887335
*A popular local gastropub, tipped for "good and consistent food", and a "friendly, happy atmosphere".*
/ **Details:** *www.appletreegerrardscross.co.uk; 10 pm.*

**Indigo Bar And Grill**  £34  ❶
Indigo Hs, Oxford Rd  SL9 7AL
(01753) 883100
*A town-centre Indian/pan-Asian which attracts consistently positive reports; it's especially tipped, though, for its "stunningly fresh grills".*
/ **Details:** *www.indigobarandgrill.co.uk.*

**Maliks**  £43  ❶❸❸
14 Oak End Way  SL9 8BR  (01753) 880888
*"Quite pricey, but well worth it", this "high-quality" Indian – spin-off from the famous Cookham establishment of the same name – is "several notches above your standard curry house". / **Details:** www.maliks.co.uk; 10.45 pm.*

**Three Oaks**  £46  ❶
Austenwood Ln  SL9 8NL  (01753) 899 016
*"Just what the area needed" – this "smart" new gastropub is a "friendly" sort of destination, tipped for the "consistently high standards" of its "interesting" and "varied" English menu.*
/ **Details:** *www.thethreeoaksgx.co.uk.*

| GLASGOW, CITY OF GLASGOW | 9–4C |
|---|---|

**Café Gandolfi**  £40  ④❷❶
64 Albion St  G1 1NY  (0141) 552 6813
*"The chattering classes of Glasgow continue to pack out" this "soothing" but superbly characterful Merchant City café (with bar above); the "haggis, neeps and tatties" are particularly good, and the wine list "'could keep you enthralled for hours".*
/ **Details:** *www.cafegandolfi.com; 11 pm; no booking, Sat.*

**Crabshakk**  £42  ❷❷❷
Finnestone  G3 8TD  (0141) 334 6127
*"It feels like a caff", but this "cramped, funky and tiny" three-year-old is one of the city's hottest spots, thanks to its "ravishing lobster, langoustines, clams, squid…"; "booking is essential" (but "you can drop in for a seat at the bar"). / **Details:** www.crabshakk.com; 12 am; closed Mon & Sun D; no Amex.*

Stravaigin

Ubiquitous Chip

Cafe Gandolfi

**Gamba** £57 ❶❷❸
225a West George St  G2 2ND
(0141) 572 0899
*"Fish to die for!"; some fans claim Derek
Marshall's "relaxed" city-centre basement is
"even better than Sheekey's" – even if it lacks
the glamour of its London rival, all reports
confirm that the food here is simply "excellent".
/ Details: www.gamba.co.uk; 10 pm; closed Sun L.*

**Mother India** £36 ❶❸❸
28 Westminster Ter  G3 7RU  (0141) 221
1663
*"Indian tapas-size dishes" ("not the usual fare at
all") come "freshly cooked " and with "superb
flavours" at this "top-value" spot, near the
university; the setting is "cramped", though, and
"it can be hard to get attention at busy times".
/ Details: www.motherindiaglasgow.co.uk; 10.30 pm,
Fri & Sat 11 pm, Sun 10 pm; Mon-Thu D only, Fri-Sun
open L & D.*

**La Parmigiana** £52 ⓣ
447 Great Western Rd  G12 8HH
(0141) 334 0686
*Rather fewer reports than we'd like, but this
"lovely traditional Italian" of long standing is
tipped as a "wonderful" destination, with "great
food, service and ambience"; it's "always busy",
says one fan, "and rightly so".
/ Details: www.laparmigiana.co.uk; 10 pm, Sun 6 pm.*

**Rogano** £63 ❹❷❶
11 Exchange Pl  G1 3AN  (0141) 248 4055
*A "faded" but still "stunning" Art Deco
"stalwart" of the Merchant City, where the
interior is "lovely" and the service generally
"accommodating"; fans say the seafood-led
cuisine is "interesting" too, but critics still discern
an establishment that is "resting on its laurels".
/ Details: www.roganoglasgow.com; 10.30 pm.*

**Stravaigin** £44 ❷❷❷
28 Gibson St  G12 8NX  (0141) 334 2665
*"One of Glasgow's finest relaxed dining
establishments" – Colin Clydesdale & Carol
Wright's "casual bar (upstairs) and more formal
(basement) dining room", in the West End, has a
big name locally for its "ever-changing" menu,
and in particular for its "lazy Sunday brunch".
/ Details: www.stravaigin.com; 11 pm; closed weekday
L.*

**Two Fat Ladies** £48 ❷❷❸
118a, Blythswood St  G2 4EG
(0141) 847 0088
*You can't really go wrong with the 'Two Fat
Ladies' franchise, and this city-centre outpost –
just like the original, at 88 Dumbarton Road*

G11, tel 0141 339 1944 – is a "small but
perfectly-formed" operation, where "beautifully-
cooked" fish is the highlight.
*/ Details: www.twofatladiesrestaurant.com; 10 pm,
Fri & Sat 11 pm, Sun 9 pm.*

**Two Fat Ladies
at The Buttery** £57 ❷❷❷
652 Argyle St  G3 8UF  (0141) 221 8188
*The locale (by the SECC) is "dingy", but you find
a "haven of good cheer" when you step inside
this "timeless" institution, whose "wonderful"
Victorian premises have been run by this local
seafood mini-chain in recent years; the food is
often very good too.
/ Details: www.twofatladiesrestaurant.com; 10 pm,
Sun 9 pm.*

**Ubiquitous Chip** £58 ❷❷❷
12 Ashton Ln  G12 8SJ  (0141) 334 5007
*In a period of renewal, it seems, after the death
of its founder Ronnie Clydesdale (and succession
by son, Colin), this gorgeous Glasgow "institution"
(est. 1971) is again delivering "great Scottish
food" and "fantastic" service; the wine list is still
"sensational" too (as is the "fabulous selection of
malts"). / Details: www.ubiquitouschip.co.uk; 11 pm.*

**La Luna** £46 ❷❷❸
10-14 Wharf St  GU7 1NN
(01483) 414155
*"Still prospering in hard times", this "classy and
genuine" Italian – regarded as something of an
"oasis" locally – offers "classic" fare, and
maintains an impressive following; it's quite a
"pricey" destination, though, and portions can
seem on the small side.
/ Details: www.lalunarestaurant.co.uk; 10 pm;
no Amex.*

**The Taverners** £37 ❸❷❸
High St  PO38 3HZ  (01983) 840 707
*A homely pub in a tourist-trail village that's
consistently well-rated for its "constantly
changing seasonal menu, always with a few
surprises and novelties".
/ Details: www.thetavernersgodshill.co.uk.*

**Fox and Hounds** £50 ⓣ
YO21 3RX  (01947) 893372
*"Fantastic local ingredients put together in new
and exciting ways" help win unanimous rave
reviews for Jason Davies's "unpretentious" but
"lovely" establishment, "lost down a tiny country*

lane".
/ **Details:** www.foxandhoundsgoldsborough.co.uk;
8.30 pm; D only, closed Sun-Tue; no Amex.

---

GORING-ON-THAMES, BERKSHIRE    2–2D

**Leatherne Bottel**    £54    ❷❷❶
Bridleway  RG8 0HS   (01491) 872667
"Perfect on a summer's day, with a terrace table
and a river-view" – this "magically-located"
Thames-side venue is a particular "romantic"
favourite; "affordable" lunches aside, it can be
"rather pricey" ("I've never seen so many Chablis
on a wine list"), but standards generally live up.
/ **Details:** www.leathernebottel.co.uk; 9 pm; closed
Sun D; children: 10+ for D.

**Pierreponts**    £32    ❷❸❷
High St  RG9 9AB   (01491) 874 464
"Small but perfectly formed", this "superb village
café", by the bridge, has a surprisingly big
following among reporters – all praise its
"freshly-made everything", and in particular the
"lovely" cakes. / **Details:** 2.30 pm; L only, closed
Sat & Sun; no Amex.

---

GRASMERE, CUMBRIA    7–3D

**The Jumble Room**    £46    ❷❷❷
Langdale Rd  LA22 9SU   (01539) 435188
"Tiny, but really inviting, friendly and casual" –
this "wackily-decorated" fifteen-year-old makes a
great find in the Lakes, combining its
"idiosyncratic" style with some "innovative and
delicious" modern cuisine.
/ **Details:** www.thejumbleroom.co.uk; 9.30 pm; closed
Mon, Tue, Wed L & Thu L. **Accommodation:** 3
rooms, from £180.

---

GRASSINGTON, NORTH YORKSHIRE    8–4B

**The Grassington House
Hotel**    £41    ❶❷❸
5 The Sq  BD23 5AQ   (01756) 752406
In the heart of a Dales village, the Rudden
family's "well-run" establishment offers
"innovative" food, a "sensibly-priced" wine list
and "friendly service" – it inspires a good
number of reports, all of them very positive.
/ **Details:** www.grassingtonhousehotel.co.uk; 9.30pm
(Mo-Sa) 7.30pm (Su). **Accommodation:** 7 rooms,
from £85.

---

GREAT DUNMOW, ESSEX    3–2C

**The Starr**    £52    ❶
Market Pl  CM6 1AX   (01371) 874321
Praise is somewhat qualified for this large, town-
centre inn-conversion of over 30 years' standing;
it's tipped, though, as "not bad for an area bereft
of decent places" – perhaps new ownership in

2012 will return it to its former glories.
/ **Details:** www.the-starr.co.uk; 8m E of M11, J8 on
A120; 9.30 pm; closed Mon & Sun D; no Amex.
**Accommodation:** 8 rooms, from £45.

---

GREAT GONERBY, LINCOLNSHIRE    5–3D

**Harry's Place**    £80    ❷❶④
17 High St  NG31 8JS   (01476) 561780
"The world's smallest and best" – Harry and
Caroline Hallam's off-beat 10-seater has
occupied their front room for a quarter of a
century; the choice is "narrow" but his
"wonderful" cooking and her "real attention"
consistently deliver "evenings to remember";
even fans, though, note it's "expensive".
/ **Details:** on B1174 1m N of Grantham; 9.30 pm;
closed Mon & Sun; no Amex; booking essential; children:
5+.

---

GREAT LONGSTONE, DERBYSHIRE    5–2C

**The White Lion**    £37    ❶
Main St  DE45 1TA   (01629) 640252
"More gastro- than pub" nowadays, this family-
run inn is tipped by all reporters as offering a
"very comfortable dining experience" (and in an
area "not over-provided with good restaurants"
either). / **Details:** www.whiteliongreatlongstone.co.uk;
9 pm, Sun 8 pm; no Amex.

---

GREAT MILTON, OXFORDSHIRE    2–2D

**Le Manoir aux
Quat' Saisons**    £166    ❶❶❷
Church Rd  OX44 7PD   (01844) 278881
"Totally exceptional in every way (including the
prices)", Raymond Blanc's "gorgeous" country
retreat ("arrive early to wander around the
gardens") delivers what many reporters consider
"the UK's finest dining experience" – with such
"attention to detail", it's "THE destination for
that special occasion". / **Details:** www.manoir.com;
from M40, J7 take A329 towards Wallingford; 9.15 pm;
booking: max 12; SRA-83%. **Accommodation:** 32
rooms, from £550.

---

GREAT MISSENDEN, BUCKINGHAMSHIRE 3–2A

**The Nags Head**    £47    ❶
London Rd  HP16 0DG   (01494) 862200
A "super pub, with a superb beer garden", tipped
for its "interesting and varied menu, that's well
prepared and presented".
/ **Details:** www.nagsheadbucks.com; off the A413;
9.30 pm, Sun 8.30 pm. **Accommodation:** 5 rooms,
from £95.

**GRESFORD, WREXHAM**                    5–3A

**Pant-yr-Ochain**          £40   ❸❷❶
Old Wrexham Rd  LL12 8TY
(01978) 853525
*"Rather like having your own country club"; this
"atmospheric" former manor house, in its own
grounds (with lake!), is nowadays a "very
comfortable" and "friendly" gastropub, offering
an "ever-changing" menu which almost
invariably satisfies.*
*/ Details: www.brunningandprice.co.uk/pantyrochain;
1m N of Wrexham; 9.30 pm, Sun 9 pm.*

**GRINDLETON, LANCASHIRE**              5–1B

**The Duke Of York Inn**    £40   ❷❷❸
Brow Top  BB7 4QR   (01200) 441266
*"Great cooking, great value"; all reports confirm
that this "consistent" country inn is a major local
favourite, thanks not least to its "varied seasonal
menus, beautifully executed".*
*/ Details: www.dukeofyorkgrindleton.com; 9 pm, Sun
7.30 pm; closed Mon.*

**GRINSHILL, SHROPSHIRE**               5–3A

**The Inn at Grinshill**    £50   ❶
The High St  SY4 3BL   (01939) 220410
*A pretty inn, in a smart village, attracting high
praise (albeit from a small number of reporters)
for its "well-presented" and "good-value" cuisine
– "either in the 'fine-dining' room or in the much
more rustic pub".*
*/ Details: www.theinnatgrinshill.co.uk; 9.30 pm; closed
Mon & Sun D; no Amex.* **Accommodation:** *6
rooms, from £90.*

**GUERNSEY, CHANNEL ISLANDS**

**Da Nello**              £43   ❷❶❸
46 Lower Pollet St  GY1 1WF
(01481) 721552
*A real "gem", this '70s Italian, in St Peter Port,
has stood up to the passing of the years much
better than most of its mainland peers; it
remains a "rock-solid performer".*
*/ Details: www.danello.gg; 10 pm.*

**Le Petit Bistro**       £44   ❷❹❶
56 Le Pollet  GY1 1WF   (01481) 725055
*"Cramped" and "intimate", this "popular local
French bistro", in St Peter Port, offers "authentic"
cuisine which impresses all reporters with its
"innovation" and "variety".*
*/ Details: www.petitbistro.co.uk; 10 pm, 10.30 pm
Fri & Sat; closed Sun.*

**GUILDFORD, SURREY**                   3–3A

**Cau**                   £44   ❸❹❸
274 High St  GU1 3JL   (01483) 459777
*"Decent steak comes to Surrey!"; the backers of
the Gaucho chain are behind this new
Argentinian 'concept', and the outcome is "much
as you'd expect, given the parentage"; all reports
agree that it offers "enjoyable casual dining, if a
little bit noisy". / Details: www.caurestaurants.com;
11 pm, Sun 10.30 pm.*

**Rumwong**               £41   ❷❸❸
18-20 London Rd  GU1 2AF
(01483) 536092
*This "classy" spot (est. 1978) "hits the mark
every time" for those in search of "great and
affordable" Thai scoff; beware Saturday nights,
though – "frantic!" / Details: www.rumwong.co.uk;
10.30 pm; closed Mon; no Amex.*

**The Thai Terrace**      £38   ❷❷❷
Castle Car Pk, Sydenham Rd  GU1 3RW
(01483) 503350
*OK, it's "on top of a multi-story car park", but
this "well-run" Thai boasts "great views over the
skyline"; it "always seems to be full" (and can
feel "conveyor-belt-like"), but most reports
acclaim its "high-class" cooking and overall
"good value". / Details: 10.30 pm; closed Sun;
no Amex.*

**GULLANE, EAST LOTHIAN**               9–4D

**La Potinière**          £51   ❶
Main St  EH31 2AA   (01620) 843214
*Not as many reports as we would like on Keith
Marley and Mary Runciman's ambitious small
restaurant (run by them for 10 years, but
originally est. 1975); it's still tipped, though, for
for food that's not just of "high quality", but
"always fascinating" too.*
*/ Details: www.la-potiniere.co.uk; 20m E of
Edinburgh, off A198; 8.30 pm; closed Mon, Tue &
Sun D; no jeans or trainers; booking essential.*

**GULWORTHY, DEVON**                    1–3C

**Horn of Plenty**        £68   ❹❷❷
PL19 8JD   (01822) 832528
*Few, and up-and-down, reports on this once-
famous restaurant, in a "gorgeous" setting
overlooking the Tamar Valley; fans do acclaim
Scott Patton's "fantastic" food, but there are too
many "disappointing" reports to make it a safe
recommendation.*
*/ Details: www.thehornofplenty.co.uk; 3m W of
Tavistock on A390; 8.45 pm; no jeans or trainers.*
**Accommodation:** *10 rooms, from £125.*

---

HALE, CHESHIRE                    5–2B

**Earle**                    **£46**    **❸❷❸**
4 Cecil Rd  WA15 9PA   (0161) 929 8869
*"A great neighbourhood eatery"; this "buzzing" suburban establishment may offer a menu that sounds rather "unadventurous", but it has many fans who are impressed by the "presentation and flavours" of the cuisine.*
/ **Details:** *www.earlerestaurant.co.uk; 9.30 pm, Sun 8 pm; closed Mon L.*

---

HALIFAX, WEST YORKSHIRE          5–1C

**Shibden Mill Inn**         **£47**    **T**
Shibden Mill Fold  HX3 7UL
(01422) 365840
*Tipped for its "ambitious and well-executed pub food", this "beautifully-located" inn is a "cosy" spot in winter, and has "nice gardens" for the summer too.* / **Details:** *www.shibdenmillinn.com; off the A58, Leeds/Bradford road; 9.15 pm, Sun 7.30 pm.*
**Accommodation:** *11 rooms, from £105.*

---

HAMBLETON, RUTLAND              5–4D

**Finch's Arms**             **£37**    **④④❷**
Oakham Rd  LE15 8TL   (01572) 756575
*A "splendid place for lunch, overlooking Rutland Water", this stylishly rustic inn, with its large terrace, is a particular hit in summer; it has a fair few critics, however, who find it "overpriced" and "pretentious".* / **Details:** *www.finchsarms.co.uk; 9.30 pm, Sun 8 pm.* **Accommodation:** *10 rooms, from £100.*

**Hambleton Hall**           **£89**    **❶❷❷**
LE15 8TH   (01572) 756991
*It's "perhaps a little traditional for some tastes", but otherwise it's hard to fault Tim Hart's "fabulous" country house hotel, overlooking Rutland Water – Aaron Patterson's "outstanding", "classical" food and the "welcoming" service are simply, for many reporters, "as good as it gets".*
/ **Details:** *www.hambletonhall.com; near Rutland Water; 9.30 pm; SRA-54%.* **Accommodation:** *17 rooms, from £265.*

---

HARDWICK, CAMBRIDGESHIRE        3–1B

**The Blue Lion**            **£43**    **T**
74 Main St  CB23 7QU   (01954) 210328
*Under new management, a pub that's already being tipped for its "extremely good" food (with some "particularly interesting" vegetarian options); "at heart, though, it remains a village pub, and doesn't mind muddy walkers and dogs pitching up for lunch".*

/ **Details:** *www.bluelionhardwick.co.uk; Mon-Thu 9 pm, Fri & Sat 9.30, Sun 8.00; no Amex.*

---

HAROME, NORTH YORKSHIRE         8–4C

**The Pheasant Hotel**       **£52**    **❸❷❸**
YO62 5JG   (01439) 771241
*"The only reason to eat here is if the Star is full"; it's not that there's anything particularly wrong with this "more austere" inn, just that it is "suicidally close" to its parent establishment, and offers food that's "very similar, but just a bit less interesting!"* / **Details:** *www.thepheasanthotel.com; 9 pm; no Amex; Essential for weekends.*
**Accommodation:** *14 rooms, from £150.*

**The Star Inn**             **£60**    **❷❷❷**
YO62 5JE   (01439) 770397
*This is "Britain's best gastropub", say fans of this "beautiful and atmospheric" inn, where chef/patron Andrew Pern uses local ingredients to simply "brilliant" effect; its ratings do fluctuate now and again though, and a few reporters this year found it "disappointing, after all the hype".*
/ **Details:** *www.thestaratharome.co.uk; 3m SE of Helmsley off A170; 9.30 pm, Sun 6 pm; closed Mon L & Sun D; no Amex.* **Accommodation:** *8 rooms, from £150.*

---

HARROGATE, NORTH YORKSHIRE      5–1C

**Bettys**                   **£45**    **❸❷❷**
1 Parliament St  HG1 2QU   (01423) 814070
*"Better than the Ritz!"; for "an elegant afternoon tea" in particular, this famous institution remains "something extra-special", and it's also "a winner for breakfast, lunch or dinner"; it's in the good-but-pricey category, however, and be prepared to "queue around the block".*
/ **Details:** *www.bettysandtaylors.co.uk; 9 pm; no Amex; no booking.*

**Drum & Monkey**            **£44**    **❸❸❸**
5 Montpellier Gdns  HG1 2TF
(01423) 502650
*"Back to its old high standards", say fans, this quirky institution is "a real favourite for fish and seafood", which "never disappoints"; for the occasional critic, though, the food "somehow still lacks the 'edge' it used to have".*
/ **Details:** *www.drumandmonkey.co.uk; 10 pm; closed Sun D; no Amex; booking: max 10.*

**Graveley's Fish & Chip
Restaurant**                 **£29**    **❶❷❸**
8-12 Cheltenham Pde  HG1 1DB
(01423) 507093
*"We've tried all the 'names' for fish 'n' chips, and this is the best!" – this "friendly" spot doesn't inspire many reports, but all rate it as*

"outstanding".
/ **Details:** www.graveleysofharrogate.com; 9 pm, Fri & Sat 10 pm, Sun 8 pm.

**Hotel du Vin et Bistro** £46 ④❷❸
Prospect Pl HG1 1LB (01423) 856800
"You never know if it's going to be on form or not!"; sadly, the cooking is the most random element at this outpost of the hotel-and-bistro chain – the "fantastic" wine list ("more a wine book") and "stylish" ambience both seem pretty reliable! / **Details:** www.hotelduvin.com; 9.45 pm, Fri & Sat 10 pm. **Accommodation:** 48 rooms, from £110.

**Mirabelles** £47 ❷❷❸
28a, Swan Rd HG1 2SE (01423) 565551
"Yorkshire meets Alsace", at this recent Gallic arrival, where – even with "one or two rough edges" – chef Lionel Strub's "absolutely beautiful" dishes have instantly won an enthusiastic following. / **Details:** closed Mon & Sun.

**Orchid** £42 ❷❸❸
28 Swan Rd HG1 2SE (01423) 560425
"Absolutely sensational" pan-Asian food ensures this "first-class" hotel-restaurant is very "popular" – "it's not a cheap night out, but you still need to book way in advance"; "fantastic-value Sunday buffet".
/ **Details:** www.orchidrestaurant.co.uk; 10 pm; closed Sat L. **Accommodation:** 28 rooms, from £115.

**Quantro** £46 ❶
3 Royal Pde HG1 2SZ (01423) 503034
"Stylish" and "friendly", this "consistently good" restaurant, near Valley Gardens, is primarily tipped for its "astoundingly good" set lunch menu. / **Details:** www.quantro.co.uk; 10 pm, Sat 10.30 pm; closed Sun; children: no under 4's in evening.

**Sasso** £42 ④④❸
8-10 Princes Sq HG1 1LX (01423) 508 838
This is "a real gem", say fans of this family-run town-centre spot, which offers a "contemporary twist on traditional Italian cuisine" (including some "fine pasta dishes"); sterner critics, though, would rate it somewhere closer to "OK".
/ **Details:** www.sassorestaurant.co.uk.

**Sukhothai** £37 ❸❸❸
17-19 Cheltenham Pde HG1 1DD (01423) 500 869
"Easily the best of the local Thais, and there are plenty to choose from!" – this "slightly glitzy" establishment pleases most reporters, and hard-core fans insist the fare is truly "awesome".
/ **Details:** www.thaifood4u.co.uk; 11 pm; Mon-Thu D only, Fri-Sun open L & D.

**Van Zeller** £65 ❷❷④
8 Montpellier St HG1 2TQ (01423) 508762
"Interesting food, presented with precision" makes Tom Van Zeller's "fantastic" three-year-old – backed by Pied à Terre owner David Moore – "the best in Harrogate"; the setting is "not that atmospheric", but the food is "impressively imaginative".
/ **Details:** www.vanzellerrestaurants.co.uk; 9.45 pm; closed Mon; booking advised.

**Incanto**
**The Old Post Office** £46 ❷❸❸
41 High St, Harrow On The Hill HA1 3HT (020) 8426 6767
Generally rated a "very good Italian", this "perennial favourite" has occasionally seemed a touch "uneven" in recent times; let's hope that the reporter who says "the new chef is improving the food" has it right.
/ **Details:** www.incanto.co.uk; 10.30 pm; closed Mon & Sun D; SRA-59%.

**Old Etonian** £39 ④❸❸
38 High St, Harrow On The Hill HA1 3LL (020) 8422 8482
"Forty years under the same owner, and offering a welcome step back in time!" – this "very '70s" French restaurant still generally pleases; "sit on the terrace – you get a great view of the Chilterns". / **Details:** www.oldetonian.com; 10.30 pm; closed Sat L & Sun D.
**Accommodation:** 13 rooms, from £70.

**The Gray Ox Inn** £40 ❷❸❷
15 Hartshead Ln WF15 8AL (01274) 872845
"A perfect Yorkshire pub" – nowadays "more of a restaurant" – with a "lovely, olde-worlde" interior, where the "traditional food with a modern twist" is of "consistent high quality", and "well presented" too.
/ **Details:** www.grayoxinn.co.uk/.

**The Pier at Harwich** £54 ④④❸
The Quay CO12 3HH (01255) 241212
"In an idyllic situation, steps from the water", the Milsom family's hotel offers a lively ground floor fish 'n' chip bistro, and a grander restaurant upstairs; critics can find the latter "over-rated".
/ **Details:** www.milsomhotels.com; 9.30 pm, Sat 10 pm; no jeans. **Accommodation:** 14 rooms, from £117.

| HASSOP, DERBYSHIRE | 5–2C |
|---|---|

**Hassop Hall**   £ 49   ❷❶❷
DE45 1NS   (01629) 640488
"A top Peaks destination for a romantic dinner";
the style of the cuisine may seem a little "retro",
but prices are "keen" and no one doubts the
Chapman family's welcome to their "elegant"
and "lovely" country house hotel is "unfailing".
/ **Details:** www.hassophall.co.uk; on the B6001
Bakewell - Hathersage Road, Junction 29 of M1; 9 pm;
closed Mon L, Sat L & Sun D. **Accommodation:** 13
rooms, from £95.

| HASTINGS, EAST SUSSEX | 3–4C |
|---|---|

**Jali Chatsworth Hotel**   £ 33   ❶
Carlisle Parade   TN34 1JG   (01424) 457300
"A different Indian experience" – the dining
room of this seafront hotel is tipped for "quality
ingredients and cooking", and most particularly
for "the best curry for miles around".
/ **Details:** www.jalirestaurant.co.uk.

**The Mermaid Café**   £ 24   ❷❸❸
2 Rock-a-Nore Rd   TN34 3DW
(01424) 438100
Looking for "the best fish 'n' chips in Hastings"?
– this locally-celebrated spot is reporters' top tip
hereabouts. / **Details:** 7.30 pm; no credit cards;
no booking.

**Webbe's Rock-a-Nore**   £ 41   ❸❸❸
1 Rock-a-Nore Rd   TN34 3DW
(01424) 721650
Part of Paul Webbe's small local chain – this
harbour-side three-year-old "puts an emphasis
on local fish from an MSC-certified fishery"; one
or two reporters feel "it could be better", but
most applaud its "good treatment of excellent
ingredients".
/ **Details:** www.webbesrestaurants.co.uk; 9.30 pm.

| HATFIELD PEVEREL, ESSEX | 3–2C |
|---|---|

**The Blue Strawberry**   £ 46   ❸❸❸
The St   CM3 2DW   (01245) 381333
This village-restaurant of nearly two decades'
standing remains a hot spot locally; most
reporters tip the food as of "top quality", though
doubters can find it a touch "unadventurous".
/ **Details:** www.bluestrawberrybistro.co.uk; 3m E of
Chelmsford; 10 pm; closed Sun D.

| HAWKEDON, SUFFOLK | 3–1C |
|---|---|

**The Queen's Head**   £ 40   ❷❷❷
Rede Rd   IP29 4NN   (01284) 789 218
A "quintessential English pub", in "a beautiful
location overlooking the rolling hills of west

Suffolk" – all reports attest to its "fantastic"
grub, and its "friendly" atmosphere too.
/ **Details:** www.hawkedonqueen.co.uk.

| HAWKHURST, KENT | 3–4C |
|---|---|

**The Great House**   £ 42   ❹❷❷
Gills Grn   TN18 5EJ   (01580) 753119
"An old Wealden house" provides the
"characterful" setting for this "busy" gastropub;
it's no great foodie haunt, but it offers a "good
variety" of dishes that's "regularly updated".
/ **Details:** www.elitepubs.com/the_greathouse;
9.30 pm; no Amex.

| HAWORTH, WEST YORKSHIRE | 5–1C |
|---|---|

**Weaver's**   £ 41   ❷❷❷
15 West Ln   BD22 8DU   (01535) 643822
"The food was simple and delicious, and the
service charm itself" – typical of the praise for
the Rushworth family's restaurant-with-rooms, by
the Brontë Parsonage Museum, which is
currently on quite a 'high'.
/ **Details:** www.weaversmallhotel.co.uk; 1.5m W on
B6142 from A629, near Parsonage; 8.30 pm; closed
Mon, Sat L & Sun; children: 5+ on Sat.
**Accommodation:** 3 rooms, from £110.

| HAYWARDS HEATH, WEST SUSSEX | 3–4B |
|---|---|

**Jeremy's at Borde Hill**   £ 52   ❶❷❷
Balcombe Rd   RH16 1XP   (01444) 441102
"Consistently a delight"; Jeremy Ashpool's "highly
professional" rural destination "always offers a
fantastic gastronomic experience", from its "ever-
changing" menu; "if you're going for lunch,
combine with a visit to the fine gardens next
door" (overlooked in summer by the restaurant's
terrace). / **Details:** www.jeremysrestaurant.com; Exit
10A from the A23; 10 pm; closed Mon & Sun D;
no Amex.

| HEATON, TYNE AND WEAR | 8–2B |
|---|---|

**Sky Apple Cafe**   £ 26   ❷❹❹
182 Heaton Rd   NE6 5HP   (01912) 092571
A "quirky" spot offering "very good vegetarian
food, beautifully presented"; it can sometimes
seem a touch "pricey", though and service is
"not always especially welcoming".
/ **Details:** www.skyapple.co.uk; 10 pm; closed Sun;
no credit cards.

| HEBDEN BRIDGE, WEST YORKSHIRE | 5–1C |
|---|---|

**Rim Nam**   £ 30   ❶
New Rd, Butlers Whf   HX7 8AD
(01422) 846 888
"Well worth an hour's drive from Manchester",
says a hard-core supporter – this rather "noisy"

restaurant is tipped, albeit by a rather small fan club, as offering "the best Thai food west of the Pennines!"
/ **Details:** www.rimnamthairestaurant.co.uk; midnight; D only, closed Mon.

**The Feathers Inn** £42 ❶❷④
Hedley-on-the-Hill NE43 7SW
(01661) 843607
"Good honest food well-sourced and well-cooked!" – reporters give a massive thumbs-up to this "fabulous" but "unpretentious" old village pub; the word is out, though – it can be "very busy" at peak times.
/ **Details:** www.thefeathers.net; 8.30 pm; closed Mon & Sun D; no Amex.

**Black Swan** £60 ❶
Market Pl YO62 5BJ (01439) 770466
An 'historic inn-turned-boutique hotel' – recently returned to individual ownership; it is perhaps not yet a gastronomic destination in itself, but is tipped for food that's "always consistent".
/ **Details:** www.blackswan-helmsley.co.uk; 9.30 pm.
**Accommodation:** 45 rooms, from £130.

**Feversham Arms** £66 ❷❸❸
1-8 High St YO62 5AG (01439) 770766
"A delightful inn with excellent food" (and a swimming pool – open air! – too); tip for top enjoyment? – "look out for one of their stay-and-eat deals on the web, as otherwise it can seem a bit pricey". / **Details:** www.fevershamarmshotel.com; 9.30 pm; no trainers; children: 12+ after 8 pm.
**Accommodation:** 33 rooms, from £260.

**The Cock** £48 ❸❸❸
47 High St PE28 9BJ (01480) 463609
Not far from the A1, this "great country pub", by the River Ouse, is a "characterful" sort of place, hailed as a "haven for the stressed traveller".
/ **Details:** www.thecockhemingford.co.uk; off the A14; follow signs to the river; 9 pm, Fri & Sat 9.30 pm, Sun 8.30 pm; children: 5+ at D.

**Hotel du Vin et Bistro** £51 ❶
New St RG9 2BP (01491) 848400
This well-located outpost of the Gallic hotel-and-bistro chain is generally tipped as offering an "enjoyable" dining experience (even if there is a

suspicion in some quarters that "it rather trades on the group's name").
/ **Details:** www.hotelduvin.com; 10 pm, Fri & Sat 10.30 pm. **Accommodation:** 43 rooms, from £110.

**Luscombes at the Golden Ball** £59 ④❸❸
Lower Assendon RG9 6AH
(01491) 574157
A "charming" place – more restaurant than pub – offering "consistently good" food, and striking many first-time visitors as a "great find"; as ever, some reporters sense an establishment where "OK" food comes at high prices.
/ **Details:** www.luscombes.co.uk; 10.30 pm, Sun 9 pm; no Amex.

**Duke Of Cumberland** £50 ❷❸❷
GU27 3HQ (01428) 652280
"A super country gastropub, led by robust modern cooking", set in beautiful countryside, and with a "nice garden" too.

**The Butchers Arms** £53 ④④❸
38 Towngate HD9 1TE (01484) 682361
On a good day, you get "great, reasonably-priced food", at this "proper local", in a "beautiful" Pennines village; hit a day when le patron is off-duty, though, and standards can notably slip.
/ **Details:** www.thebutchersarmshepworth.co.uk; 10 pm, Sun 9 pm; no Amex.

**Café at All Saints** £25 ❶
All Saints Church, High St HR4 9AA
(01432) 370415
"A top cappuccino in an amazing church" – the sort of recommendation which makes this "unusual" eatery a top local tip; "all food home-made on the premises, using the best ingredients". / **Details:** www.cafeatallsaints.co.uk; L only; closed Sun; no Amex; no booking; children: 6+ upstairs.

**Castle House Restaurant**
**Castle House Hotel** £47 ❶
Castle St HR1 2NW (01432) 356321
"Quite sophisticated, for a small county town"; the dining room of this townhouse-hotel is tipped as a "lovely" all-rounder.
/ **Details:** www.castlehse.co.uk; 9.30 pm, Sun 9 pm.
**Accommodation:** 24 rooms, from £150.

| HERNE BAY, KENT | 3–3D |
|---|---|

**Le Petit Poisson**   **£40**   ❸❸④
Pier Approach, Central Parade  CT6 5JN
(01227) 361199
*"Delicious fresh fish at a far better price than neighbouring Whitstable!" – so say fans of this "smashing" seafood restaurant, "right on the beach"; it's consistently praised for its "short" but "ever-changing" menu.*
/ ***Details:*** *www.lepetitpoisson.co.uk; 9.30 pm; closed Mon & Sun D; no Amex.*

| HESSLE, EAST YORKSHIRE | 6–2A |
|---|---|

**Artisan**   **£72**   ❷❷❸
22 The Weir  HU13 0RU   (01482) 644906
*"Run by the Johns family, an excellent restaurant about which the only real complaint is that it is usually fully-booked!" – all reports confirm that the cuisine of the chef-patron, formerly of Winteringham Fields, is "immaculate".*
/ ***Details:*** *www.artisanrestaurant.com; 8.30 pm; D only, closed Mon & Sun; children: 10+ D.*

| HETTON, NORTH YORKSHIRE | 5–1B |
|---|---|

**The Angel Inn**   **£50**   ❷❷❷
BD23 6LT   (01756) 730263
*"One of the first fine-dining pubs in the country, and still one of the best" – this famous rural inn is "splendid in all respects", not least its "first class seafood", and "incredible wine list at bargain prices"… "but is it beginning to rest on its laurels just a bit?"*
/ ***Details:*** *www.angelhetton.co.uk; 5m N of Skipton off B6265 at Rylstone; 9 pm; D only, ex Sun open L only.* ***Accommodation:*** *9 rooms, from £140.*

| HEXHAM, NORTHUMBERLAND | 8–2A |
|---|---|

**Bouchon Bistrot**   **£40**   ❸❸❸
4-6 Gilesgate  NE46 3NJ   (01434) 609943
*"An unexpected find in these parts", this "timeless" Gallic bistro generally pleases with its "classic", "well-executed" dishes.*
/ ***Details:*** *www.bouchonbistrot.co.uk; 9.30 pm; closed Mon & Sun; no Amex.*

| HIGH WYCOMBE, BUCKINGHAMSHIRE | 3–2A |
|---|---|

**The Old Queens Head**   **£43**   🅣
Hammersley Ln  HP10 8EY   (01494) 813371
*This "pretty" Tudor inn, with a rambling, much-beamed interior, is a top tip in this part of the world for "above-average pub fare in a very pleasant atmosphere"; food and service standards, though, can 'dip' at busy times.*
/ ***Details:*** *www.oldqueensheadpenn.co.uk; 9.30 pm, Fri & Sat 10 pm.*

| HINDON, WILTSHIRE | 2–3C |
|---|---|

**The Lamb Inn**   **£36**   ④④④
High St  SP3 6DP   (01747) 820573
*For fans, this rural-inn outpost of London's Boisdale empire is a "lovely place to stay, and to eat at"; it attracts surprisingly little survey feedback, however, some of which is rather ambivalent.* / ***Details:*** *www.lambathindon.co.uk; 2 minutes from the A350, 5 minutes from the A303; 9.30 pm, Sun 9 pm.* ***Accommodation:*** *19 rooms, from £75.*

| HINTLESHAM, SUFFOLK | 3–1D |
|---|---|

**Hintlesham Hall**   **£61**   ❷❸❸
Duke St  IP8 3NS   (01473) 652334
*This "quietly elegant" country house hotel of the old school doesn't inspire a huge number of reports nowadays, but most (if not quite all) of these praise its "beautifully-presented" dishes in "classic" style.* / ***Details:*** *www.hintleshamhall.com; 4m W of Ipswich on A1071; 9.30 pm; jacket at D; children: 12.* ***Accommodation:*** *33 rooms, from £150.*

| HINTON ST GEORGE, SOMERSET | 2–3A |
|---|---|

**Lord Poulett Arms**   **£44**   ❷❸❷
TA17 8SE   (01460) 73149
*"A wonderful gastropub in a lovely village"; all reports confirm it's a cosy place where the food is of "high quality", and "good value" too.*
/ ***Details:*** *www.lordpoulettarms.com; 9 pm; no Amex.* ***Accommodation:*** *4 rooms, from £85.*

| HITCHIN, HERTFORDSHIRE | 3–2B |
|---|---|

**Hermitage**   **£40**   🅣
20-21 Hermitage Rd  SG5 1BT
(01462) 433603
*A top tip for "great setting and atmosphere", this "loft-style" former nightclub is also consistently praised for the "good food" produced from its large open kitchen.*
/ ***Details:*** *www.hermitagerd.co.uk; closed Mon.*

| HOLKHAM, NORFOLK | 6–3C |
|---|---|

**The Victoria**   **£35**   🅣
Park Rd  NR23 1RG   (01328) 711008
*Fans tip it for its "lovely atmosphere, good food and helpful staff", but the Holkham Estate's PR-friendly coastal hotel attracts flak too, for a menu some reporters find "limited" and "unsatisfying"; indeed, cynics feel "the place survives on its 'name' and its Hooray following".*
/ ***Details:*** *www.holkham.co.uk; on the main coast road, between Wells-next-the Sea and Burnham Overy*

*Staithe; 8.45 pm; no Amex; booking essential.*
**Accommodation:** 10 rooms, from £125.

---

HOLT, NORFOLK                                    6–3C

**Byfords**                    **£41**   🅣
1-3 Shirehall Plain  NR25 6BG
(01263) 711400
*An "excellent menu for breakfast" is a top tip at
this prettily-housed all-day, all-week
café/restaurant (plus deli and B&B); it's "always
busy". / Details: www.byfords.org.uk; 9.30 pm.*
**Accommodation:** 16 rooms, from £145.

**The Pigs**                   **£43**   ❸④④
Norwich Rd  NR24 2RL   (01263) 587634
*"A pub mainly given over to being a restaurant";
"there's lots of porky stuff on the menu",
naturally, but the "guilty pleasure" of the
"heavenly" pudding trolley is arguably the top
culinary attraction; kids' facilities are "amazing"
too. / Details: www.thepigs.org.uk; 9 pm.*
**Accommodation:** 10 rooms, from £110.

---

HONITON, DEVON                                   2–4A

**Combe House**                **£74**   ❸❷❶
Gittisham  EX14 3AD   (01404) 540400
*This "lovely, unpretentious and relaxed country
house hotel", in "beautiful Devon countryside",
makes a "delightful and romantic" destination;
the cooking is "well above the average for such
places" too, although it can seem "dull"
compared to the location.
/ Details: www.combehousedevon.com; on the
outskirts of Honiton; not far from the A30, A375, 303;
9.30 pm. Accommodation: 15 rooms, from £215.*

**The Holt**                   **£41**   🅣
178 High St  EX14 1LA   (01404) 47707
*"Somewhere between a pub, a tapas bar and a
restaurant… " – this riverside operation, owned
by the Otter Brewery, is tipped for a "compact"
but "imaginative" menu (which changes
regularly). / Details: www.theholt-honiton.com; 9 pm,
Fri & Sat 9.30 pm; closed Mon & Sun.*

---

HOOK, HAMPSHIRE                                  2–3D

**Old House at Home**          **£47**   🅣
Newham Grn  RG27 9AH   (01256) 762222
*For "freshly-prepared gastropub fare", this
"attractive old pub" is tipped for its "reasonably-
priced" selections.*

---

HORDLE, HAMPSHIRE                                2–4C

**The Mill at Gordleton**      **£49**   ④④❶
Silver St  SO41 6DJ   (01590) 682219
*"Get a table outside on a sunny day, and the*

ambience is second to none", say fans of this
restaurant "by a lovely little stream", where the
(simple) food is "delicious" too; for critics, though,
the food "never lives up", and service is
"lukewarm".
/ **Details:** www.themillatgordleton.co.uk; on the A337,
off the M27; 9.15 pm, Sun 8.15 pm; no Amex.*
**Accommodation:** 8 rooms, from £150.

---

HORNDON ON THE HILL, ESSEX          3–3C

**The Bell Inn**               **£44**   ❷❷❷
High Rd  SS17 8LD   (01375) 642463
*This "hugely welcoming inn" has been owned by
John and Christine Vereker for over 40 years;
thanks to its "fresh and interesting daily-
changing menu", "amazing-value" wine list and
"wonderful selection of cask ales", it's always
"full of hustle and bustle".
/ Details: www.bell-inn.co.uk; signposted off B1007,
off A13; 9.45 pm; booking: max 12.*
**Accommodation:** 15 rooms, from £50.

---

HORSHAM, WEST SUSSEX                     3–4A

**Camellia Restaurant**
**South Lodge Hotel**         **£56**   ④❸❸
Brighton Rd  RH13 6PS   (01403) 891711
*The more traditional of the two restaurants at
this grand country house hotel has a "wonderful
terrace" with "magnificent views"; fans say it has
"good food and service to match", but critics can
find standards "just slightly disappointing".
/ Details: www.southlodgehotel.co.uk; 9.30 pm.*
**Accommodation:** 89 rooms, from £195.

**The Pass Restaurant**
**South Lodge Hotel**         **£86**   ❷❶④
Brighton Rd  RH13 6PS   (01403) 891711
*"The best eating experience ever!"; this
"refreshingly inspirational approach to a chef's-
table style experience" (22 covers) still doesn't
inspire a huge volume of reports, but they all
extol Matthew Gillen's "superbly accomplished"
cuisine, and the "exceptional" service too.
/ Details: www.southlodgehotel.co.uk; 9 pm; closed
Mon & Tue; booking essential. Accommodation: 89
rooms, from £235.*

**Restaurant Tristan**         **£56**   ❶❸❷
3 Stans Way, East St  RH12 1HU
(01403) 255688
*"A remarkable restaurant, with superb food",
located in a "nicely-beamed" 16th-century
building; the reports on Tristan Mason's
establishment are all very positive, but there is a
caveat – service, though "personable", is
"sometimes rather slower than you would
expect". / Details: www.restauranttristan.co.uk;
9.30 pm; closed Mon & Sun.*

**WABI** **£52** ❸❸❸
38 East St RH12 1HL (01403) 788 140
*"A rare find – a decent out-of-town Japanese!";
an ex-Nobu chef delivers an "exciting fusion of
flavours", at this "contemporary-style" spot; even
fans, though, can find results a little up-and-
down. / Details: www.wabi.co.uk; 10.45 pm; closed
Mon & Sun.*

**HOUGH ON THE HILL, LINCOLNSHIRE**
**6–3A**

**Brownlow Arms** **£46** ❶
NG32 2AZ (01400) 250234
*"An intimate country gastropub", tipped for its
"wide selection of well-cooked dishes"; for the
area, though, it can sometimes seem "a bit
expensive". / Details: www.brownlowarms.com; on
the Grantham Road; 9.15 pm; closed Mon,
Tue–Sat D only, closed Sun D; no Amex; children: 10+.
Accommodation: 5 rooms, from £98.*

**HOVE, EAST SUSSEX** **3–4B**

**The Foragers** **£30** ❷❷❷
3 Stirling Pl BN3 3YU (01273) 733134
*"There's never a problem in choosing something
good", at this popular Hove hang out, serving
"excellent home-cooked gastro-fare", much of it
living up to the pub's name (and with a big
emphasis on sustainability and local sourcing).
/ Details: www.theforagerpub.co.uk; 10 pm; closed
Sun D; children: 12+ after 8 pm.*

**HUDDERSFIELD, WEST YORKSHIRE** **5–1C**

**Bradley's** **£35** ❸❹❹
84 Fitzwilliam St HD1 5BB (01484) 516773
*Celebrating two decades in business, this
"always-reliable" bistro may offer nothing
startling on the food front, but almost all reports
concur that it's a "reliable" sort of destination,
where "good value for money" is assured.
/ Details: www.bradleyscatering.co.uk; 10 pm; closed
Mon, Sat L & Sun; no Amex.*

**Eric's** **£49** ❶
73-75 Lidget St HJ3 3JP (01484) 646416
*"A newish restaurant, in a parade of shops just
outside the town"; this Lindley spot is consistently
tipped for its "very good and well-presented"
dishes. / Details: www.ericsrestaurant.co.uk.*

**HUNSDON, HERTFORDSHIRE** **3–2B**

**The Fox and Hounds** **£42** ❷❸❸
2 High St SG12 8NH (01279) 843999
*"Ambitious, restaurant-orientated cooking" is
"served with minimal fuss", at this "high-quality"
gastropub – don't miss the "amazing" bread
(which you can even buy to take home!).
/ Details: www.foxandhounds-hunsdon.co.uk; off the
A414, 10 min from Hertford; 10 pm.*

**HUNTINGDON, CAMBRIDGESHIRE** **3–1B**

**Old Bridge Hotel** **£51** ❸❷❸
1 High St PE29 3TQ (01480) 424300
*John Hoskin's former coaching inn may be a
"very busy and buzzing" sort of place, but it's
not the "competent" food which is the main
attraction, but rather this Master of Wine's
"impressive" list – "they have an Enomatic
system, and you can pre-taste in the wine shop".
/ Details: www.huntsbridge.com; off A1, off A14;
10 pm. Accommodation: 24 rooms, from £150.*

**HURLEY, BERKSHIRE** **3–3A**

**Black Boys Inn** **£47** ❹❺❹
Henley Rd SL6 5NQ (01628) 824212
*Decidedly "spotty" service seems to have
contributed to quite a slide in satisfaction with
this rustic restaurant-with-rooms; that's a real
shame – if you hit a good day, the food can be
"fantastic". / Details: www.blackboysinn.co.uk;
9 pm; closed Sun D; no Amex. Accommodation: 8
rooms, from £85.*

**The Olde Bell** **£52** ❸❷❷
High St SL6 5LX (01628) 825881
*Attached to a "stunning old inn" (Britain's second
oldest), and set "in some lovely countryside", this
"relaxed" dining room consistently impresses with
its "delicious" food, and its "attentive but
unobtrusive service".
/ Details: www.theoldebell.co.uk; 9.45 pm; closed
Sun D. Accommodation: 48 rooms, from £119.*

**HURWORTH, COUNTY DURHAM** **8–3B**

**The Bay Horse** **£48** ❷❷❷
45 The Grn DL2 2AA (01325) 720 663
*"Interesting and tasty food, in a classic small-
village-pub setting" – Jonathan Hall and Marcus
Bennett's much "classier than average"
revamped inn realises a straightforward formula
to a remarkably high and consistent standard.
/ Details: www.thebayhorsehuworth.com; 9.30 pm,
Sun 8.30 pm; no Amex.*

**HYTHE, KENT** **3–4D**

**Everest Inn** **£37** ❶
32-34 High St CT21 5AT (01303) 269 898
*Not many reports, but this Indian/Nepalese
establishment (which has a twin in Blackheath,
London) is strongly tipped for its "beautiful" and
"individual" cuisine.
/ Details: www.everestinn.co.uk.*

**Hythe Bay** £42 🅣
Marine Pde CT21 6AW (01303) 267024
*Particularly tipped for the "most spectacular views over Dover Harbour", an establishment where most reporters say the "simple, well-prepared fish" is "very good" too.*
/ **Details:** *www.thehythebay.co.uk; 9.30 pm.*

**Bettys** £40 ❷❷❷
32-34 The Grove LS29 9EE
(01943) 608029
*"It may be pricey, but you get value and a sense of occasion", when you visit this outpost of the famous teahouse chain; "the queues are shorter than at some branches" too.*
/ **Details:** *www.bettysandtaylors.com; 5.30 pm; no Amex; no booking.*

**The Box Tree** £70 ❶❸④
35-37 Church St LS29 9DR
(01943) 608484
*This "quaintly luxurious" (rather "dated") stalwart of provincial fine dining has regained its reputation for "excellent" cuisine under Simon Gueller; occasionally "condescending" service can grate though, and Marco Pierre White's apparent recent re-involvement with his 'alma mater' "has had no discernible influence".*
/ **Details:** *www.theboxtree.co.uk; on A65 near town centre; 9.30 pm; closed Mon & Sun D; no Amex; no jeans or trainers; children: 8+ Fri & Sat D.*

**The Far Syde** £42 ❸❸❸
1-3 New Brook St LS29 8DQ
(01943) 602030
*"Good, local cuisine for many years" – Gavin Beedhan's town-centre bistro is hailed by practically all reporters for its "consistent and reasonably-priced" food.*
/ **Details:** *www.thefarsyde.co.uk; 10 pm; closed Mon & Sun; no Amex.*

**Ilkley Moor Vaults** £34 ❸❷❸
Stockeld Rd LS29 9HD (01943) 607012
*"Honest and intelligent local food" is served by "helpful young staff" at this "family-friendly" spot, which inspires unanimously positive reports.*
/ **Details:** *www.ilkleymoorvaults.co.uk; 9 pm, Sun 7 pm; closed Mon.*

**The Howard Arms** £42 🅣
Lower Grn CV36 4LT (01608) 682226
*"A lovely rural gastropub", tipped as "worth hunting down" for its good standards across the board, and perhaps in particular for its "lovely Cotswold location and great terrace".*
/ **Details:** *www.howardarms.com; 8m SW of Stratford-upon-Avon off A4300; 9.30 pm; no Amex.*
**Accommodation:** *8 rooms, from £145.*

**Chez Roux**
**Rocpool Reserve** £50 ❶❷❸
Culduthel Rd IV2 4AG (01463) 240089
*"Superb food in a stylish setting"; this outpost of the Roux empire, with its "nice location by the River Ness", is hailed by almost all reporters for its "superlative" cuisine.*
/ **Details:** *www.rocpool.com; 9.30 pm.*
**Accommodation:** *11 rooms, from £210.*

**The Mustard Seed** £39 ❸❸❷
16 Fraser St IV1 1DW (01463) 220220
*In a "wonderfully atmospheric" Georgian church, with views over the River Ness, a venture that's been a local linchpin for over a decade, and where the food is invariably rated "decent" or better.*
/ **Details:** *www.themustardseedrestaurant.co.uk; 10 pm.*

**Rocpool** £50 ❷❷❷
1 Ness Walk IV3 5NE (01463) 717274
*Surprisingly "precise" and "complex" cooking, using "consistently excellent local produce", helps make this "buzzy" riverside brasserie a real hit with almost all who comment on it.*
/ **Details:** *www.rocpoolrestaurant.com; 10 pm; closed Sun L , open Sun evenings June-Sept only.; no Amex.*

**Baipo** £36 ❷❸④
63 Upper Orwell St IP4 1HP
(01473) 218402
*"A more authentic taste of Thailand than virtually all so-called Thai restaurants you find… and not just in Ipswich!" – locals, in particular, love this "great-value" destination, "even if it could be a bit more comfortable".*
/ **Details:** *www.baipo.co.uk; 10.45 pm; closed Mon L & Sun; no Amex.*

**Bistro on the Quay** £36 🅣
3 Wherry Quay IP4 1AS (01473) 286677
*Nicely located in a converted warehouse on the waterfront, a "good-value" bistro tipped for its "well presented" cuisine; set menus offer "a particularly good deal".*
/ **Details:** *www.bistroonthequay.co.uk; 9.30 pm; closed Sun D.*

**Mariners at Il Punto** £42 ❸❸❷
Neptune Quay IP4 1AX (01473) 289748
*"A little bit of France, in a delightful boat" – the Crépy family's nicely-restored naval vessel, in the*

marina, makes a "compelling" venue; foodwise it's "not spectacular, but still possibly the best bet locally". / **Details:** www.marinersipswich.co.uk; 9.30 pm; closed Mon & Sun; no Amex.

**Trongs** £ 34 ❷⓿❸
23 St Nicholas St IP1 1TW
(01473) 256833
"One of Ipswich's few top-quality restaurants", this (Vietnamese-run) Chinese is "always first-class in every department"; "it's always busy, so make sure you book". / **Details:** 10.30 pm; closed Sun; booking essential.

IRBY, MERSEYSIDE 5–2A

**Da Piero** £ 48 ❷⓿❸
5 Mill Hill Rd CH61 4UB (0151) 648 7373
"Real Sicilian food is skilfully prepared from first-rate ingredients and served with friendliness and pride", at this "proper, small, simple and charming" family-run Italian; unsurprisingly, it's usually "crowded". / **Details:** www.dapiero.co.uk/; 11pm; closed Mon.

JERSEY, CHANNEL ISLANDS

**Bohemia**
**The Club Hotel & Spa** £ 74 ❷❷❸
Green St, St Helier JE2 4UH
(01534) 876500
"Shaun Rankin's food just gets better" – that's the (almost) universal view on this "chic" St Helier design-hotel dining room, where the cuisine "exploits the outstanding local produce" to deliver some "fantastic" flavour combinations; STOP PRESS – he's off to set up on his own in 2013! / **Details:** www.bohemiajersey.com; 10 pm; closed Sun; no trainers. **Accommodation:** 46 rooms, from £185.

**Green Island Restaurant** £ 44 ❷❷❸
St Clement JE2 6LS (01534) 857787
"One of the best upmarket bistros", offering a "constantly-changing menu with an excellent choice of local produce"; even fans, though, are prone to noting that it's "not cheap". / **Details:** www.greenisland.je; 9.30 pm; closed Mon & Sun D; no Amex.

**Longueville Manor** £ 87 ❷⓿❷
Longueville Rd, St Saviour JE2 7WF
(01534) 725501
The style may be a little "passé" for some tastes, but feedback on this "beautiful" hotel on the fringe of St Helier has been impressively upbeat in recent times – the food is often "fantastic", and "nothing is too much trouble" for the staff. / **Details:** www.longuevillemanor.com; head from St. Helier on the A3 towards Gorey; less than 1 mile from

St. Helier; 10 pm; no jeans or trainers. **Accommodation:** 31 rooms, from £220.

**Ocean Restaurant**
**Atlantic Hotel** £ 80 ❸❸④
Le Mont de la Pulente, St Brelade JE3 8HE
(01534) 744101
For fans, this liner-style chamber, with ocean-views from some tables, is "the best dining room on the island", and Mark Jordan is touted locally as a "chef to watch"; the odd critic, however, finds the food "good but unexceptional", and service so-so. / **Details:** www.theatlantichotel.com; 10 pm; no jeans or trainers. **Accommodation:** 50 rooms, from £150 - 250.

**The Oyster Box** £ 41 ❷❸❷
St Brelade's Bay JE3 8EF (01534) 743311
"Why go to the Med?"; on a sunny day, it's hard to beat this smart but informal restaurant, right by the beach in "dreamy" St Brelade's Bay; the odd critic, though, does find the prices on the high side – "the next door Crab Shack (same owner) is a cheap and cheerful lunchtime alternative". / **Details:** www.oysterbox.co.uk; 9 pm; closed Mon L; no Amex.

**Suma's** £ 50 ❸❷❷
Gorey Hill, Gorey JE3 6ET (01534) 853291
"Great seafood, plus lovely views of Gorey Harbour" reward those who secure terrace tables at this first-floor restaurant; "the menu seems to have changed of late, now offering tempting light, modern food far removed from the old more rustic style".
/ **Details:** www.sumasrestaurant.com; underneath castle in Gorey Harbour; 10 pm; closed Sun D; booking: max 12.

KENILWORTH, WARWICKSHIRE 5–4C

**Bosquet** £ 53 ❷⓿❸
97a Warwick Rd CV8 1HP
(01926) 852463
"The local standard-bearer for high-quality cuisine"; the Ligniers have now been in charge for over three decades, but the standards of their "top-class cooking in the style of south west France" rarely wavers.
/ **Details:** www.restaurantbosquet.co.uk; 9.15 pm; closed Mon, Sat L & Sun; closed 2 weeks in Aug.

**Petit Gourmand** £ 44 ❸❸❸
101-103 Warwick Rd CV8 1HP
(01926) 864567
A local "star turn" – this richly-furnished Gallic restaurant is a "popular" destination, unanimously hailed by reporters for its "solid bistro cooking" from a "limited but good-quality

menu". / **Details:** www.petit-gourmand.co.uk; 9.45 pm; closed Mon & Sun.

---

KENTON, GREATER LONDON     3–2A

**Blue Ginger**     **£35**   ⊕
383 Kenton Rd   HA3 0XS   (020) 8909 0100
A top tip for those in search of "bargain Indian food" in this part of the world; a Chinese menu is also available.
/ **Details:** http://www.bgrestaurant.com/contact.html; 11 pm; closed Mon L.

---

KESTON, KENT     3–3B

**Lujon**     **£48**   ❷❸❸
6 Commonside   BR2 6BP   (01689) 855501
A smart (if sometimes "slightly noisy") local restaurant, where the "fantastic" food is often compared to that of Chapter One (Locksbottom), where the chef formerly worked; the "concise" wine list offers "a good selection, at reasonable prices". / **Details:** www.lujon.co.uk; midnight; closed Mon, Tue & Sun D.

---

KESWICK, CUMBRIA     7–3D

**Lyzzick Hall**     **£50**   ❷❷❸
CA12 4PY   (017687) 72277
The wine list – "a real treat for Iberian fans" – hints at the heritage of the family who've long owned this country house hotel, where the "tasty modern British cooking" comes with a distinctive Mediterranean influence; "stunning views" too, especially from the terrace.
/ **Details:** www.lyzzickhall.co.uk.

---

KETTLESHULME, CHESHIRE     5–2B

**The Swan Inn**     **£45**   ⊕
Macclesfield Rd   SK23 7QU
(01663) 732943
An "atmospheric" 15th-century Peak District freehouse, tipped for a "daily-changing menu", where the "extensive" range of choices always features fish.
/ **Details:** www.verynicepubs.co.uk/swankettleshulme/; 8.30 pm, Thu-Fri 7 pm, Sat 9 pm, Sun 4 pm; closed Mon L; no Amex.

---

KEYSTON, CAMBRIDGESHIRE     3–1A

**The Pheasant
at Keyston**     **£49**
Loop Rd   PE28 0RE   (01832) 710241
A well-known gastropub which reverted to the ownership of the Huntsbridge group during our survey year – in the circumstances, we've felt it best to leave it un-rated.
/ **Details:** www.thepheasant-keyston.co.uk; 1m S of

A14 between Huntingdon & Kettering, J15; 9.30 pm; closed Mon & Sun D.

---

KIBWORTH BEAUCHAMP, LEICESTERSHIRE 5–4D

**Firenze**     **£46**   ❷❷❷
9 Station St   LE8 0LN   (0116) 279 6260
"A small island of culinary excellence in the cold sea of the East Midlands" – the Poli family's "classy" but "buzzy" venture is a "smooth operation", offering "authentic Italian cooking and interesting wine". / **Details:** www.firenze.co.uk; 10 pm; closed Mon & Sun; no Amex.

---

KIBWORTH HARCOURT, LEICESTERSHIRE5–4D

**Boboli**     **£40**   ❸❸❸
88 Main St   LE8 0NQ   (0116) 2793303
"Baby brother to the Poli family's flagship, Firenze, with a more rustic approach some will prefer" – for a "speedy and cheerful" meal, the "good-value" Italian "staples" it offers are approved by all who report on it.
/ **Details:** www.bobolirestaurant.co.uk; 9.30 pm; no Amex.

---

KINGHAM, GLOUCESTERSHIRE     2–1C

**Daylesford Café**     **£41**   ④④❸
GL56 0YG   (01608) 731700
"Not much sign of recession-hit folk here…" – this "chic" canteen in a converted barn (with deli/kitchen shop attached) is a "beautiful" bit of urbs-in-rure that goes down particularly well with the "local 4x4 set"; its "very fresh" fare generally pleases, though service can be rather up-and-down. / **Details:** www.daylesfordorganic.com; Mon-Wed 5 pm, Thu-Sat 6 pm, Sun 4pm; L only.

---

KINGHAM, OXFORDSHIRE     2–1C

**The Kingham Plough**     **£46**   ❸④④
The Green   OX7 6YD   (01608) 658327
"Notting Hill comes to the country!", at Emily Watkins's "rustic" inn; it takes different people different ways – fans love its "deeply ambitious" cooking and "comfy" style, but critics say the food "doesn't always deliver".
/ **Details:** www.thekinghamplough.co.uk; 8.30 pm, Fri & Sat 8.45 pm, Sun 8 pm; no Amex.
**Accommodation:** 7 rooms, from £90.

---

KINGSTON UPON THAMES, SURREY   3–3A

**The Canbury Arms**     **£44**   ❷❷❷
49 Canbury Park Rd   KT2 6LQ
(020) 8255 9129
"Honest home-cooked food at a fair price, friendly staff, great atmosphere, a handy location, and plenty of parking" – that's the deal

*that's making a huge success of this "excellent" gastropub; "it's better, though, to eat in the main building than in the conservatory".*
/ **Details:** www.thecanburyarms.com; 9 pm, Fri & Sat 10 pm.

**fish! Kitchen** £45 ❸④⑤
56-58 Coombe Rd KT2 7AF
(020) 8546 2886
*"Piping hot, fresh and crispy" fish 'n' chips ensures this "cramped" bistro is "always popular"; ambience, though, is "definitely lacking".* / **Details:** www.fishkitchen.com; 10 pm; closed Mon & Sun.

**Frère Jacques** £46 **T**
10-12 Riverside Walk KT1 1QN
(020) 8546 1332
*Tipped for its "great riverside location", a "popular middle-of-the-road Gallic brasserie", generally hailed for its "good value for money".*
/ **Details:** www.frerejacques.co.uk; 10 pm; no Amex.

**Roz ana** £41 **T**
4-8 Kingston Hill KT2 7NH
(020) 8546 6388
*A "gourmet-Indian", in Norbiton, that's highly popular locally; it's tipped for "nice regional Indian cooking", which includes "the most amazing puds"; there's a cocktail bar too.*
/ **Details:** www.roz-ana.com; 10.30 pm, Fri & Sat 11 pm, Sun 10 pm.

**Hipping Hall** £66 ❷❷❷
Cowan Bridge LA6 2JJ (01524) 271187
*"Fabulous food in a fabulous location"; this "romantic" 15th-century hall maintains a low profile (and can sometimes be a little "quiet"), but most reporters remain impressed by its "amazing" standards, twinned with relatively "reasonable" prices.*
/ **Details:** www.hippinghall.com; 9.15 pm; closed weekday L; no Amex; no trainers; booking essential; children: 10+. **Accommodation:** 9 rooms, from £200.

**The Mason's Arms** £55 ❷❶❷
EX36 4RY (01398) 341231
*"Fantastic food in the heart of Exmoor"; it helps that Mark Dodson, le patron of this "beautifully-located" inn, used to head up the kitchen at the Waterside Inn (Bray)!*
/ **Details:** www.masonsarmsdevon.co.uk; 9 pm; closed Mon & Sun D; children: 5+ after 6pm.

**Belle Époque** £50 ❸④❶
60 King St WA16 6DT (01565) 633060
*A "stunning interior" in "real Belle Époque style" makes it easy for this remarkable Art Nouveau landmark to win fans – if it were not for the "smug complacency" to which it has sometimes succumbed in recent years, it could again become a famous destination.*
/ **Details:** www.thebelleepoque.com; 1.5m from M6, J19; 9.30 pm; closed Sat L & Sun D; booking: max 6, Sat. **Accommodation:** 7 rooms, from £100.

**Falcondale Hotel** £35 ❷❸❷
Falcondale Drive SA48 7RX
(01570) 422910
*"A lovely country house hotel", set in "beautiful countryside", and enjoying "magnificent views"; it is acclaimed not only as a "super-romantic retreat", but also for its "fabulous" cuisine.*
/ **Details:** www.thefalcondale.co.uk; 8.30 pm.
**Accommodation:** 19 rooms, from £149.

**Simply French** £84 **T**
27a St Georges Quay LA1 1RD
(01524) 843199
*Not a great deal of commentary this year on this authentic Gallic bistro of over 15 years' standing; it's still tipped, though, for the "good value of the prix-fixe menus".*
/ **Details:** www.quitesimplyfrench.co.uk; 9.30 pm, Sun & Mon 9 pm; D only, ex Sun open L & D; no Amex.

**Langar Hall** £52 ❸❷❷
Church Ln NG13 9HG (01949) 860559
*"A warm welcome always awaits", at Imogen Skirving's "superb" country house hotel, where she (with her staff) injects a real "sense of occasion" (without stuffiness) into the dining experience; standards are "well maintained" in the kitchen too.* / **Details:** www.langarhall.com; off A52 between Nottingham & Grantham; 9.30 pm; no Amex; no trainers. **Accommodation:** 13 rooms, from £100.

**Northcote** £68 ❶❷❸
Northcote Rd BB6 8BE (01254) 240555
*"Continuing to set the standard in the North West", this "amazingly consistent" manor house restaurant-with-rooms provides "year-on-year, an unbeatable regional food experience", featuring*

an "outstanding", locally-sourced menu, prepared by chef Lisa Allen, and a hugely impressive wine list too. / **Details:** www.northcote.com; M6, J31 then A59; 9.30 pm; no trainers. **Accommodation:** 14 rooms, from £230.

---

LAPWORTH, WARWICKSHIRE          5–4C

**The Boot**                    £ 42    **T**
Old Warwick Rd  B94 6JU   (01564) 782464
A popular local inn, tipped for its "ever-reliable" standards, and "handy for the M40" too; the bar (or its terrace), though, is sometimes preferred to the main restaurant.
/ **Details:** www.lovelypubs.co.uk; 10 pm, Sun 9 pm; no Amex.

---

LAVANT, WEST SUSSEX             3–4A

**The Earl of March**           £ 48    **❸❹❸**
Lavant Rd  P018 0BQ   (01243) 533993
For most reporters, this popular and "wonderfully-located" gastropub, deserves acclaim for its "excellent local food"; the occasional critic, though, finds it "expensive" for what it is. / **Details:** www.theearlofmarch.com; 9.30 pm.

---

LAVENHAM, SUFFOLK               3–1C

**The Angel**                   £ 55    **❹❹❹**
Market Pl  CO10 9QZ   (01787) 247388
"Nigh on the oldest room in this lovely town" is now part of Marco Pierre White's 'Wheeler's' brand; there is some praise for its "unfussy" steaks and seafood, but to numerous locals – who find it "average" and hugely "over-rated" – his arrival has been a major let-down.
/ **Details:** www.maypolehotels.com; on A1141 6m NE of Sudbury; 9.15 pm. **Accommodation:** 9 rooms, from £110.

**Great House**                 £ 51    **❶❷❷**
Market Pl  CO10 9QZ   (01787) 247431
Nearly 30 years in business, the Crépy family's "Gallic oasis" occupies a prime position in "the most perfect medieval town in England"; there's the odd quibble, of course, but most reporters say this is just a "fabulous" place, offering "outstanding" cuisine.
/ **Details:** www.greathouse.co.uk; follow directions to Guildhall; 9.30 pm; closed Mon & Sun D; closed Jan; no Amex. **Accommodation:** 5 rooms, from £95.

**Swan Hotel**                  £ 53    **T**
High St  C010 9QA   (01787) 247477
A 15th-century inn described by one reporter as a "popular tourist hotel", and tipped by most, if not quite all, reporters as a "good all-rounder".
/ **Details:** www.theswanatlavenham.co.uk; 9.30 pm;

no jeans or trainers; children: 12+ at D.
**Accommodation:** 49 rooms, from £105.

---

LEAMINGTON SPA, WARWICKSHIRE    5–4C

**La Coppola**                  £ 42    **❷❸❷**
86 Regent St  CV32 4NS   (01926) 888 873
A "superb" town-centre Italian , which serves "an extensive menu with panache and charm"; "there are never any bargain menus as such… but it always seems to be full!"
/ **Details:** www.lacoppola.co.uk; 10 pm, Sun 9 pm.

**Oscars French Bistro**        £ 42    **❸❷❸**
39 Chandos St  CV32 4RL   (01926) 452807
"A friendly bistro, offering genuinely French food that's uncomplicated but well-sourced"; the lunchtime offers find particular favour.
/ **Details:** www.oscarsfrenchbistro.co.uk; 9.30 pm; closed Mon & Sun.

---

LEEDS, WEST YORKSHIRE           5–1C

**Aagrah**                      £ 32    **❷❷❸**
Aberford Rd  LS25 2HF   (0113) 287 6606
"Still one of the best modern Indian restaurants", this "busy" city-centre outpost of the eminent local chain wins unanimous praise for its "delicious" food, and "great value" too.
/ **Details:** www.aagrah.com; from A1 take A642 Aberford Rd to Garforth; 11.30 pm, Sun 10.30 pm; D only.

**Akbar's**                     £ 28    **❷❹❹**
16 Greek St  LS1 5RU   (0113) 242 5426
"Family naans are a particular favourite", at this Indian "oasis" – the central Leeds version of the Bradford original; it's consistently well-rated, although there's the odd fear that its "evident popularity" can lead to a "conveyor belt" experience. / **Details:** www.akbars.co.uk; midnight; D only.

**Anthony's**                   £ 62    **❸❹❺**
19 Boar Ln  LS1 6EA   (0113) 245 5922
For "molecular gastronomy without the Bull(i)", many fans still praise Anthony Flynn's "excellent" city-centre spot which, they say, has been "truly back on form" of late; critics, though, see clear drift since its 2004 debut – "it used to be odd they didn't have a Michelin star, but nowadays it's clear why they don't!"
/ **Details:** www.anthonysrestaurant.co.uk; 9.30 pm; closed Mon & Sun; no Amex.

**Art's**                       £ 35    **❸❸❸**
42 Call Ln  LS1 6DT   (0113) 243 8243
Near the Corn Exchange, the city's original trendy, informal spot is still going strong; it's mainly the "really good lunchtime platters" which excite reporter attention nowadays, but the food

at other times can also be "interesting".
/ **Details:** www.artscafebar.com; 10 pm .

**Bibis Italianissimo**   £41   ⑤⑤⑤
Criterion Pl, Swinegate  LS1 4AG
(0113) 243 0905
This vast place may be big news locally, but no
reporter has a good word to say about this ultra-
"glitzy" Art Deco-style "pastiche of an Italian
restaurant", near the station – most feedback
says it's "dire". / **Details:** www.bibisrestaurant.com;
11.30 pm; closed Mon; no shorts; no booking, Sat.

**Brasserie Forty 4**   £43   ❶
44 The Calls  LS2 7EW   (0113) 234 3232
Not quite the 'destination' it once was, this
veteran canalside bistro is still tipped as a
"pleasant" and "good-value" operation, where
the food is "interesting" and "well-presented".
/ **Details:** www.brasserie44.com; 10 pm; closed Sun.
**Accommodation:** 41 rooms, from £90.

**Chaophraya**   £46   ④④④
20a, First Floor, Blayds Ct  LS2 4AG
(0113) 244 9339
This "busy" shopping-mall outpost of a small
Northern chain is still praised for its "first-class
Thai food, and value for money too"; it can be a
bit of a "zoo", though, and critics find "standards
down, and prices up in recent times… and there
are too many happy-birthday drum-rolls!"
/ **Details:** www.chaophraya.co.uk; in Swinegate;
10.30 pm.

**Create**   £37   ❷❷❸
31 King St  LS1 2HL   (0113) 242 0628
This may be a social-enterprise restaurant, but
"no feeling of worthiness" pervades this
"friendly" city-centre spot, where the food is
usually "really good"; the lunch menu offers
"particularly good value".
/ **Details:** www.foodbycreate.co.uk/restaurant;
10.30 pm; closed Mon D & Sun; no Amex.

**The Cross Keys**   £42   ❸❸❸
107 Water Ln  LS11 5WD   (0113) 243 3711
"The best Sunday lunch in Leeds" continues to
be the stand-out attraction of this "family-
friendly" city-centre gastroboozer; it's "always
packed" – "book well in advance".
/ **Details:** www.the-crosskeys.com; 10 pm.

**Flying Pizza**   £37   ④④❸
60 Street Ln  LS8 2DQ   (0113) 266 6501
A famous Headingley pizzeria, now taken over
by the San Carlo empire; reviews are mixed –
the middle-course view is that it's "nice enough,
but not really worth the hype or prices";
important style tip – "don't forget the Bentley".

/ **Details:** www.theflyingpizza.co.uk; 11 pm, Sun
10 pm; no shorts.

**Fourth Floor Café**
**Harvey Nichols**   £46   ❷❷❷
107-111 Briggate  LS1 6AZ
(0113) 204 8000
"A good lunch choice, if perhaps a bit pricey";
this elevated department store dining room often
impresses with its "excellent" food; major
supporting attraction – "a big wine list, with
some unusual gems".
/ **Details:** www.harveynichols.com; 10 pm; L only, ex
Thu-Sat open L & D; SRA-52%.

**Fuji Hiro**   £24   ❸④④
45 Wade Ln  LS2 8NJ   (0113) 243 9184
More mixed reviews this year on this popular
"cheap 'n' cheerful" noodle-bar, in the city-centre;
most still praise its "simple food which tastes
great, at a good price", but a couple of
refuseniks found it plain "disappointing".
/ **Details:** 10 pm, Fri & Sat 11 pm; need 5+ to book.

**La Grillade**   £38   ❸❸❸
Wellington St  LS1 4HJ   (0113) 245 9707
"Everywhere in Leeds seems to be a steakhouse
nowadays, but nowhere does it as well as
La Grillade!" – this "whitewashed underground
room with lots of alcoves" may strike critics as
"rather '80s", but it's a "discreet" Gallic spot
that's consistently well reviewed, especially for
business. / **Details:** www.lagrillade.co.uk; 10 pm, Sat
10.30 pm; closed Sat L & Sun.

**Hansa's**   £29   ❶❶❸
72-74 North St  LS2 7PN   (0113) 244 4408
"Actually like the vegetarian food you might find
in India!" – Mrs Hansa Dhabhi's long-established,
city-centre Gujarati has been on particularly
good form of late, and is praised for its "light",
"zingy" and "delicate" dishes, with "lovely
spicing". / **Details:** www.hansasrestaurant.com;
10 pm, Fri & Sat 11 pm; D only, ex Sun L only.

**Kendells Bistro**   £44   ❷❸❷
St Peters square  LS9 8AH   (0113) 243 6553
"Low-lit, and with candles everywhere", this city-
centre bistro does the "'very French' thing very
well – especially as Mr Kendell is thoroughly
English! – and the menu "offers some real
treats"; "great pre-theatre menu".
/ **Details:** www.kendellsbistro.co.uk; 9 pm, Fri & Sat
10 pm; D only, closed Mon & Sun; no Amex; booking
essential.

**Little Tokyo**   £42   ❷❸❸
24 Central Rd  LS1 6DE   (0113) 243 9090
"Always consistently good", "freshly-prepared"
and "good-value" – all reporters concur on the

virtues of the cuisine at this "pleasing" city-centre Japanese; "excellent" Bento boxes a highlight. / **Details:** 10 pm, Fri & Sat 11 pm; need 8+ to book.

**The Piazza By Anthony**
**The Corn Exchange** £42 ④④⑤
Corn Exchange, Call Ln LS1 7BR
(0113) 247 0995
Fans vaunt the Italianate cuisine as "interesting", but reports on this "too big and cold" dining facility, on the cavernous lower level of the (fabulous) old Corn Exchange building, are notably up-and-down – "Anthony has spread himself too thin, and it shows".
/ **Details:** www.anthonysrestaurant.co.uk; 10 pm, Sun 9 pm, Fri & Sat 10.30 pm; no Amex.

**Red Chilli** £38 ❷④④
6 Great George St LS1 3DW
(01132) 429688
"Best Chinese in town (despite the basement location)" – this city-centre fixture will, say fans, "knock your socks off" with its "eclectic menu delving into regional cuisine" (including chilli-hot Sichuan and Beijing dishes); it's "always busy".
/ **Details:** www.redchillirestaurant.co.uk; 10.30 pm, Fri & Sat 11.30 pm.

**The Reliance** £37 ❷❸❸
76-78 North St LS2 7PN (0113) 295 6060
"Inventive menus, with realisation that's generally spot-on" contribute to the "winning formula" of this boho-chic city-centre gastroboozer.
/ **Details:** www.the-reliance.co.uk; 10 pm, Thu-Sat 10.30 pm, Sun 9.30 pm; no booking.

**Salvo's** £43 ❸❸④
115 Otley Rd LS6 3PX (0113) 275 5017
"Following an extensive refit, Headingley's favourite Italian has come back stronger than ever" – the majority view on this long-running local institution; occasional critics, though, simply see a "loss of charm", and find prices "greedy".
/ **Details:** www.salvos.co.uk; 10.30 pm, Fri & Sat 11 pm, Sun 9 pm; no booking at D.

**San Carlo** £45 ❸④❷
6-7 South Pde LS1 5QX (0113) 246 1500
"The food is good, but it's the atmosphere you go for" – that's the consensus on this "beautifully decorated" city-centre outpost of the ever-successful San Carlo franchise (occasionally "abrupt" service notwithstanding).
/ **Details:** www.sancarlo.co.uk/leeds; 11 pm.

**Sous le Nez en Ville** £44 ❷❷❷
Quebec Hs, Quebec St LS1 2HA
(0113) 244 0108
"An utterly reliable stand-by, for which it's always best to book" – this "cosy" and "authentic" city-

centre basement operation is "still the best place in Leeds for lunch", and its early-evening menu has long been known as a "real bargain"; "classy" wines too. / **Details:** www.souslenez.com; 10 pm, Sat 11 pm; closed Sun.

**Sukhothai** £36 ❷⓪④
8 Regent St LS7 4PE (0113) 237 0141
Fans of this "always-thriving" Chapel Allerton spot acclaim "amazing" cooking "like you'd find in Thailand" and "well-intentioned" staff; critics, though, can find the setting rather "sardine-like"; also in Headingley. / **Details:** www.sukhothai.co.uk; 11 pm; Mon-Thu D only, Fri-Sun open L & D; no Amex.

**Bobby's** £24 ❶
154-156 Belgrave Rd LE4 5AT (
0116) 266 0106
Not a huge amount of feedback of late on this landmark Indian veggie, on the Golden Mile; it's still tipped, though, for its "genuine" cuisine, and "excellent sweetmeats" in particular.
/ **Details:** www.eatatbobbys.com; 10 pm; no Amex.

**Hotel Maiyango** £40 ❷❷❷
13-21 St Nicholas Pl LE1 4LD
(0116) 251 8898
"The new star in Leicester city-centre dining"; this boutique-hotel dining room may occupy an "unprepossessing" former office block, but – with its "eccentric but very comfortable Moroccan styling" – it's "certainly now the best restaurant in town", serving some "excellent" modern British fare. / **Details:** www.maiyango.com.

**Kayal** £35 ❷❷❸
153 Granby St LE1 6FE (0116) 255 4667
"The best curry house in town!" – this "unprepossessing" ("but inside very comfortable") outfit, near the station, is "unusual compared with most of Leicester's 100+ curry houses, in its focus on Keralan veggie and seafood dishes" – food that's "light, delicate, fragrant, spicy and remarkably moreish".
/ **Details:** www.kayalrestaurant.com; 11 pm, Sun 10 pm.

**The Tiffin** £36 ❸❷❸
1 De Montfort St LE1 7GE (0116) 247 0420
"Quite expensive by Leicester standards, but worth it for an excellent culinary experience" – this "consistently good" Indian, near the De Montfort Hall, inspires only positive reports.
/ **Details:** www.the-tiffin.co.uk; 10.45 pm; closed Sat L & Sun.

### LEIGH-ON-SEA, ESSEX 3–3C

**Simply Seafood** £49 **T**
High St SS9 2ER (01702) 716645
The name does not lie! – it's "the food that
'sells'" this restaurant located between a railway
line and the sea; the location may leave a little to
be desired, but all-round reactions are generally
positive. / **Details:** www.simplyseafood.co.uk; 9 pm;
closed Mon.

### LEIGHTON BUZZARD, BEDFORDSHIRE 3–2A

**The Kings Head** £55 **T**
Ivinghoe LU7 9EB (01296) 668388
A grand 17th-century inn that's "one of the few
where you can enjoy genuine Aylesbury duck";
it's tipped by fans as nothing short of
"exquisite". / **Details:** www.kingsheadivinghoe.co.uk;
3m N of Tring on B489 to Dunstable; 9.30 pm; closed
Sun D; jacket & tie required at D.

### LEINTWARDINE, SHROPSHIRE 5–4A

**Jolly Frog** £47 **T**
The Todden SY7 0LX (01547) 540298
Fans still find "wonderful food, charming service
and eccentric surroundings", at this bistro-style,
rural gastropub – there is some suggestion in
recent reports, however, that the place isn't
coping with its popularity.
/ **Details:** www.jollyfrogpub.co.uk; 9.30 pm; closed
Mon; no Amex.

### LETHERINGSETT, NORFOLK 6–3C

**Kings Head** £39 **❸❷❷**
Holt Rd NR25 7AR (01263) 712691
"Part of the 'Flying Kiwi' chain, and quite possibly
the best of the lot!" – this "lovely" gastropub
(with microbrewery) offers a good range of
"generously-portioned" fare, and a "really
interesting" wine list too.
/ **Details:** www.letheringsettkingshead.co.uk; 9.30 pm;
no Amex.

### LEWES, EAST SUSSEX 3–4B

**Bill's Produce Store** £36 **❷❸❸**
56 Cliffe High St BN7 2AN
(01273) 476918
"As the empire grows" – Bill's is now a Richard
Caring production – this famous deli/diner
"doesn't have quite the high standards" it once
did; it remains a "bustling" spot, though, and still
does "some of the best coffee around".
/ **Details:** www.bills-website.co.uk; 10.30 pm, Fri-Sat
11.30 pm; no Amex.

### LIFTON, DEVON 1–3C

**The Arundell Arms Hotel** £59 **❷❷❸**
PL16 0AA (01566) 784666
The ambience is "locked in time", but that's part
of the appeal of this "wonderful country hotel"
(owned by a famous angler, and whose special
feature is access to 20 miles of fishing); both bar
and restaurant win praise for "unbelievable
value, given the quality of the food".
/ **Details:** www.arundellarms.com; 0.5m off A30,
Lifton Down exit; 9.30 pm; no Amex; no jeans or shorts.
**Accommodation:** 21 rooms, from £179.

### LINCOLN, LINCOLNSHIRE 6–3A

**Browns Pie Shop** £39 **T**
33 Steep Hill LN2 1LU (01522) 527330
"A busy and cheerful spot in an historic
location"; as you might hope, it is tipped as
"THE place for a wonderful pie"!
/ **Details:** www.brownspieshop.co.uk; 9.30 pm, Sun
8 pm; no Amex.

**Jew's House Restaurant** £43 **T**
15 The Strait LN2 1JD (01522) 524851
Not as many reports as we'd like on this prettily-
located restaurant in one of the city's oldest
buildings; they are all positive, though, and it is
tipped for its "imaginative" cuisine, with lunches,
in particular, offering "top value".
/ **Details:** www.jewshouserestaurant.co.uk; 9.30 pm;
closed Mon & Sun.

**The Old Bakery** £45 **④④❸**
26-28 Burton Rd LN1 3LB (01522) 576057
"This has always been one of the most reliable
restaurants in Lincoln, but sadly the chef now
sees himself as a local celebrity" – this
restaurant-with-rooms still has some big fans for
its "fantastic home-made food", but even they
can find the style "haughty", "fussy" or "OTT"!
/ **Details:** www.theold-bakery.co.uk; 9 pm; closed Mon;
no jeans. **Accommodation:** 4 rooms, from £55.

**The Wig & Mitre** £35 **④④❷**
30-32 Steep Hill LN2 1TL (01522) 535190
Not quite the institution it once was, but this
"fine old building" has a "great location" near
the Cathedral, and fans still tip it as a "cheap 'n'
cheerful" place, where "good food is served".
/ **Details:** www.wigandmitre.com; 10 pm, Fri & Sat
10.30 pm, Sun 10 pm.

## LINLITHGOW, WEST LOTHIAN 9–4C

**Champany Inn** £75 ⊤
EH49 7LU (01506) 834532
*For those in search of an "awesomely indulgent menu", this famous (and famously pricey) steakhouse-inn also boasts an "awesome" cellar to go with it; even the cheaper 'chop and ale house', though, is hailed by fans for "the best steak in Scotland". / Details: www.champany.com; 2m NE of Linlithgow on junction of A904 & A803; 10 pm; closed Sat L & Sun; no jeans or trainers; children: 8+.* **Accommodation:** *16 rooms, from £125.*

## LITTLE ECCLESTON, LANCASHIRE 5–1A

**The Cartford Inn** £33 ⊤
Cartford Ln PR3 0YP (01995) 670 166
*A "deservedly popular" pub/restaurant-with-rooms, by the Cartford Toll Bridge, tipped for its "good food", "comfortable surroundings" and "friendly and enthusiastic staff". / Details: www.thecartfordinn.co.uk; 9 pm; closed Mon L.*

## LITTLE WILBRAHAM, CAMBRIDGESHIRE 3–1B

**The Hole In The Wall** £44 ❸④④
2 High St CB21 5JY (01223) 812282
*Masterchef runner-up Alex Rushmer is behind the stoves of this "middle-of-nowhere" inn, not far from Cambridge; many reporters do acclaim it as a "fantastic find" with "very serious" cooking, but others have found the cuisine "below expectations". / Details: www.holeinthewallcambridge.co.uk; 9 pm; closed Mon & Sun D; no Amex.*

## LITTLEHAMPTON, WEST SUSSEX 3–4A

**East Beach Cafe** £41 ⊤
Sea Rd, The Promenade BN17 5GB
(01903) 731903
*"Worth visiting for the position and building" – this extraordinary modern structure offers "very acceptable" cooking, with an emphasis on seafood; good sea-views too. / Details: www.eastbeachcafe.co.uk; 8.30 pm.*

## LIVERPOOL, MERSEYSIDE 5–2A

**Chaophraya** £42 ❸❸❸
5-6 Kenyon Steps L1 3DF (0151) 707 6323
*"A welcome development"; this Liverpool One outpost of the Northern chain of rather stylised Thai restaurants is hailed by all reporters as "much better than you'd expect". / Details: www.chaophraya.co.uk; 10.30 pm.*

**Delifonseca** £39 ❷❷❸
12 Stanley St L1 6AF (0151) 255 0808
*"The best places for lunch"; these all-day deli/dining rooms – by Brunswick Dock, and in the city-centre – remain massively popular, thanks to their "tasty" Portuguese-influenced scoff (from blackboards published daily online); gripes? – the style is "café-like", and regulars can find menu choice "limited". / Details: www.delifonseca.co.uk; 9 pm, Fri & Sat 9.30 pm; closed Sun D.*

**Gulshan** £33 ⊤
544-548 Aigburth Rd L19 3QG
(0151) 427 2273
*By the cricket ground, a grand curry house of over a quarter of a century's standing, still sometimes tipped for "the best Indian food" locally; there's a "welcoming" atmosphere too (and, upstairs, a "fabulous cocktail bar"). / Details: www.gulshan-liverpool.com; 11 pm; D only; no shorts.*

**Host** £36 ❸❷❸
31 Hope St L1 9XH (0151) 708 5831
*"All manner of Asian food" – offering "fresh and exciting flavours" – is served up by "friendly" and "helpful" staff at this "lively" offshoot of 60 Hope Street (nearby); its "great value" is proclaimed by practically all of the many reporters who comment on it. / Details: www.ho-st.co.uk; 11 pm, Sun 10 pm.*

**The Italian Club Fish** £42 ❸❸❸
128 Bold St L1 4JA (0151) 707 2110
*"Consistent cooking in an informal setting at very reasonable prices" – that's the formula that makes this "Italo-Glaswegian" outfit, near Central Station, one of the city-centre's top all-rounders; "try to sit at the back". / Details: www.theitalianclubfish.co.uk; 10 pm, Sun 9 pm; closed Mon L; no Amex.*

**The London Carriage Works**
**Hope Street Hotel** £54 ④④④
40 Hope St L1 9DA (0151) 705 2222
*The menu at this stylish boutique-hotel dining room can offer some "great combinations" (and it is twinned with a "varied and interesting" wine list); service can be "unpredictable", though, and – for harsher critics – the whole performance is "very tired". / Details: www.thelondoncarriageworks.co.uk; 10 pm, Sun 9 pm; no shorts.* **Accommodation:** *89 rooms, from £150.*

**Lunya** £41 ❸❸❸
18-20 College Ln L1 3DS (0151) 706 9770
*For "a taste of Spain", Peter Kinsella's "well-*

stocked deli", in the heart of Liverpool One, inspires only positive reports (and a good number of 'em too) for its "varied and unusual" tapas. / **Details:** www.lunya.co.uk; 11 pm, Sun 10 pm.

**Mei Mei**  £33  ○
9-13 Berry St L1 9DF  (0151) 707 2888
Tipped as "on a par with the best in Manchester" (not a bad endorsement, when you're talking about Asian restaurants), an inexpensive city-centre (fringe) spot, noted for its "popularity with the Chinese community". / **Details:** 11.30 pm, Fri & Sat midnight, Sun 10 pm; no Amex.

**The Monro**  £41  ❷❷❸
92-94 Duke St L1 5AG  (0151) 707 9933
"Perhaps the city's best gastropub" – convenience for Liverpool One and the "reasonably-priced" menu help it attract a "noisy, fun-loving crowd". / **Details:** www.themonro.com; 9.30 pm, Sun 7.30 pm; no Amex; no trainers.

**Panoramic**
**Beetham West Tower**  £50  ❹❹❶
Brook St L3 9PJ  (0151) 236 5534
"Stunning views of the city and the Mersey" ("when it isn't raining or encased in fog") are, of course, the "main attraction" of a visit to this landmark, 34th-floor dining room; some (but not all) reporters insist that the food is "very good" too – as you would expect, it is certainly "expensive". / **Details:** www.panoramicliverpool.com; 9.30 pm, Sun 5 pm; no trainers.

**Puschka**  £49  ❷❷❷
16 Rodney St L1 2TE  (0151) 708 8698
"Liverpool's's undiscovered gem!"; currently firing on all cylinders, this "cosy" ("slightly cramped") spot, in the city's Georgian Quarter, offers some "adventurous and interesting" food, and "very friendly" service too. / **Details:** www.puschka.co.uk; 10 pm, Sun 9 pm; D only.

**The Quarter**  £34  ❸❸❸
7-15 Falkner St L8 7PU  (0151) 707 1965
This "trendy eatery, popular with students" serves "good pasta" and so on; "laid-back" lunchtimes are more relaxing, though, than the sometimes "noisy" evenings. / **Details:** www.thequarteruk.com; 11 pm, Sun 10.30 pm.

**Salt House**  £37  ❸❸❸
Hanover Sq L1 3DW  (0151) 706 0092
"Super tapas and an interesting Spanish wine list" inspire many upbeat reports on this "bright"

year-old bar/restaurant, in the city-centre. / **Details:** www.salthousetapas.co.uk; 10.30 pm.

**San Carlo**  £45  ❹❸❷
41 Castle St L2 9SH  (0151) 236 0073
"Good food, priced for WAGs" – the usual San Carlo formula is seen in its purest "glitzy" form at this "wonderfully buzzy" city-centre spot; "you spot a footballer every time!" / **Details:** www.sancarlo.co.uk; 11 pm.

**The Side Door**  £42  ○
29a, Hope St L1 9BQ  (0151) 707 7888
Early days under new ownership, but this "intimate" restaurant in a Georgian house is tipped for "fabulous food and great service" – more reports please! / **Details:** www.thesidedoor.co.uk; 10 pm, Sun 4 pm; closed Sun D.

**60 Hope Street**  £57  ❸❸❹
60 Hope St L1 9BZ  (0151) 707 6060
In a "smart" townhouse near the Anglican cathedral, the city's longest-established fine dining restaurant is, say fans, still "easily the best"; the odd off-day is not unknown, though, and even fans who proclaim "great food and service" can find ambience "lacking" at quiet times. / **Details:** www.60hopestreet.com; 10.30 pm; closed Sat L.

**Spire**  £43  ❷❸❸
1 Church Rd L15 9EA  (0151) 734 5040
"Unfailingly delicious food in friendly and informal surroundings" – that's the deal that makes this "small suburban restaurant", in Wavertree, "the best in town", so far as some reporters are concerned; critics, though, say "there's not enough imagination to make it truly top-notch"; good lunchtime offer. / **Details:** www.spirerestaurant.co.uk; Mon-Thu 9 pm, Fri & Sat 9.30 pm; closed Mon L, Sat L & Sun.

**Tai Pan**  £29  ❷❸❹
WH Lung Bldg, Great Howard St L5 9TZ
(0151) 207 3888
"A large Chinese restaurant above an even larger Chinese supermarket"; weekend dim sum is something of a local cult, so arrive early or be prepared to queue. / **Details:** 11.30 pm, Sun 9.30 pm.

LLANDEWI SKIRRID, MONMOUTHSHIRE2–1A

**The Walnut Tree**  £60  ❶❷❸
NP7 8AW  (01873) 852797
"Back to its best!"; thanks to Shaun Hill's "outstanding" cooking, ("neither too hearty nor too fussy"), this "busy" gastropub, in "gorgeous" countryside, has re-established itself as "the best

restaurant in Wales" – even those who found the dining room "a bit cold" had "a fantastic experience overall".
/ **Details:** www.thewalnuttreeinn.com; 3m NE of Abergavenny on B4521; 10 pm; closed Mon & Sun. **Accommodation:** 5 rooms, from £180.

---

LLANDRILLO, DENBIGHSHIRE          4–2D

**Tyddyn Llan**          **£78**   ❷❷❷
LL21 0ST   (01490) 440264
"Impressive but unpretentious" cuisine and "professional" service have carved out a big reputation for Bryan & Susan Webb's "classy yet unstuffy" gastronomic "hide-away" in "the beautiful hills of North Wales"; critics, though, can find the style a touch "old-fashioned".
/ **Details:** www.tyddynllan.co.uk; on B4401 between Corwen and Bala; 9 pm; (Mon-Thu L by prior arrangement only); no Amex; booking essential breakfast & weekday L. **Accommodation:** 13 rooms, from £120.

---

LLANDUDNO, CONWY          4–1D

**Bodysgallen Hall**          **£67**   ⓣ
LL30 1RS   (01492) 584466
Just outside the town, an intriguingly-sited Elizabethan manor house, in beautiful gardens – the food is something of a supporting attraction, but the overall experience is very pleasant; there's also a bistro – 1620.
/ **Details:** www.bodysgallen.com; 2m off A55 on A470; 9.15 pm, Fri & Sat 9.30 pm; closed Mon; no jeans or trainers; children: 6+. **Accommodation:** 31 rooms, from £179.

**Jaya**          **£35**   ⓣ
36 Church Walks  LL30 2HN   (01492) 818 198
An upmarket B&B (claiming to offer 'the only truly authentic home cooked Indian food in North Wales'); fans tip it for its "delightful" and ever-evolving menu, incorporating East African influences. / **Details:** www.jayarestaurant.co.uk; 10 pm; closed Mon & Tue.

**St Tudno Hotel**          **£48**   ❸❷❷
Promenade  LL30 2LP   (01492) 874411
You won't find a formula much more "traditional" than that of this Victorian-style townhouse hotel near the pier of this characterful resort; the new chef's cooking, though, is hailed in most reports as "unexpectedly good".
/ **Details:** www.st-tudno.co.uk; 9.30 pm; no shorts; children: 6+ after 6.30 pm. **Accommodation:** 18 rooms, from £100.

---

LLANFRYNACH, POWYS          2–1A

**White Swan**          **£45**   ⓣ
Brecon LD3 7BZ   (01874) 665276
"Set in the beautiful Brecon Beacons", a 17th-century coaching inn tipped for good cooking generally, and some "superb Welsh lamb daily specials" in particular.
/ **Details:** www.the-white-swan.co.uk; 9 pm; closed Mon & Tue; no Amex; booking essential.

---

LLANGOLLEN, DENBIGHSHIRE          5–3A

**Corn Mill**          **£40**   ❹❸❷
Dee Ln  LL20 8PN   (01978) 869555
It's the dramatic and "lovely" location of this attractive gastropub – overhanging the foaming waters of the Dee – that makes it of real interest; the food, though, does have its fans.
/ **Details:** www.cornmill-llangollen.co.uk; 9.30 pm, Sun 9 pm.

---

LLANWDDYN, POWYS          4–2D

**Lake Vyrnwy Hotel**          **£57**   ⓣ
Lake Vyrnwy  SY10 0LY   (01691) 870692
An "old-fashioned" country house hotel with "one of the best settings in the UK" – the lake it overlooks was created by the same Victorian engineers who built the house; it hasn't attracted much feedback of late, but fans still tip its all-round "comfortable" charms.
/ **Details:** www.lakevyrnwyhotel.co.uk; on B4393 at SE end of Lake Vyrnwy; 9.15 pm; no shorts. **Accommodation:** 52 rooms, from £120.

---

LLANWRTYD WELLS, POWYS          4–4D

**Carlton Riverside**          **£53**   ❸❸④
Irfon Cr  LD5 4SP   (01591) 610248
Mary Ann & Alan Gilchrist's "relaxing" traditional-style riverside restaurant-with-rooms is praised for its "interesting" and "well-presented" cooking; even the least impressed reporters concede that the food is "sound".
/ **Details:** www.carltonriverside.com; 8.30 pm; D only, closed Sun; no Amex. **Accommodation:** 5 rooms, from £75.

---

LOCH LOMOND, DUNBARTONSHIRE 9–4B

**Martin Wishart**
**Cameron House**          **£93**   ❷❷❷
G83 8QZ   (01389) 722504
Outpost of leading Edinburgh chef Martin Wishart, this stylish restaurant, attached to a lochside country house hotel, is a "great special-occasion restaurant", offering "an exceptional tasting menu"; the occasional critic, though, can find it "hugely overpriced".

/ **Details:** www.martinwishartlochlomond.co.uk; over
Erskine Bridge to A82, follow signs to Loch Lomond;
9.45 pm. **Accommodation:** 129 rooms, from £215.

---

LOCHINVER, HIGHLAND                    9–1B

**The Albannach**            **£74**   ❶❷❸
IV27 4LP   (01571) 844407
A remote boutique hotel which wins the highest
ratings for its "beautifully precise cuisine" – "it
never fails to make a fantastic impression in
food, wines, hospitality, professionalism and
charm!" / **Details:** www.thealbannach.co.uk; one
sitting; D only, closed Mon; no Amex; children: 12+.
**Accommodation:** 5 rooms, from £290.

---

LOCKSBOTTOM, KENT                     3–3B

**Chapter One**             **£53**   ❶❷❸
Farnborough Common  BR6 8NF
(01689) 854848
"Superb food, bettered by not many in London"
has won a simply enormous fan club for this
"classy" and "comfortable" – but still quite
"reasonably-priced" – suburban spot; if there is a
criticism of chef Andrew McLeish's menu, it's that
it can strike regulars as a touch "static".
/ **Details:** www.chaptersrestaurants.com; Sun-Thu
9.15 pm, Fri & Sat 9.45 pm; no trainers; booking:
max 12.

---

LONG CRENDON, BUCKINGHAMSHIRE 2–2D

**The Angel**               **£51**   ❶
47 Bicester Rd  HP18 9EE   (01844) 208268
"A bistro-pub in an archetypal English village",
tipped as an "efficient and friendly" sort of place
that's "ever-reliable... but always the same!"
/ **Details:** www.angelrestaurant.co.uk; 2m NW of
Thames, off B4011; 9.30 pm; closed Sun D; no Amex.
**Accommodation:** 4 rooms, from £95.

**The Mole & Chicken**      **£43**   ❸❸❷
Easington  HP18 9EY   (01844) 208387
Prettily "tucked-away", a "lovely old pub" whose
"no-nonsense" fare generally impresses; the prix-
fixe lunch menu offers "great value".
/ **Details:** www.themoleandchicken.co.uk; follow signs
from B4011 at Long Crendon; 9.30 pm, Sun 9 pm.
**Accommodation:** 5 rooms, from £110.

---

LONG WHITTENHAM, OXFORDSHIRE 2–2D

**The Vine and Spice**      **£40**   ❷❸④
High St  OX14 4QH   (01865) 409 900
"Effectively, an Indian gastropub!" – "lighter-than
normal" dishes, with "very well-balanced spicing",
are all part of the package that makes this a
"very pleasant" all-rounder.
/ **Details:** www.thevineandspice.co.uk; 10.30 pm.

---

LOUGHBOROUGH, LEICESTERSHIRE   5–3D

**The Hammer and Pincers £50**   ❸❷❸
5 East Rd  LE12 6ST   (01509) 880735
"Run by a delightful couple", this "reliable"
gastropub pleases all reporters with its "good
food at very reasonable prices" (and in an area
that's otherwise "something of a gastronomic
desert"). / **Details:** www.hammerandpincers.co.uk;
9.30 pm, Sun 6 pm; closed Sun D; no Amex.

---

LOWER BOCKHAMPTON, DORCHESTER,
DORSET                                  2–4B

**Yalbury Cottage**         **£49**   ❷❸❷
DT2 8PZ   (01305) 262382
"Wonderful food is lovingly served in Ariane &
Jamie Jones's pretty thatched restaurant-with-
rooms" – all reporters agree it's an "informal yet
comfortable" destination that "deserves wider
recognition". / **Details:** www.yalburycottage.com;
9 pm; closed Mon, Tue–Sat D only, closed Sun D;
no Amex. **Accommodation:** 8 rooms, from £95.

---

LOWER FROYLE, ALTON, HAMPSHIRE  2–3D

**The Anchor Inn**          **£48**   ④❸❸
GU34 4NA   (01420) 23261
"Well-presented, and with bags of flavour", the
food at this "very welcoming" and stylish
gastropub (with rooms) invariably satisfies
reporters.
/ **Details:** www.anchorinnatlowerfroyle.co.uk; 9.30 pm,
Sun 9 pm. **Accommodation:** 5 rooms, from £120.

---

LOWER HARDRES, KENT                   3–3D

**The Granville**           **£38**   ❷❸❸
Street End  CT4 7AL   (01227) 700402
"Arguably the best value within striking distance
of Canterbury" – the "straightforward" food at
this friendly "beacon in the desert surrounding
the town" pleases all who comment on it.
/ **Details:** 9 pm; closed Sun D; no Amex.

---

LOWER ODDINGTON, GLOUCESTERSHIRE
2–1C

**The Fox Inn**             **£44**   ❷❸❷
GL56 0UR   (01451) 870555
"A pub restaurant that puts many restaurants to
shame"; this "classic Cotswold boozer" (with
garden), "in a sleepy village", is highly rated for
its "confidently realised" traditional fare, which
includes some truly "excellent" puddings.
/ **Details:** www.foxinn.net; on A436 near
Stow-on-the-Wold; 10 pm, Sun 9.30 pm; no Amex.
**Accommodation:** 3 rooms, from £75.

---

**LOWER PEOVER, KNUTSFORD, CHESHIRE** 5–2B

**Bells of Peover** £39 🌐
The Cobbles WA16 9PZ (01565) 722269
Staff with surprisingly serious cvs are now
installed at an inn that's long been celebrated
locally as a foodie destination; not many reports
as yet, but fans tip the cuisine as of consistently
"great quality". / **Details:** www.thebellsofpeover.com; opp St Oswald's
church, off B5081; 9.30 pm, Sun 8 pm; closed Mon.

---

**LUDLOW, SHROPSHIRE** 5–4A

**La Bécasse** £83 ❷❸❸
17 Corve St SY8 1DA (01584) 872325
Thanks to Will Holland's "fabulous", locally-
sourced cooking, this panelled outpost of the '10
in 8' empire has become Ludlow's best-known
culinary destination; desperation to please
restaurant-inspectors, though, may account for
the rather "finicky" style, and sometimes "stuffy"
atmosphere. / **Details:** www.labecasse.co.uk; 9 pm,
Sat 9.30 pm; closed Mon, Tue L & Sun D; no Amex;
no trainers.

**Green Café, Ludlow Mill
on the Green** £33 ❷❷❸
Dinham Millennium Grn SY8 1EG
(01584) 879872
"No everyday place in Ludlow comes close to
this quality", say fans of this "model café", which
has "a delightful setting overlooking the river";
Clive Davis's "deceptively simple" food is "well-
prepared and makes a fantastic cheap lunch";
"great with kids" too.
/ **Details:** www.ludlowmillonthegreen.co.uk; closed
Mon, L only Tue-Sun; no Amex.

**Mr Underhill's** £84 ❶❶❷
Dinham Weir SY8 1EH (01584) 874431
"Great hosts, great food"; no-one has a bad word
to say about Chris & Judy Bradley's "charming"
restaurant-with-rooms, which "has a wonderful
location by the banks of the Teme" – "it really is
hard to imagine how the dining experience here
could be made much more pleasant!"
/ **Details:** www.mr-underhills.co.uk; 8.15 pm; D only,
closed Mon & Tue; no Amex; children: 8+.
**Accommodation:** 6 rooms, from £140.

---

**LUPTON, CUMBRIA** 7–4D

**The Plough Inn** £39 ❸❸❸
Cow Brow LA6 1PJ (01539) 567 700
Much survey feedback on this "dramatically-
refurbished inn" – an offshoot of the Punch Bowl
(Crosthwaite), (and "handily located a couple of
miles off the M6"); most reports say it's a
"special" place offering "great food at great

prices", but there is the odd critic for whom the
experience is a big let-down.
/ **Details:** www.theploughatlupton.co.uk; 9 pm.
**Accommodation:** 5 rooms, from £95.

---

**LYDDINGTON, RUTLAND** 5–4D

**Marquess of Exeter** £42 ❹❸❸
52 Main St LE15 9LT (01572) 822 477
"A bit barn-like", the dining area may be, but
Brian Baker's "tastefully restored", "light and
airy" gastropub is a "cheerful" place, which is
"sound" foodwise ("you know exactly what to
expect"), and "fairly priced" too.
/ **Details:** www.marquessexter.co.uk; 9.30 pm, Sun
9 pm; no Amex. **Accommodation:** 17 rooms,
from £99.50.

---

**LYDFORD, DEVON** 1–3C

**The Dartmoor Inn** £46 ❷❸❸
Moorside EX20 4AY (01822) 820221
On the edge of the moor, "a former coaching inn
that's more a restaurant nowadays", and one
which "makes impressive use of local produce"
too; "the set lunch is a steal".
/ **Details:** www.dartmoorinn.com; on the A386
Tavistock to Okehampton road; 9.30 pm; closed
Mon L & Sun D. **Accommodation:** 3 rooms,
from £95.

---

**LYME REGIS, DORSET** 2–4A

**Harbour Inn** £41 ❹❹❸
Marine Pde DT7 3JF (01297) 442299
"A reliable staple of Lyme Regis" – this
"relaxing" inn "right by the sea" makes a "fun"
spot for some "good-value" grub, including "great
fish". / **Details:** www.harbourinnlymeregis.co.uk;
9 pm; closed Sun D.

**Hix Oyster and
Fish House** £53 ❷❹❶
Cobb Rd DT7 3JP (01297) 446910
"The setting is to die for", at Mark Hix's "bright"
clifftop venture, which has "spectacular views
over Lyme Regis bay"; "there are the occasional
low notes" – service can be "unpolished" and
some prices are "silly" – but "all in all, this is a
tremendous seafood restaurant".
/ **Details:** www.restaurantsetcltd.co.uk; 10 pm.

---

**LYMINGTON, HAMPSHIRE** 2–4C

**Egan's** £45 ❷❸❸
24 Gosport St SO41 9BE (01590) 676165
All reports on this "long-standing bistro" are in
complete accord – "John Egan continues to
deliver exceptionally good food, and at
remarkably reasonable prices too".

/ **Details:** 10 pm; closed Mon & Sun; no Amex; booking: max 6, Sat.

---

LYMM, CHESHIRE                    5–2B

**The Church Green**     £54  🔵
Higher Ln  WA13 0AP   (01925) 752068
A former Dorchester Grill head chef adds gloss to this village-restaurant in the Footballer Belt, which benefits from some pleasant al fresco tables; it inspires somewhat mixed reviews, but is still tipped for "standard" fare that "can be very good… if you hit the right day".
/ **Details:** www.aidenbyrne.co.uk; 9.30 pm, Fri & Sat 10 pm, Sun 7.45 pm; no Amex.

---

LYNDHURST, HAMPSHIRE              2–4C

**Lime Wood**     £69  🔵
Beaulieu Rd  SO43 7FZ   (02380) 287168
The "ambitious" main dining room of this "beautifully-located" New Forest country house hotel seems to be dropping off the culinary map; all feedback this year, however, spoke of "top-notch" results. / **Details:** www.limewood.co.uk; 9.30 pm; SRA-71%. **Accommodation:** 30 rooms, from £295.

**Lime Wood (Scullery)**     £48  🔵
Beaulieu Rd  SO43 7FZ   (02380) 287168
"Plain food, served in an appealing way" wins consistent praise for the "very attractive" No. 2 restaurant at this country house hotel, tipped for its "very friendly" service, and "great value for money" too. / **Details:** www.limewood.co.uk; 9.30 pm. **Accommodation:** 30 rooms, from £295.

---

MADINGLEY, CAMBRIDGESHIRE         3–1B

**Three Horseshoes**     £51  ④⑤❸
High St  CB23 8AB   (01954) 210221
With its "lovely conservatory", this "picturesque" pub has long been a classic day-out bolt hole for Cambridge undergrads and their parents; many reports this year though complain of "tired", or "hit and miss" meals – the patron has recently returned to the stoves, so let's hope for a return to past standards!
/ **Details:** www.threehorseshoesmadingley.co.uk; 2m W of Cambridge, off A14 or M11; 9.30 pm, Sun 8.30 pm.

---

MAIDENHEAD, BERKSHIRE             3–3A

**Boulters Riverside Brasserie**     £51  ④④❷
Boulters Lock Island  SL6 8PE
(01628) 621291
An unusual venue, perched over the Thames, where fans insist that the food is "usually very good"; not everyone is quite convinced, though, so first-timers may wish to check out the cheaper terrace bar. / **Details:** www.boultersrestaurant.co.uk; 9.30 pm; closed Mon & Sun D; no Amex.

**The Royal Oak**     £68  ❸❷❷
Paley St  SL6 3JN   (01628) 620541
'Parkie's pub' is everything you might hope of "a well-run stockbroker-belt gastroboozer"; it may be no bargain, but it "combines friendly pub atmosphere and fabulous food".
/ **Details:** www.theroyaloakpaleystreet.com; 9.30 pm, Fri & Sat 10 pm; closed Sun D; children: 3+ .

---

MAIDENSGROVE, OXFORDSHIRE         2–2D

**Five Horseshoes**     £45  🔵
RG9 6EX   (01491) 641282
A characterful "hikers' pub", tipped for its "lovely location" in the heart of the Chilterns, and "above-average food" too.
/ **Details:** www.thefivehorseshoes.co.uk; off B481 between Nettlebed & Watlington; 9.30 pm, Sun 8.30 pm; no Amex; booking essential.

---

MALMESBURY, WILTSHIRE             2–2C

**The Old Bell Hotel**     £54  🔵
Abbey Row  SN16 0BW   (01666) 822344
"The overall ambience makes it well worth a visit" – the 'oldest hotel in England' still generally wins praise for its "well-cooked and presented" fare, not least "some of the best desserts going".
/ **Details:** www.oldbellhotel.com; 9 pm, Fri & Sat 9.30 pm. **Accommodation:** 33 rooms, from £125.

---

MANCHESTER, GREATER MANCHESTER5–2B

**Akbar's**     £27  ❸❸❸
73-83 Liverpool Rd  M3 4NQ   (0161) 834 8444
"The queues are worth it", say fans of this large and "buzzing" city-centre spot, who praise its "reasonably-priced Pakistani fare" ("amazing, given the numbers served"); there are quite a few critics, though, for whom it's just "big, and bog-standard". / **Details:** www.akbars.co.uk; 11 pm, Fri & Sat 11.30 pm; D only; need 10+ to book.

**Albert's**     £44  ④④④
120-122 Barlow Moor Rd  M20 2PU
(0161) 434 8289
"Spacious and upmarket", this West Didsbury "cocktail-brasserie" is of particular note for its "great al fresco tables"; it's particularly popular with reporters as an "excellent-value" lunchtime rendezvous – evenings can be "very noisy".
/ **Details:** www.albertsdidsbury.com; 10 pm; no Amex.

**Albert's Shed**　　£45　④❸❷
20 Castle St　M3 4LZ　(0161) 839 9818
A popular destination for "a night out with
friends" (or a "good-value set lunch"), this large
Castlefields venue benefits particularly from its
"lovely" canalside setting.
/ **Details:** www.albertsshed.com; 10 pm, Fri
10.30 pm, Sat 11 pm, Sun 9.30 pm; no Amex.

**Armenian Taverna**　　£36　❸❸❸
3-5 Princess St　M2 4DF　(0161) 834 9025
"Cosily retro, but with surprisingly fresh food" –
this "idiosyncratic", but "very friendly and
welcoming" city-centre basement fixture is "still
going strong"; "I must have been eating here for
35 years, and I've never had a bad or
unenjoyable meal!"
/ **Details:** www.armeniantaverna.co.uk; 11 pm; closed
Mon, Sat L & Sun L.

**Aumbry**　　£52　❷❷❸
2 Church Ln　M25 1AJ　(0161) 7985841
"Deserving national recognition", say fans, this
"quirky" Prestwich "treasure" is proving one of
Manchester's most notable arrivals of recent
years; there's always work to do, though –
consistency can sometimes slip and, by local
standards, portions can appear rather "small".
/ **Details:** www.aumbryrestaurant.co.uk; 9.30 pm;
closed Mon, Tue L, Wed L, Thu L & Sun; no Amex;
SRA-67%.

**Australasia**　　£54　❸❸❷
1 Spinningfields　M3 3AP　(0161) 831 0288
"A bit like London's Zuma" (if minus the
oligarchs), this "trendy" and "interesting"
subterranean pan-Oriental is, say fans, "a breath
of fresh air" – "just what Manchester has been
waiting for"; perhaps inevitably, critics can find it
a bit "wannabe" – "to avoid the drinking crowd,
and the DJ, go for lunch".
/ **Details:** www.australasia.uk.com; midnight; no Amex.

**Azzurro**　　£36　🅣
242 Burton Rd　M20 2LW　(0161) 448 0099
In West Didsbury, this is sometimes tipped as
"the most authentic Italian in south Manchester"
(and offering "interesting specials, particularly
fish and seafood"); reports, though, are fewer
than we would like, and a little uneven.
/ **Details:** www.azzurrorestaurant.com; 11 pm; D only,
Fri & Sat; no Amex.

**Chaophraya,**　　£46　❸❸❷
Chapel Walks　M2 1HN　(0161) 832 8342
A "cracking" city-centre Thai, which is praised to
the skies by locals and visitors alike for its
"brilliant" cooking and "lovely" buzz; it occupies

a "spacious" (and "recently glammed-up")
setting. / **Details:** www.chaophraya.co.uk; 10.30 pm.

**Croma**　　£30　❸❷❷
1-3 Clarence St　M2 4DE　(0161) 237 9799
"Brilliant for a simple night out"; it may be
something of a "PizzaExpress clone", but this
"always-welcoming" spot, by the Town Hall, is a
real "stalwart", and its "no-fuss" formula remains
extremely popular; also in Chorlton and
Prestwich. / **Details:** www.cromapizza.co.uk; 10 pm,
Fri & Sat 11 pm.

**Dimitri's**　　£45　❸❸❸
1 Campfield Arc　M3 4FN　(0161) 839 3319
"Back to its best after the recent expansion", this
long-established semi al-fresco Greek – adjacent
to a Victorian arcade – is a good choice for a
group night out, or "the sort of lunch that goes
on all afternoon"; there is now also an offshoot
in Didsbury. / **Details:** www.dimitris.co.uk;
11.30 pm.

**Dough**　　£33　❷❷❸
75-77 High St　M4 1FS　(0161) 8349411
"Ticking all the boxes on quality and value", this
"quite basic" Northern Quarter pizzeria offers
some "intriguing" options – "not all of them
work, but when they do, they're a cut above".
/ **Details:** www.doughpizzakitchen.co.uk; 11 pm.

**East Z East**
**Hotel Ibis**　　£34　❷❸④
Charles St　M1 7DG　(0161) 244 5353
The décor may not excite much ("yet another
sterile attempt at 'Footballers' Wives'"), but – on
the food and service fronts – this "big" and
"busy" Pakistani/Northern Indian inspires
impressively positive reports.
/ **Details:** www.eastzeast.com; 11.15 pm, Fri & Sat
11.45 pm, Sun 10.45 pm; D only.

**Evuna**　　£42　❸❷④
Deansgate　M3 4EW　(0161) 819 2752
On the fringe of the city-centre, a tapas bar
whose biggest attraction is its "incredible"
Spanish wine list; not everyone feels the food
lives up, but service is unusually "good and
attentive", and the lunchtime and early-evening
menus are a "bargain".
/ **Details:** www.evuna.com; 11 pm, Sun 9 pm.

**The French Restaurant**
**Midland Hotel**　　£70　🅣
Peter St　M60 2DS　(0161) 236 3333
"Tucked-away" inside a famous late-Victorian
hotel, this once-celebrated grand dining room
(think London's Ritz, scaled down) attracts few
comments nowadays; fans, though, tip it as a

Aumbry

Katsouris

Sam's Chop House

venue offering "quality all the way".
/ **Details:** www.qhotels.co.uk; 10.30 pm, Fri & Sat
11 pm; D only, closed Mon & Sun; no jeans or trainers;
children: no children . **Accommodation:** 312 rooms,
from £145.

### Gaucho                                    £66  ❸④④
2a St Mary's St  M3 2LB   (0161) 833 4333
London's steakhouse boom not yet having
reached Manchester, this "glitzy" outpost of the
Argentinian-themed chain quite possibly does
still offer "the best steaks" hereabouts; critics,
though, proclaim this a somewhat "tired"
formula, charging "killer" prices.
/ **Details:** www.gauchorestaurants.com; 10.30 pm,
Fri & Sat 11 pm.

### Glamorous                                 £31  ❷④④
Wing Yip Bus' Centre, Oldham Rd  M4 5HU
(0161) 839 3312
Food that's "notably better than you get in
Chinatown", say fans, makes it worth the trip to
this "HK-style" outfit, above the Ancoats outpost
of the Wing Yip supermarket empire; the cuisine
may occasionally have its faults, say critics, but
even they concede a visit here "is always cheap
and fun".
/ **Details:** www.glamorous-restaurant.co.uk.

### Great Kathmandu                           £27  ❷❸④
140 Burton Rd  M20 1JQ   (0161) 434 6413
"The top curry for miles, but not a place to
linger" – this "traditional" Nepalese curry house
in West Didsbury ("not actually an Indian, but
with the best Madras ever") is hailed by most
reporters as "superb".
/ **Details:** www.greatkathmandu.com; midnight.

### Green's                                   £40  ❷❸❸
43 Lapwing Ln  M20 2NT   (0161) 434 4259
"A great veggie, where carnivores will not be
disappointed!"; although this West Didsbury
fixture is "bigger nowadays, it's lost none of its
intimacy". / **Details:** www.greensdidsbury.co.uk;
10.30 pm; closed Mon L; no Amex.

### Grill on the Alley                        £47  ❸❷❸
5 Ridgefield  M2 6EG   (0161) 833 3465
"Straightforward food, well presented"; just off
St Anne's Square, this "buzzy" ("noisy") but
"intimate" spot rarely gives cause for complaint,
and its steaks in particular are "tip-top".
/ **Details:** www.blackhouse.uk.com; 11 pm.

### Gurkha Grill                              £33  ❷④④
194-198 Burton Rd  M20 1LH
(0161) 445 3461
Not many reports this year, on this long-
established West Didsbury spot, but fans still say
its "quality" Nepalese cooking and "helpful"

service put it amongst Manchester's better curry
houses. / **Details:** www.gurkhagrill.com; midnight,
Fri & Sat 1 pm; D only.

### Jem & I                                   £42  ❷❸❸
1c School Ln  M20 6RD   (0161) 445 3996
Very consistent reports on this "rock-solid"
Didsbury bistro – it may not inspire the same
volume of reports as the Lime Tree (where Jem
formerly worked), but satisfaction with the
cooking is very much in the same league.
/ **Details:** www.jemandirestaurant.co.uk; 10 pm, Fri &
Sat 10.30 pm.

### Katsouris Deli                            £11  ❷④④
113 Deansgate  M3 2BQ   (0161) 819 1260
"Hard to get a seat, as it's always absolutely
packed" – this city-centre (and Bury) café is
"deservedly popular" for its "great sarnies" and
its "amazing-value" platters. / **Details:** L only;
no Amex.

### Koh Samui                                 £36  ❸④⑤
16 Princess St  M1 4NB   (0161) 237 9511
The basement setting near Chinatown is
arguably a tad "dingy", but this city-centre
oriental wins high praise from reporters; the
lunch deal, in particular, is "a steal".
/ **Details:** www.kohsamuirestaurant.co.uk; 11.30 pm;
closed Sat L & Sun L.

### The Lime Tree                             £43  ❶❷❷
8 Lapwing Ln  M20 2WS   (0161) 445 1217
"It's no mean achievement to be so consistently
great!" – this "unpretentious" but "ever-popular"
West Didsbury brasserie (est. 1987) is "streets
ahead of many more expensive places in the
city-centre"; it's not aiming for culinary fireworks,
it's just "always tip-top quality".
/ **Details:** www.thelimetreerestaurant.co.uk; 10 pm;
closed Mon L & Sat L.

### Little Yang Sing                          £37  ❸④④
17 George St  M1 4HE   (0161) 228 7722
Slightly up-and-down reports of late, but this
offshoot of the city's best-known oriental is "still
one of Chinatown's better stand-bys"; indeed,
hard-core supporters insist it's "better than its
big brother". / **Details:** www.littleyangsing.co.uk;
11.30 pm, Fri midnight, Sat 12.30 am, Sun 10.45 pm.

### Livebait                                  £44  ❶
22 Lloyd St  M2 5WA   (0161) 817 4110
Now bought out by its management, this ex-
chain outlet is still Manchester city-centre's only
fish-restaurant of any note – even detractors
consider it "improved", and it is generally tipped
for its "reliable" and "flavoursome" food.
/ **Details:** www.livebaitmanchester.com; 10.30 pm, Sat
11 pm, Sun 9 pm.

**The Mark Addy**  £42  ❸④⑤
Stanley St M3 5EJ  (0161) 832 4080
*Down by the Irwell, a "rather rough-around-the-edges" gastroboozer, where local hero Robert Owen-Brown presides over the stoves; he trained at St John (London), and the "big flavours" of his "sometimes unusual" British dishes generally impress reporters. / Details: www.markaddy.co.uk; 9 pm, Fri & Sat 10 pm, Sun 6 pm; closed Sun D; no Amex.*

**Michael Caines**
**ABode Hotel**  £66  ❸④④
107 Piccadilly M1 2DB  (0161) 200 5678
*With its "innovative" and "tasty" food ("albeit in rather small portions"), this subterranean operation, near Piccadilly Station, still strikes many reporters as an "accomplished" destination; but – leaving the "excellent-value" lunch menu out of account – the experience can seem "pretentious" and "pricey" too. / Details: www.michaelcaines.com; 10 pm; closed Sun; no shorts; 8+ to go through Events.*
**Accommodation:** *61 rooms, from £79.*

**Mr Thomas's**
**Chop House**  £39  ❸❸❷
52 Cross St M2 7AR  (0161) 832 2245
*"Old-fashioned English dishes done well in a classic Victorian tiled pub"; this city-centre institution continues its steady all-round performance, and remains a – perhaps 'the' – city-centre business lunch venue par excellence. / Details: www.tomschophouse.com; 9.30 pm, Sun 8 pm.*

**The Northern Quarter**  £45  ④④❸
108 High St M4 1HQ  (0161) 832 7115
*"Becoming a 'standard'" in this trendy part of town – a neighbourhood spot offering a menu of "good-value" staples. / Details: www.tnq.co.uk; 10.30 pm, Sun 7 pm.*

**Piccolino**  £40  ❸❷❸
8 Clarence St M2 4DW  (0161) 835 9860
*"Part of a chain, but you wouldn't really think so" – this "smart" city-centre Italian makes a "useful rendezvous for both business and pleasure"; "there's been more competition of late", says one reporter, "and they have had to up their game". / Details: www.piccolinorestaurants.co.uk/manchester; 11 pm, Sun 10 pm.*

**Red Chilli**  £25  ❷④④
70-72 Portland St M1 4GU
(0161) 236 2888
*"Interesting, tasty and genuine" dishes have made quite a name for this city-centre Sichuanese/Cantonese (which has a "huge"*

*offshoot near the university at 403-419 Oxford Road, tel 0161 273 1288); it's a "busy" place, though, and staff sometimes "fail to cope". / Details: www.redchillirestaurant.co.uk; 11 pm; need 6+ to book.*

**Room**  £45  ④❸❷
81 King St M2 4AH  (0161) 839 2005
*In the heart of Victorian Manchester, the main room on the 'piano nobile' of this impressive former gentleman's club makes a "stunning" setting for a restaurant and bar; the food ("traditional British with some quirky twists") plays rather a supporting role. / Details: www.roomrestaurants.com; 10 pm, Sat 11 pm; closed Sun.*

**Rosso**  £46  ⑤④❸
43 Spring Gdns M2 2BG  (0161) 8321400
*Fans adore the "great atmosphere" of the restaurant in this "beautiful old marbled bank", co-owned by Rio Ferdinand; foodwise though "there's very little to get excited about", and as to the service? – "as soon as a famous footballer comes in, they all get diverted". / Details: www.rossorestaurants.com; 11 pm.*

**Sam's Chop House**  £45  ❷❸❸
Back Pool Fold, Chapel Walks M2 1HN
(0161) 834 3210
*"Real old-fashioned British food" – generally "well-cooked", and served in "enormous portions" – draws quite a following to this pubbily-styled city-centre basement; especially popular with "local office-folk", it's a "very busy" venue. / Details: www.samschophouse.com; 9.30 pm, Sun 8 pm.*

**San Carlo**  £40  ④④❷
40 King Street West M3 2WY
(0161) 834 6226
*Just about "the most popular spot in town" – this "vibrant" ("bedlam!") Italian, near House of Fraser, is a "good all-rounder" with "an exceptional buzz"; even fans can find it "variable", though, and critics are scathing – "as so often in Manchester, quality is inversely proportional to the number of LV handbags!" / Details: www.sancarlo.co.uk; 11 pm.*

**San Carlo Cicchetti**  £45  ❷④❸
42 King Street West M3 2QG
(0161) 839 2233
*A location on the ground floor of House of Fraser (Kendal's to old-timers) has done little to dim the appeal of San Carlo's 'Italian tapas' spin-off; with its "classily laid-back style" and "wonderful range of dishes", it has quickly become a major local hang-out. / Details: www.sancarlocicchetti.co.uk.*

**Second Floor Restaurant
Harvey Nichols** £56 ❷❸❸
21 New Cathedral St M1 1AD
(0161) 828 8898
Especially for lunch, this department store dining room is arguably "the bet bet in a city-centre starved of fine dining"; it may be no bargain, but the cooking invariably impresses, and the wine list is "amazing".
/ **Details:** www.harveynichols.com; 9.30 pm; closed Mon D & Sun D; SRA-60%.

**Stock** £50 ④❸❷
4 Norfolk St M2 1DW (0161) 839 6644
Everyone agrees the setting (in the former Stock Exchange) is "lovely", but reports on the food at this city-centre Italian come in every possible degree of (dis)satisfaction.
/ **Details:** www.stockrestaurant.co.uk; 10 pm; closed Sun.

**Tai Pan** £33 ❷④④
81-97 Upper Brook St M13 9TX
(0161) 273 2798
"Consistently good, especially for dim sum" – this "very busy" Chinese restaurant, above a Longsight cash-and-carry, is unanimously hailed by reporters for its "very broad and well-prepared" menu, and at "very good prices" too.
/ **Details:** 11 pm, Sun 9.30 pm.

**Tai Wu** £32 ❷❷④
44 Oxford Rd M1 5EJ (0161) 236 6557
This "large and busy" restaurant, near Chinatown, impresses all reporters with its "wonderful" food in "generous" portions; the setting is a touch "sterile", though, and the downstairs buffet "best avoided".
/ **Details:** www.tai-wu.co.uk; 2.45 am.

**Tampopo** £30 ❸❷❸
16 Albert Sq M2 5PF (0161) 819 1966
"One of the best Wagamama-clones!" – right by the Town Hall, it's "always a good choice for a quick bite" ("ideal pre-theatre"), and "rather buzzier" than the famous chain too.
/ **Details:** www.tampopo.co.uk; 11 pm, Sun 10 pm; need 7+ to book.

**Teacup on
Thomas Street** £22 ❷❷❷
53-55 Thomas St M4 1NA
(0161) 832 3233
The name (almost) says it all about this "beautiful" Northern Quarter "hidden gem", which offers a "mouthwateringly massive display of artisan pies, cakes and tarts"; "well-priced light lunches" too.
/ **Details:** www.teacupandcakes.com.

**This & That** £12 ❶❸⑤
3 Soap St M4 1EW (0161) 832 4971
OK, it looks ultra-"cheap 'n' cheerful", but you get a "massive depth of flavour" in the curries ("freshly-made daily") at this famous Northern Quarter "canteen", where the "rice-and-three-for-a-fiver" is the stuff of Mancunian legend.
/ **Details:** www.thisandthatcafe.co.uk; 4 pm, Fri & Sat 8 pm; no credit cards.

**Wing's** £51 ❷❶❸
1 Lincoln Sq M2 5LN (0161) 834 9000
"A bit pricey, but well worth it", this "slick" (and "celeb-friendly") Chinese, near the Town Hall, is simply the best restaurant in central Manchester of any type; "from the style and quality of service, you'd think you were at a top restaurant in Paris!" / **Details:** www.wingsrestaurant.co.uk; 11 pm; closed Sat L; children: 11+ after 8 pm Mon-Fri, 21+ D.

**Yang Sing** £42 ❷❸④
34 Princess St M1 4JY (0161) 236 2200
"The top dim sum in the North"; Harry Yeung's warehouse-style Chinatown institution has had its ups and downs over the years (est. 1977), but it continues to be Manchester's most famous – and for many reporters best – dining destination. / **Details:** www.yang-sing.com; 11.30 pm, Sat 12.15 am, Sun 10.30 pm.

**MANNINGTREE, ESSEX** 3–2C

**Lucca Enoteca** £35 ❶
39-43 High St CO11 1AH (01206) 390044
"A really good Italian in an out-of-the-way location"; this "jewel in Essex's crown" is of particular note for its "great" pizzas ("one is good enough for two") – salads and puddings, though, are "very good" too.
/ **Details:** www.luccafoods.co.uk; 9.30 pm, Fri & Sat 10 pm; no Amex.

**MARGATE, KENT** 3–3D

**The Ambrette** £45 ❶❷❸
44 King St CT9 1QE (01843) 231 504
"Simply the best Indian food I have ever had!" – fans do not stint in their praise for the "innovative" and "well-spiced" fare on offer at Dev Biswal's "delightful" restaurant in the Old Town; "if you visit Margate, you must come here at least once!". / **Details:** www.theambrette.co.uk; 9.30 pm, Fri & Sat 10 pm; closed Mon.

**Turner Contemporary** £28 ❷④❷
The Rendez Vous CT9 1HG
(01843) 233022
"Remarkably good cooking" and "amazing" views win recommendations for this "bustling"

*year-old gallery café, particularly as a brunch destination; now if only they could just sort out the sometimes "shoddy" service…*

**The Harrow at**
**Little Bedwyn**          £73    ❶❷❷
Little Bedwyn  SN8 3JP   (01672) 870871
"An absolute gastronomic gem in the heart of the Wiltshire countryside" – the Jones's small restaurant combines "very modern and clean-flavoured cuisine" with an "amazing", "innovative" wine list; the "lunch-with-two-glasses" formula comes particularly highly recommended.
/ **Details:** www.theharrowatlittlebedwyn.co.uk; 9 pm; closed Mon, Tue & Sun; no Amex; no trainers.

**Adam Simmonds**
**Danesfield House**          £91    ❸❸❸
Henley Rd  SL7 2EY   (01628) 891010
"Superb… everything is put together with such imagination and precision", says one of the fans of this "majestic" country house dining experience; critics do find results "patchy", though, and – even with the "breathtaking" gardens/Thames views – the experience can feel surprisingly "sterile".
/ **Details:** www.danesfieldhouse.co.uk; 3m outside Marlow on the A4155; 9.30 pm; closed Mon, Tue L, Wed L & Sun; no jeans or trainers.
**Accommodation:** 62 rooms, from £159.

**Aubergine**
**Compleat Angler**          £73    ❸❷❸
Marlow Bridge  SL7 1RG   (01628) 405405
"A change of management but not of chef has improved this once-ordinary place into a pretty decent destination!" – at last, this famous and "impressive"-looking landmark is beginning to live up to its "fabulous" riverside location, though prices do remain "very Marlow".
/ **Details:** www.atozrestaurants.com; 10.30 pm, Sun 9.30 pm; no shorts. **Accommodation:** 64 rooms, from £150.

**Hand & Flowers**          £74    ❷❸④
West St  SL7 2BP   (01628) 482277
Tom Kerridge's simple inn has become a big deal since it won a second Michelin star, and "it's ever-harder to get a table"; not all reporters are quite convinced it can stand the strain, but – despite recurrent complaints of "over-salting" – most reporters feel the "refined" cuisine "deserves its reputation".
/ **Details:** www.thehandandflowers.co.uk; 9.30 pm;

*closed Sun D.* **Accommodation:** 4 rooms, from £140.

**The Royal Oak**          £42    ⓣ
Frieth Rd, Bovingdon Grn  SL7 2JF   (01628) 488611
A popular pub-cum-restaurant, tipped for food that's "always reliable" – "you could call it 'samey', but others prefer to use the word 'guaranteed'!"
/ **Details:** www.royaloakmarlow.co.uk; 9.30 pm, Fri & Sat 10 pm.

**The Vanilla Pod**          £64    ❶❸❸
31 West St  SL7 2LS   (01628) 898101
"Intense flavours and wonderful combinations" characterise the "consistently excellent" contemporary French cuisine at Michael MacDonald's "extremely comfortable" restaurant, "in a small house in the centre of the town"; shame service can sometimes be on the "chilly" side. / **Details:** www.thevanillapod.co.uk; 10 pm; closed Mon & Sun.

**Black Sheep**
**Brewery Bistro**          £34    ⓣ
Wellgarth  HG4 4EN   (01765) 680101
"A bistro in a brewery, what more could you want?" – this large café offers "simple" fare that's generally reliable, as well as the great beer you would expect. / **Details:** www.blacksheep.co.uk; 9 pm; Sun-Wed L only, Thu-Sat L & D; no Amex.

**Samuel's**
**Swinton Park Hotel**          £71    ❷❷❶
HG4 4JH   (01765) 680900
"Everything was superb", says a fan of the dining experience at this "stunning" venue – part of a large, castellated country house hotel; there is the odd quibble, but the general view is that Simon Crannage's cuisine "goes from strength to strength". / **Details:** www.swintonpark.com; 9.30 pm, Fri & Sat 10 pm; closed Mon L; no jeans or trainers; booking: max 8; children: 8+ at D; SRA-84%.
**Accommodation:** 32 rooms, from £185.

**Verveine Fishmarket**          £53    ❶❷❸
98 High St  SO41 0QE   (01590) 642176
Fishmongers in this quaint seaside village created this "small but professional" seafood operation a couple of years ago; the fish is always "beautifully-cooked" – "innovative", but "without too much elaboration".
/ **Details:** www.verveine.co.uk; 9.30 pm; closed Mon & Sun; no Amex.

## MILTON KEYNES, BUCKINGHAMSHIRE 3–2A

**Jaipur** £38 ❸❸❸
599 Grafton Gate East MK9 1AT
(01908) 669796
*This vast, purpose-built Indian (also serving other Asian cuisine), near the railway station, is "the pick of Milton Keynes" restaurant-wise – the food's good, the building is "fantastic", and staff "make you feel special every time".*
/ **Details:** *www.jaipur.co.uk; 11.30 pm, Sun 10.30 pm; no shorts.*

## MISTLEY, ESSEX 3–2D

**Mistley Thorn Hotel** £39 ❸❸❸
High St CO11 1HE (01206) 392 821
*It's not just the "lovely setting in a pretty village, overlooking the Stour" that makes Sherri Singleton's gastropub-with-rooms of note – it's long been popular for its "excellent seafood selection". / **Details:** www.mistleythorn.com; 9.30 pm; no Amex. **Accommodation:** 8 rooms, from £80.*

## MOLD, FLINTSHIRE 5–2A

**Glasfryn** £41 ❶
Raikes Ln CH7 6LR (01352) 750500
*"A solid member of the Brunning & Price chain" (a range of classy North Western gastropubs) – an establishment that's popular "both at lunch (Civic Centre) and dinner (Theatr Clwyd)".*
/ **Details:** *www.glasfryn-mold.co.uk; 9.30 pm, Sun 9 pm.*

## MORETON-IN-MARSH, GLOUCESTERSHIRE 2–1C

**Horse & Groom** £43 ❸❹❸
Upper Oddington GL56 0XH
(01451) 830584
*"A gem in the Gloucestershire countryside"; this "casual" gastroboozer continues to be a consistent crowd-pleaser, thanks to its "boldly-flavoured" dishes.*
/ **Details:** *www.horseandgroom.uk.com; 9 pm; no Amex. **Accommodation:** 7 rooms, from £89.*

## MORSTON, NORFOLK 6–3C

**Morston Hall** £83 ❷❸❷
Main Coast Rd NR25 7AA (01263) 741041
*Galton Blackiston's "very relaxed" coastal country house hotel remains "a perfect spot" for most reporters, thanks to his "fabulous", locally-sourced cuisine; even fans can find it "very, very expensive" though, and doubters find it "competent but lacking wow-factor".*
/ **Details:** *www.morstonhall.com; between Blakeney &*

*Wells on A149; 8 pm; D only, ex Sun open L & D. **Accommodation:** 13 rooms, from £310.*

## MOULSFORD, OXFORDSHIRE 2–2D

**The Beetle & Wedge Boathouse** £45 ❹❹❶
Ferry Ln OX10 9JF (01491) 651381
*A "beautiful setting on the banks of the Thames" – the stretch immortalised in the 'Wind in the Willows' – underpins the popularity of this cosy former boathouse; the food? – it's "OK but nothing special".*
/ **Details:** *www.beetleandwedge.co.uk; on A329 between Streatley & Wallingford, take Ferry Lane at crossroads; 9.45 pm. **Accommodation:** 3 rooms, from £100.*

## MOULTON, NORTH YORKSHIRE 8–3B

**Black Bull** £51 ❸❹❸
DL10 6QJ (01325) 377289
*"Gorgeous food, especially fish, in a quirky but classy pub setting" – that's still the deal at this celebrated pub, seemingly most popular amongst those who dine in the (genuine) "fun and comfy" Pullman carriage attached; overall, though, feedback is a bit up-and-down, and much more limited than once it was.*
/ **Details:** *www.blackbullmoulton.com; 1m S of Scotch Corner; 9.30 pm, Fri & Sat 10 pm; closed Sun D.*

## MOUSEHOLE, CORNWALL 1–4A

**Cornish Range** £41 ❶
6 Chapel St TR19 6SB (01736) 731488
*A pleasant restaurant-with-rooms, in a back street near the harbour (with its own courtyard garden), tipped for its sometimes "amazing" fish dishes. / **Details:** www.cornishrange.co.uk; on coast road between Penzance & Lands End; 9.30 pm, 9 pm in Winter; no Amex. **Accommodation:** 3 rooms, from £80.*

**2 Fore Street** £42 ❶
2 Fore St TR19 6PF (01736) 731164
*Cute, but "a little cramped" – this bistro near the harbour offers the "predominantly fish" menu you might expect, and all reports confirm that it's "very well executed".*
/ **Details:** *www.2forestreet.co.uk; 9.30 pm. **Accommodation:** 2 rooms, from £250 pw.*

## MURCOTT, OXFORDSHIRE 2–1D

**The Nut Tree Inn** £49 ❶❷❷
Main St OX5 2RE (01865) 331253
*It may be "in the middle of nowhere", but Michael North & Imogen Young's "idyllic" thatched pub makes "an amazing find in a tiny*

village"; the food is "amazing", and there are "fabulous" wine-matching opportunities too.
/ **Details:** www.nuttreeinn.co.uk; 9 pm.

---

MUTHILL, PERTH AND KINROSS          9–3C

**Barley Bree**          **£42**    ❷❷❸
6 Willoughby St  PH5 2AB   (01764) 681451
"Edging towards fine dining without being pretentious", this "rustic" restaurant, in a "charming" hotel, has become an "established favourite" for visitors from Gleneagles and elsewhere; it's "popular with shooting parties" too. / **Details:** www.barleybree.com; 9 pm Wed-Sat, 7.30pm Sun; closed Mon & Tue; no Amex.
**Accommodation:** 6 rooms, from £105.

---

NAILSWORTH, GLOUCESTERSHIRE     2–2B

**Wild Garlic**          **£46**    ❷❷❸
3 Cossacks Sq  GL6 0DB   (01453) 832615
Matthew Beardshall's "useful" small restaurant (with rooms), is tipped for cooking that's invariably "very competent", and sometimes "superb". / **Details:** www.wild-garlic.co.uk; 9.30 pm, Sun 2.30 pm; closed Mon, Tue, Wed L & Sun D; no Amex. **Accommodation:** 3 rooms, from £75.

---

NANTGAREDIG, CARMARTHENSHIRE  4–4C

**Y Polyn**          **£42**    ❷❷❸
SA32 7LH   (01267) 290000
You'll "need the SatNav", but it's worth the effort of seeking out this "surprisingly good" rural gastropub, with its "well-executed comfort food dishes" – a place that's "always reliable, and where the service always makes you feel good".
/ **Details:** www.ypolyn.co.uk; 9 pm; closed Mon & Sun D.

---

NETHER BURROW, CUMBRIA          7–4D

**The Highwayman**          **£42**    ❷❸❷
LA6 2RJ   (01524) 273338
"A fantastic welcome, and a good hearty meal" – standards seem to be on the up at this "consistently good" outpost of the Northcote-based Ribble Valley Inns chain.
/ **Details:** www.highwaymaninn.co.uk; 8.30 pm, Fri & Sat 9 pm, Sun 8 pm; closed Mon.

---

NETHER WESTCOTE, OXFORDSHIRE   2–1C

**The Feathered Nest Inn**   **£59**   ❷❸❷
OX7 6SD   (01993) 833 030
"Thought I'd died and gone to gastropub heaven!" – this "off-the-beaten-track" inn offers "superb, inventive and local" food and "excellent" wines, and all in a "stunning" Cotswold setting.

/ **Details:** www.thefeatherednestinn.co.uk; 9.30 pm; closed Mon & Sun D.

---

NEW MILTON, HAMPSHIRE          2–4C

**Vetiver**
**Chewton Glen**          **£81**    ❸❷❷
Christchurch Rd  BH25 6QS
(01425) 275341
"What a treat" – this swanky country house hotel is acclaimed by some reporters as the "UK's finest" and it's undoubtedly an "impressive" and "beautiful" destination; its restaurant (re-launched in recent times) is "solidly excellent" nowadays – a bargain, however, it is not…
/ **Details:** www.chewtonglen.com; on A337 between New Milton & Highcliffe; 10 pm; SRA-75%.
**Accommodation:** 58 rooms, from £310.

---

NEWARK, NOTTINGHAMSHIRE          5–3D

**Café Bleu**          **£45**    ❶
14 Castle Gate  NG24 1BG
(01636) 610141
A "competent" bistro, still regarded as "the best place locally"; even some reporters for whom it's a favourite, though, perceive standards to be slipping, and it no longer inspires nearly as much feedback as once it did.
/ **Details:** www.cafebleu.co.uk; 9.30 pm; closed Mon & Sun D; no Amex.

---

NEWBURY, BERKSHIRE          2–2D

**The Crab at Chieveley**   **£57**   ❷❸❷
Wantage Rd  RG20 8UE   (01635) 247550
"Superb fish in an unlikely location" – the formula that's made a big hit of this "homely" thatched former inn; some reports, though, do suggest it's "patchy" – "when it's good, it's very good but…" / **Details:** www.crabatchieveley.com; M4 J13 to B4494 – 0.5 mile on right; 9.30 pm.
**Accommodation:** 13 rooms, from £99.

---

**Yew Tree Inn**          **£55**
Hollington Cross, Andover Rd  RG20 9SE
(01635) 253360
A popular inn, relaunched shortly before this guide went to press; the owners are a company with former Gordon Ramsay Holdings head chef Mark Askew at the helm – should be one to watch. / **Details:** www.yewtree.net; off the A343, near Highclere Castle; 9 pm; booking essential.
**Accommodation:** 7 rooms, from £120.

NEWCASTLE UPON TYNE, TYNE AND WEAR
8–2B

**Blackfriars Restaurant   £48   Ⓣ**
Friars St  NE1 4XN   (0191) 261 5945
This "peaceful monastic courtyard" is certainly
top tip for those in search of a "beautiful
location" in the heart of the city – most reports
speak of "good food from local ingredients" too,
but a couple of off-days were also recorded this
year. / **Details:** www.blackfriarsrestaurant.co.uk;
10 pm; closed Sun D.

**Broad Chare   £44   ❸❸❸**
25 Broad Chare  NE1 3DQ   (019) 1211
2144
Just off the Quayside, the gastropub offshoot of
the Terry Laybourne empire offers, say fans,
"hearty food cooked to gourmet standards" –
there is the occasional dissenter, but it's a
package that impresses most reporters across
the board. / **Details:** www.thebroadchare.co.uk;
10 pm; closed Sun D; no Amex.

**Café 21**
**Fenwick   £32   ❸❸❸**
39 Northumberland St, First Floor  NE1 7DE
(0191) 260 3373
"A great lunch venue, and handy for the shops"
– this department store "haven from shopping"
is also recommended for brunch or a snack at
any time. / **Details:** www.cafetwentyone.co.uk; 0;
L only.

**Café 21   £62   ❷❷❷**
Trinity Gdns  NE1 2HH   (0191) 222 0755
Perennially "setting the Newcastle standard" –
Terry Laybourne's "bustling" flagship, just off the
Quayside, continues to be the city's most
commented-on destination, thanks not least to its
"confident" cuisine; lunch and early-evening
menus offer particularly "good value".
/ **Details:** www.cafetwentyone.co.uk; 10.30 pm, Sun
9 pm.

**Café Royal   £44   ❸❸❸**
8 Nelson St  NE1 5AW   (0191) 231 3000
"For a coffee break when shopping in
Newcastle" this grand café, by Grainger Market,
is something of a classic; since the recent "total
refurbishment", though, there's a feeling that
standards – particularly of pastries and bread –
are not all they used to be.
/ **Details:** www.sjf.co.uk; 6 pm; L only; no booking, Sat.

**Caffè Vivo   £43   ❸❸❷**
29 Broad Chare  NE1 3DQ   (0191) 232
1331
"A classy place on the Quayside" – Terry

Laybourne's "well-judged" Italian, attached to a
theatre, is thought a "handy spot" by all who
comment on it; "creeping prices" remain a
source of concern for some visitors, so look out
for the lunch and pre-theatre deals.
/ **Details:** www.caffevivo.co.uk; 10 pm; closed Mon &
Sun.

**Dabbawal   £32   ❷❸❸**
69-75 High Bridge  NE1 6BX   (0191) 232
5133
"A new restaurant serving 'Indian street food'
with a difference" – the "subtle" and
"beautifully-executed" cuisine of this city-centre
spot, just off Grey Street, pleases all who
comment on it. / **Details:** www.dabbawal.com;
10.30 pm; closed Sun.

**David Kennedy's Food Social**
**The Biscuit Factory   £40   ❷❷❸**
Shieldfield  NE2 1AN   (0191) 2605411
David Kennedy made quite a name at the
former Black Door, and his eponymous new
operation – in a "boho location", by an art
gallery – is already winning a strong, if still small,
reporter following with its "local food, well
cooked and presented".
/ **Details:** www.foodsocial.co.uk; 9.30 pm; closed
Sun D.

**Francesca's   £32   ❹❸❷**
Manor House Rd  NE2 2NE   (0191) 281
6586
"As busy and bustly as ever", this "cheap 'n'
cheerful" Jesmond Dene pizzeria is quite the
local institution; fans insist the pizzas are "the
best in Newcastle", but it's arguably the
"fantastic-value" prices that are the key draw.
/ **Details:** 9.30 pm; closed Sun; no Amex; no booking.

**Jesmond Dene House   £59   ❹❹❸**
Jesmond Dene Rd  NE2 2EY   (0191) 212
6066
Terry Laybourne's Arts & Crafts country house is
a "lovely" place in a "fantastic" location; its
cuisine can be "variable", however, and even
some who feel it's a "lovely" place baulk at the
"sky-high prices".
/ **Details:** www.jesmonddenehouse.co.uk; 9.30 pm,
Fri & Sat 10 pm. **Accommodation:** 40 rooms,
from £144.

**Pan Haggerty   £49   ❷❷❸**
21 Queen St  NE1 3UG   (0191) 221 0904
"A great little restaurant, not far from the
Quayside, offering great English food, and some
traditional, 'local' specials too" – it's a destination
that all reporters agree is "enjoyable" and "good
value". / **Details:** www.panhaggerty.com; 9.30 pm;
closed Sun D.

**Pani's**  £30  ④❸❸
61-65 High Bridge  NE1 6BX  (0191) 232 4366
"Italy-on-Tyne"; this "fantastically buzzy" Sardinian café is one of the "friendliest" places – "always fun and lively", and mega-popular for a "cheap 'n' cheerful" bite; the odd critic, though, finds the food a tad "uninspiring".
/ **Details:** www.paniscafe.co.uk; 10 pm; closed Sun; no Amex; no booking at L.

**Paradiso**  £33  ④❶❸
1 Market Ln  NE1 6QQ  (0191) 221 1240
Living up to its name, for most reporters, this city-centre Mediterranean café/bar/restaurant is a warehouse-style operation with "unfailingly delightful" staff; the food is not really the main event, but it rarely disappoints.
/ **Details:** www.paradiso.co.uk; 10.30 pm, Fri & Sat 10.45 pm; closed Sun.

**Sachins**  £36  ⊤
Forth Banks  NE1 3SG  (0191) 261 9035
"Consistent top quality, and good value for money too" – that's the appeal of this long-established spot, near Central Station, offering "great Indian food, Punjabi-style".
/ **Details:** www.sachins.co.uk; 11.15 pm; closed Sun.

**Six**
**Baltic Centre**  £50  ④④❸
Gateshead Quays, South Shore Rd  NE8 3BA (0191) 440 4948
An "unparalleled view" ("especially from the loos!") helps make this top-floor dining room of a Gateshead arts centre a "unique" location; critics, though, can find it a "noisy" place, with a kitchen that "sometimes skimps", and staff who seem "a bit pleased with themselves".
/ **Details:** www.sixbaltic.com; 9.30 pm, Fri & Sat 10 pm; closed Sun D.

**A Taste of Persia**  £27  ❷❷❸
14 Marlborough Cr  NE1 4EE  (0191) 221 0088
"It doesn't look much from the outside, but the food is amazingly good, and comes at stunningly low prices", at this "top-notch" family-run Persian (which has a sibling in Jesmond); if you're in a group, ask about the lavishly decorated 'traditional room'.
/ **Details:** www.atasteofpersia.com; 11 pm; closed Sun.

**Tyneside Coffee Rooms**
**Tyneside Cinema**  £24  ④❸❷
10 Pilgrim St  NE1 6QG  (0191) 227 5520
It's the "great atmosphere at any time of day" that makes it especially worth seeking out this

genuine Art Deco institution; as a venue for "a coffee and a snack", it remains "hard to beat" – "be prepared to queue".
/ **Details:** www.tynesidecinema.co.uk; 9 pm; no Amex.

**Thai Street Cafe**  £31  ⊤
26-28 High St  CB8 8LB  (01638) 674123
A town-centre establishment, tipped for its "wonderful, authentic Thai fare"; the lunch menu is "cheap and delicious" – evenings are livelier and pricier. / **Details:** www.thaistreetcafe.co.uk.

**Llys Meddyg**  £51  ❸④❸
East St  SA42 0SY  (01239) 820008
"Innovative" food is presented with a "sense of theatre", at this "gem" of a restaurant-with-rooms, which offers a number of dining areas, including a "wonderful garden".
/ **Details:** www.llysmeddyg.com; 9 pm; D only, closed Mon & Sun; no Amex. **Accommodation:** 9 rooms, from £100.

**Crooked Billet**  £33  ❸❷❸
2 Westbrook End  MK17 0DF (01908) 373936
The wine list (200+ choices by the glass) is the star at the Gilchrists' "wonderful" thatched inn, on the fringes of Milton Keynes; its food rating dipped a tad this year – hopefully just a blip.
/ **Details:** www.thebillet.co.uk; 9.30 pm, Fri & Sat 10 pm; D only, ex Sun open L only.

**The Dawnay Arms**  £44  ⊤
YO30 2BR  (01347) 848345
"Upmarket pub food" at "very reasonable prices" makes this Georgian inn, by the River Ouse, a top tip locally.
/ **Details:** www.thedawnayatnewton.co.uk; 9.30 pm, Sun 6 pm; closed Mon & Sun D.

**The Parkers Arms**  £40  ❶❷❷
BB7 3DY  (01200) 446236
"In rural Lancashire – a hidden gem which never disappoints"; Kathy Smith and Stosie Madi's "lovely country pub" is a "very friendly" sort of place where the "amazing locally-sourced food" is of "unbelievable quality"; there's a "small selection of excellent wines", too, at "unbelievably

low prices". / **Details:** www.parkersarms.co.uk;
8.30 pm, Sun 6.30 pm; closed Mon.
**Accommodation:** 4 rooms, from £77.

---

### NEWTOWN, CHEW MAGNA, BRISTOL 2–2B

**The Pony and Trap**  £41  ❶❷❸
BS40 8TQ  (01275) 332 627
The cuisine at Josh Eggleton's "hidden gem" is
"simple and delicious, but perfectly executed" –
however, despite all its accolades, it "remains
every inch a proper pub"!
/ **Details:** www.theponyandtrap.co.uk; 9.30 pm; closed
Mon; no Amex.

---

### NOMANSLAND, WILTSHIRE 2–3C

**Les Mirabelles**  £43  ❶❷❷
Forest Edge Rd  SP5 2BN  (01794) 390205
"Ponies graze right outside this fantastic morsel
of France, in the heart of the New Forest"; it's a
"brilliant", "traditional" spot, with well-judged
service, that wins consistent acclaim for its
"excellent menu at incredible prices".
/ **Details:** www.lesmirabelles.co.uk; off A36 between
Southampton & Salisbury; 9.30 pm; closed Mon & Sun.

---

### NORDEN, LANCASHIRE 5–1B

**Nutter's**  £51  ❶
Edenfield Rd  OL12 7TT  (01706) 650167
Approaching a decade in business, the Nutter
family's characterful manor-house restaurant,
overlooking the moors, inspired more modest
feedback this year than usual – it was
consistently well-rated nonetheless.
/ **Details:** www.nuttersrestaurant.com; between
Edenfield & Norden on A680; 9 pm; closed Mon.

---

### NORTHALLERTON, NORTH YORKSHIRE8–4B

**McCoys at the Tontine**  £57  ❷❷❶
DL6 3JB  (01609) 882 671
"Like an old friend" to its local fanclub, Eugene
McCoy's crazily-furnished country house veteran
is a notably "relaxed" destination, offering "the
same welcome to local farmers and footie stars
alike"; a "very good selection of fish dishes" is a
highlight, and the wines are well-chosen too.
/ **Details:** www.theclevelandtontine.co.uk; near
junction of A19 & A172; 9 pm, Fri & Sat 9.45 pm, Sun
8 pm. **Accommodation:** 7 rooms, from £130.

---

### NORTHAW, HERTFORDSHIRE 3–2B

**The Sun at Northaw**  £54  ❷❹❸
1 Judges Hill  EN6 4NL  (01707) 655507
"A lovely gastropub in the centre of a little
village", where the menu is "imaginative without
being pretentious", and portions are "generous"
too; service, though, can be "erratic".

/ **Details:** www.thesunatnorthaw.co.uk; 10 pm, Sun
4 pm; closed Mon & Sun D; no Amex.

---

### NORTHLEACH, GLOUCESTERSHIRE 2–1C

**Wheatsheaf Inn**  £44  ❷❸❷
GL54 3EZ  (01451) 860244
In the centre of a lovely village ("make time to
visit the church"), this "cosy" spot is one of the
Cotswold's top 'eating' pubs (and with "superb"
rooms too); the "big gardens" make "a
spectacular venue for summer dinners".
/ **Details:** 9 pm, Sat & Sun 10 pm.
**Accommodation:** 14 rooms, from £130.

---

### NORTON, NEAR MALMESBURY, WILTSHIRE 2–2B

**The Vine Tree**  £42  ❸❸❷
Foxley Rd  SN16 0JP  (01666) 837654
"A great little country pub with stunning food, in
an area where there's quite a lot of
competition"; with its "sensible" menu and its
"shady" garden, it makes a "good lunch stop off
the M4" too. / **Details:** www.thevinetree.co.uk;
9.30 pm, Fri & Sat 10 pm; closed Sun D in winter.

---

### NORWICH, NORFOLK 6–4C

**The Gunton Arms**  £44  ❷❶❶
Cromer Rd, Thorpe Mkt  NR11 8TZ
(01263) 832010
"A real north Norfolk gem" – this "very
professionally-run", three-year-old gastropub
(with rooms) is "a lovely rural inn set in a large
deer park"; "the food is cooked on an open fire
in the dining room, and local venison is a
speciality". / **Details:** www.theguntonarms.co.uk;
10 pm; no Amex. **Accommodation:** 8 rooms,
from £95.

**Last Wine Bar**  £37  ❸❸❷
70-76 St Georges St  NR3 1AB
(01603) 626626
First choice for many of the locals – this former
shoe factory is now a "busy" and "vibrant"
venue, where "you can eat in the more formal
restaurant or various bar areas"; when it comes
to wine "they know their stuff" and the food is
well-regarded too.
/ **Details:** www.thelastwinebar.co.uk; 10.30 pm; closed
Sun.

**Roger Hickman's**  £59  ❶❷❷
79 Upper St. Giles St  NR2 1AB
(01603) 633522
David Adlard's former head chef is now chef-
patron at the "intimate" Norwich address long
synonymous with 'fine dining' – almost all
reporters find this a really strong all-rounder, and

offer lavish praise for cuisine that's "creative well-balanced and well-executed".
/ **Details:** www.rogerhickmansrestaurant.com.

**Waffle House**   **£28**   🔵
39 St Giles St NR2 1JN   (01603) 612790
"A Norwich institution for over 30 years", this self-explanatory joint is tipped as destination which – "for a brunch or a snack" – is "still an old-favourite". / **Details:** www.wafflehouse.co.uk; 10 pm; no Amex; need 6+ to book.

NOSS MAYO, DEVON                    1–4C

**The Ship Inn**   **£42**   ❸❹❷
PL8 1EW   (01752) 872387
"A pretty pub on the waterfront of a pretty village" – it's "deservedly busy", thanks to its "attractive terrace" and its "beautiful" scoff ("fantastic fish 'n' chips" and the like).
/ **Details:** www.nossmayo.com; 9.30 pm, Sun 9 pm.

NOTTINGHAM, NOTTINGHAMSHIRE  5–3D

**Atlas**   **£22**   ❷❷❸
9 Pelham St NG1 2EH   (0115) 950 1295
Near the Council House, a "cheerful" sandwich bar with a major reporter-following for its "excellent variety of sandwiches", and its "wonderful coffee" too.
/ **Details:** www.atlasdeli.co.uk; 4 pm, Sat 5 pm; L only.

**Cast**   **£29**   ❹❸❸
The Playhouse, Wellington Circus NG1 5AN
(0115) 852 3898
Adjoining the Playhouse, this "reasonably-priced" establishment makes an "always-reliable" choice, especially, of course, "for a pre-theatre meal"; its terrace is a nice spot on a sunny day.
/ **Details:** www.nottinghamplayhouse.co.uk; 10 pm, Sun 6 pm; no Amex.

**Chino Latino**

**Park Plaza Hotel**   **£55**   🔵
41 Maid Marian Way NG1 6GD
(0115) 947 7444
Once oh-so-trendy, this Asian-fusion hang-out can seem a little "dated" nowadays; fans, though, still tip it for its "delicious" and "different" Asian-fusion fare, and "buzzy" atmosphere.
/ **Details:** www.chinolatino.co.uk; 10.30 pm; closed Sun.

**The Cumin**   **£35**   🔵
62-64 Maid Marian Way NG1 6BQ
(0115) 941 9941
Not as many reports as we would like, but this city-centre Indian is tipped for "excellent" food from a menu "with great variety", and "very

good" service too; "ambience is good at the front, but not so good in the back room".
/ **Details:** www.thecumin.co.uk; 10.45 pm; closed Mon L, Tue L, Sat L & Sun L.

**Delilahs**   **£29**   🔵
12 Victoria Street NG1 2EX   (0115) 948 4461
Tipped for its "very tasty" food from "excellent" ingredients, a deli/café that generates quite a lot of commentary… even though it has only 7 seats; to no one's great surprise, "it can be hard to get in!" / **Details:** www.delilahfinefoods.co.uk; 7 pm, Sun 5 pm; no Amex.

**French Living**   **£33**   ❸❷❸
27 King St NG1 2AY   (0115) 958 5885
This "very reliable" bistro "remains the benchmark for traditional French eating hereabouts"; it makes "a perfect stop for lunch or pre-theatre". / **Details:** www.frenchliving.co.uk; 10 pm; closed Sun; no Amex.

**Hart's**   **£50**   ❷❹❸
Standard Ct, Park Row NG1 6GN
(0115) 988 1900
Still the city-centre's best-known destination – Tim Hart's "classic" modern brasserie, near the castle, invariably impresses with its "consistent" cuisine and its notably "efficient" service – a formula that seems "made for business", but which "can work well for an 85th birthday party too"! / **Details:** www.hartsnottingham.co.uk; 10 pm, Sun 9 pm. **Accommodation:** 32 rooms, from £125.

**Iberico**   **£35**   ❷❸❷
The Shire Hall, High Pavement NG1 1HN
(01159) 410410
"Fabulous" tapas – from a "regularly-changing menu" and some with an "international flavour" (for instance, with Japanese influences) – have made a major local hit of this vibey bar, "in an historic cellar", in the Lace Market; the lunch deal, in particular, offers "exceptionally good value". / **Details:** www.ibericotapas.com; 10 pm; closed Sun; no Amex; children: 12+ D.

**Kayal**   **£29**   ❷❷❸
8 Broad St NG1 3AL   (0115) 941 4733
"Superb Keralan food" in "generous portions" wins high praise for this outpost of a small chain – one reporter does caution, though, that "the lack of known and usual dishes on the menu can make for a bit of a lucky dip".
/ **Details:** www.kayalrestaurant.com; 11 pm , Sun 10 pm.

**The Larder
on Goosegate**   **£ 42**   ❸④❸
1st Floor, 16 -22 Goosegate  NG1 1FE
(01159) 500111
*It's not just the location ("the original Boots!")
that makes this city-centre spot an "interesting"
find – the locally-sourced food's "seriously-
realised", and sometimes quite "original" too.
/ **Details:** www.thelarderongoosegate.co.uk; 9 pm,
Thu-Sat 10 pm; closed Mon & Sun D.*

**MemSaab**   **£ 39**
12-14 Maid Marian Way  NG1 6HS
(0115) 957 0009
*"Traditionally the best Indian in Nottingham by a
long way"; as it has recently changed hands, we
think it best not to rate it, but an early reporter
notes that "there are hopeful signs that the high
standards will be maintained".
/ **Details:** www.mem-saab.co.uk; near Castle, opposite
Park Plaza Hotel; 10.30 pm, Fri & Sat 11 pm, Sun
10 pm; D only; no shorts.*

**Mistral**   **£ 40**   ❸❸❸
2-3 Eldon Chambers  NG1 2NS   (0115) 941
0401
*A city-centre bistro tipped for its "reasonably-
priced" dishes, "pleasant" service and "good
atmosphere"; "it's part of a small chain, and this
is the best branch". / **Details:** 11 pm; no Amex.*

**Restaurant Sat Bains**   **£ 106**  ❶❷④
Lenton Ln  NG7 2SA   (0115) 986 6566
*"Fabulous food, with ambition as high as the
prices!"; Sat Bains's "thought-provoking
combinations of tastes and flavours" dazzle
practically all who report on this "truly
outstanding" venue – "don't, however, expect to
be wowed by the location" (near pylons and fly-
overs). / **Details:** www.restaurantsatbains.com;
8.30 pm; closed Mon & Sun; children: 12+.
**Accommodation:** 8 rooms, from £129.*

**Tarn Thai**   **£ 36**   ❷❷❷
9 George St  NG1 1BU   (0115) 959 9454
*"Much admired by our Thai relations when they
visited" – this "brilliant" and "authentic" spot,
"tucked-away" off the Lace Market, is a
destination which attracts consistently positive
feedback all-round. / **Details:** www.tarnthai.co.uk;
10.30 pm, Fri & Sat 11 pm.*

**Victoria Hotel**   **£ 33**   ❶
Dovecote Ln  NG9 1JG   (0115) 925 4049
*By Beeston Station, a top tip locally for "well-
made, home-cooked pub food" (from a daily-
changing menu) and a "great selection of real
ales and ciders too"; "large and cheerful garden
area under cover".*

*/ **Details:** www.victoriabeeston.co.uk; 9.30 pm,
Sun-Tue 8.45 pm; no Amex; children: 18+ after 8 pm.*

**The Wollaton**   **£ 40**   ❶
Lambourne Drive  NG8 1GR
(0115) 9288610
*"A lot better than your average pub grub, but still
at reasonable prices" – this popular, kid-friendly
gastroboozer invariably pleases those who
comment on it. / **Details:** www.thewollaton.co.uk;
9 pm, Fri & Sat 10 pm, Sun 7 pm.*

**World Service**   **£ 53**   ❷❷❷
Newdigate Hs, Castlegate  NG1 6AF
(0115) 847 5587
*It perennially has its critics, but the arrival of a
new chef has revved up the reports on this
popular and stylish city-centre venue (with cute
courtyard); it was strongly praised this year for its
"unfussy but complex" cuisine (and "exceptional-
value cocktails" too).
/ **Details:** www.worldservicerestaurant.com; 10 pm;
closed Sun D, except bank holidays; children: 10+ at D.*

| OARE, KENT | 3–3C |

**The Three Mariners**   **£ 40**   ❸④❸
2 Church Rd  ME13 0QA   (01795) 533633
*Some "delectable" fish dishes, served in "rustic"
portions, are the high point of the "good
selection of dishes" on offer at this "attractive"
village pub.
/ **Details:** www.thethreemarinersoare.co.uk; 8.30 pm,
Fri & Sat 9 pm; no Amex.*

| OBAN, ARGYLL AND BUTE | 9–3B |

**Ee-Usk**   **£ 45**   ❸❸❶
North Pier  PA34 5QD   (01631) 565666
*A harbourside location "to die for" and "willing"
service again earn high praise for this popular
waterside spot; its fish cuisine is "good and
straightforward" – even those who say it's "not
exciting" feel "they would certainly go again".
/ **Details:** www.eeusk.com; 9 pm; no Amex; children:
12+ at D .*

| OCKLEY, SURREY | 3–4A |

**Bryce's at the
Old School House**   **£ 49**   ❸❸❸
Stane St  RH5 5TH   (01306) 627430
*"Splendid fish dishes" – "well-priced too!" –
again win many fans for this "reliable" twenty-
one-year-old, in a converted schoolhouse; its
ratings, though, did dip a fraction this year.
/ **Details:** www.bryces.co.uk; 8m S of Dorking on A29;
9 pm; no Amex.*

### OLD HUNSTANTON, NORFOLK    6–3B

**The Neptune**    **£68**   ❶❷❷
85 Old Hunstanton Rd   PE36 6HZ
(01485) 532122
*"Probably the best food on the Norfolk coast";
the Mangeolle family's 18th-century coaching inn
is really beginning to make waves – "very fresh
fish dishes" make up much of a menu that's
realised with "skill, care and imagination".
/ **Details:** www.theneptune.co.uk; 9 pm; closed Mon,
Tue-Sat D only, Sun open L & D; children: 10.*
**Accommodation:** *6 rooms, from £110.*

### OLDSTEAD, NORTH YORKSHIRE    5–1D

**Black Swan**    **£57**   ❶❸❷
YO61 4BL   (01347) 868 387
*"Deserving of its accolades", this "snug"
gastropub – "tucked-away off the beaten track"
(near Byland Abbey) "goes from strength to
strength"; Adam Jackson's "terrific", locally-
sourced cuisine is "immaculately presented
without fuss or pretension".
/ **Details:** www.blackswanoldstead.co.uk; 9 pm; closed
Mon L, Tue L & Wed L; no Amex.*

### ONGAR, ESSEX    3–2B

**Smith's Brasserie**    **£58**   ❷❷❷
Fyfield Rd   CM5 0AL   (01277) 365578
*A supremely consistent performer of late, this
"top-class" destination – though best known for
its "excellent" seafood – wins praise for all
aspects of its operation; it has a new Wapping
sibling too. / **Details:** www.smithsbrasserie.com; left
off A414 towards Fyfield; 10 pm, Fri & Sat 10.30 pm;
closed Mon L; no Amex; children: 12+.*

### ONICH, HIGHLAND    9–3B

**Loch Leven**
**Seafood Café**    **£46**   ❷❷❸
PH33 6SA   (01855) 821048
*"The view across Loch Leven is stunning", from
this "friendly" waterside café; "mighty and
wonderful" seafood platters are the special
culinary draw, but the menu is "varied" and
quality is uniformly "very good" ("even for
veggies!").
/ **Details:** www.lochlevenseafoodcafe.co.uk; 9 pm;
no Amex.*

### ORFORD, SUFFOLK    3–1D

**Butley Orford**
**Oysterage**    **£37**   ❷❸⑤
Market Hill   IP12 2LH   (01394) 450277
*"Blessedly unchanged" after half a century in
business – the Pinney family's "very basic"
stalwart is "a simple, canteen-style, eat-straight-*
off-the-boat" kind of place, and "maintains its
focus on careful fish cooking with no concessions
to the 21st century"; "perfect" traditional puds
too. / **Details:** www.butleyorfordoysterage.co.uk; on
the B1078, off the A12 from Ipswich; 9 pm; no Amex.*

**The Crown & Castle**    **£48**   ❷❷❸
IP12 2LJ   (01394) 450205
*"The food gets better every time", says one of
the fans of this "fantastic" restaurant-with-rooms;
even more remarkably, given its 'celebrity' co-
ownership (Ruth Watson), it's a "solid", "no-
hype" operation where, the food is invariably
"really enjoyable".
/ **Details:** www.crownandcastle.co.uk; on main road to
Orford, near Woodbridge; 9 pm, Sat & Sun 9.15 pm;
no Amex; booking: max 10; children: 8+ at D.*
**Accommodation:** *19 rooms, from £130.*

**Jolly Sailor**    **£39**   ❶
Quay St   IP12 2NU   (01394) 450243
*In a pretty seaside village, "a great family pub",
tipped for its "terrific location by the water", well-
rated food, and good beer too.
/ **Details:** www.jollysailororford.co.uk; 9 pm; no Amex.*
**Accommodation:** *3 rooms, from £95.*

### ORPINGTON, KENT    3–3B

**Xian**    **£30**   ❶❶❷
324 High St   BR6 0NG   (01689) 871881
*"A gem in the gloom of a fading high street" –
Gary Rhodes's favourite local (we're reliably
informed) is "the best Chinese for miles and
miles around", and all reports extol his
"sensational" cooking, with "authentic textures
and flavouring". / **Details:** 11 pm; closed Mon &
Sun L.*

### OSWESTRY, SHROPSHIRE    5–3A

**Sebastian's**    **£55**   ❶
45 Willow St   SY11 1AQ   (01691) 655444
*In this under-served part of the world, this
attractive restaurant-with-rooms is a top tip for
"high-quality French-style food, always beautifully
presented", and a complementary list of "fine
wines" too. / **Details:** www.sebastians-hotel.co.uk;
9.45 pm; D only, closed Mon & Sun.*
**Accommodation:** *8 rooms, from £65.*

### OXFORD, OXFORDSHIRE    2–2D

**Al-Shami**    **£27**   ❷④④
25 Walton Cr   OX1 2JG   (01865) 310066
*"A north Oxford classic!" – this "airy" Lebanese
stalwart charges "very reasonable prices", and
continues to be much praised for its "vibrant"
and "very authentic" mezze dishes.*

/ **Details:** www.al-shami.co.uk; 11.30 pm.
**Accommodation:** 12 rooms, from £50.

**Anchor**                    £41    ❸❷❸
2 Hayfield Rd  OX2 6TT   (01865) 510282
"A reliable local that's worth travelling for"; this
"good gastropub" is hailed by (almost) all
reporters for its "decent" cooking, and "friendly"
service too. / **Details:** www.theanchoroxford.com;
9.30 pm, Sun 8.30 pm; no Amex.

**Ashmolean**
**Dining Room**              £50    ④⑤❸
Beaumont St  OX1 2PH   (01865) 553 823
"A waste of a fantastic location"; although fans
insist we "under-rate" this "amazing" rooftop
dining facility "overlooking the dreaming spires",
the volume of criticism of "pretty average" food
and "dreadful" service is too great to ignore.
/ **Details:** www.ashmoleandiningroom.com; 4 pm;
closed Mon.

**Atomic Burger**            £27    ❷❷❸
96 Cowley Rd  OX4 1JE   (01865) 790 855
"Don't be put off if über-American diner-style
isn't your thing" – this "fun" south Oxford
student bar does a "vast" and "marvellously
baffling" range of burgers that wows all
reporters – "expect sticky fingers, sauce
everywhere, and massive grins all round".
/ **Details:** www.atomicburger.co.uk; 10.30 pm;
no Amex.

**Aziz**                      £33    ❸❸❸
228-230 Cowley Rd  OX4 1UH
(01865) 794945
"Consistently better than the ever-burgeoning
universe of Identikit Cowley Road curry houses"
– this long-running spot remains an Oxford
mainstay. / **Details:** www.aziz.uk.com; 11.30 pm,
Sat midnight; closed Fri L.

**Bombay**                    £23    ❷❷④
82 Walton St  OX2 6EA   (01865) 511188
"Consistently good, and you can BYO too" – this
Jericho favourite maintains a reputation for "top-
value", and is still often tipped as "the best
Indian in Oxford". / **Details:** 11 pm; closed Fri L;
no Amex.

**Branca**                    £42    ④❷❸
111 Walton St  OX2 6AJ   (01865) 556111
"An Oxford favourite" – locals "love the buzz" of
this "noisy" Jericho fixture, which they
consistently praise for "reliably tasty, simple
Italian cuisine"; early-evening menus, in
particular, offer "good value".
/ **Details:** www.branca-restaurants.com; 11 pm;
no Amex.

**Brasserie Blanc**          £45    ❸❷❸
71-72 Walton St  OX2 6AG
(01865) 510999
The original of the burgeoning Raymond Blanc-
branded chain, this "relaxed" brasserie is one of
Oxford's most commented-on places... even if
the cuisine is more "reliable" than exciting;
excellent set deals.
/ **Details:** www.brasserieblanc.com; 10 pm, Sat
10.30 pm, Sun 9.30 pm; SRA-64%.

**Browns**                    £40    ④⑤❸
5-11 Woodstock Rd  OX2 6HA
(01865) 511995
This famous British brasserie-institution (now
part of a major chain) divides opinion – it's still a
"favourite haunt" for many reporters... even
though the food is "fairly ordinary", and service
sometimes "so bad, it's as if they were taking the
mickey!" / **Details:** www.browns-restaurants.com;
11 pm, Fri & Sat 11.30 pm, Sun 10.30 pm.

**Cherwell Boathouse**       £44    ❸❸❷
Bardwell Rd  OX2 6ST   (01865) 552746
"A lovely spot to watch the punts going by", this
"spacious" restaurant also has the benefit of an
excellent wine list, and the set meals offer "good
value" too; the food more generally? – something
of a supporting attraction.
/ **Details:** www.cherwellboathouse.co.uk; 9 pm, Fri &
Sat 9.30 pm.

**Chiang Mai**               £35    ❷❸❸
Kemp Hall Passage  OX1 4DH
(01865) 202233
Down an alleyway, just off the High, this "reliably
classy" Thai – "quirkily" housed in a very
"attractive", if "crowded" and "noisy", Tudor
building – remains "an oasis in the Oxford
desert"; main complaint? – it's "too popular"!
/ **Details:** www.chiangmaikitchen.co.uk; 10.30 pm.

**La Cucina**                £35    ❷❸❸
39-40 St Clements  OX4 1AB
(01865) 793811
In St Clement's, a "great-value" neighbourhood
restaurant that offers a "basic" pasta-and-pizza
menu – plus more ambitious "specials" – which
almost invariably satisfy.
/ **Details:** www.lacucinaoxford.co.uk; 10.30 pm.

**Edamame**                  £31    ❷❸❸
15 Holywell St  OX1 3SA   (01865) 246916
"It may be small", but this "astonishingly good"
hole-in-the-wall pleases all who report on it with
its "simple, straightforward, well-executed
Japanese food"; the queue, though, is a "pain".
/ **Details:** www.edamame.co.uk; 8.30 pm; L only, ex
Thu-Sat open L & D, closed Mon & Tue; no Amex;
no booking.

Cherwell Boathouse

Branca

Malmaison

**The Fishes** £40 🅣
North Hinksey OX2 0NA (01865) 249796
*Tipped for its "lovely setting" by a stream – with a large garden, for which you can order a picnic – this city-fringe boozer also attracts praise for its "reliable" cuisine, albeit at prices critics find rather high. / Details: www.fishesoxford.co.uk; 9.45 pm; no Amex; SRA-58%.*

**Gee's** £55 ④④❷
61 Banbury Rd OX2 6PE (01865) 553540
*The food can be "uninspired", but a "gorgeous" Victorian-conservatory-like setting makes this north Oxford restaurant "a really nice place to do business" (or to go for romance) – indeed, "in the context of the local dining scene, it's one of the best options!" / Details: www.gees-restaurant.co.uk; 10 pm, Fri & Sat 10.30 pm.*

**Jamie's Italian** £43 ④④④
24-26 George St OX1 2AE
(01865) 838383
*"Living off Jamie's name, but basically a chain outlet" – this city-centre Italian seems ever-more "a victim of its own success"; fans still value it as a "reliable and pleasant place" despite the queues, but critics say it's "over-hyped", "overpriced" and a "real disappointment". / Details: www.jamieoliver.com; 11 pm, Sun 10.30 pm; Booking 6+.*

**The Magdalen Arms** £41 ❷❸④
243 Iffley Rd OX4 1SJ (01865) 243 159
*"Best food in Oxford!"; this 'country' outpost of London's Hope & Anchor may be "a bit scruffy", but its "seasonal" and "excellent" dishes – in "huge portions" – make it really stand out in this under-provided city. / Details: www.magdalenarms.com; 10 pm, Sun 9.30 pm; closed Mon L; no Amex.*

**Malmaison** £51 ❸❸❸
3 Oxford Circle OX1 1AY (01865) 268400
*"Impressive, for a chain" – this hotel dining room particularly benefits from its setting in a "splendidly-converted prison", and "the meal-deals offer good value too". / Details: www.malmaison.com; 10 pm; 6+ need to book. Accommodation: 94 rooms, from £160.*

**My Sichuan** £32 ❶④❸
The Old School, Gloucester Grn OX1 2DA
(01865) 236 899
*"A quantum leap from most Chinese restaurants" – this "old school house, near the bus station" is again hailed for its "authentic, unusual, hot and tingly" cooking, which is "much favoured by Asian students"; communication can*

be an issue – "the pictures on the menu are a big help!" / Details: www.mysichuan.co.uk; 11 pm.

**The Nosebag** £28 ❷④❸
6-8 St Michael's St OX1 2DU
(01865) 721033
*An "Oxford institution", this "thinking person's café" is celebrated for its "wholesome food" ("home-made soups and casseroles, and delicious salads"); it's sometimes preferred "at quiet times, when you don't have to share". / Details: www.nosebagoxford.co.uk; 9.30 pm, Fri & Sat 10 pm, Sun 8.30 pm.*

**The Old Parsonage** £54 ❸❷❶
1 Banbury Rd OX2 6NN (01865) 292305
*Upping its standards a bit in recent times, this "wonderful" old building is nowadays a "thoroughly enjoyable" destination, especially when you can eat in the "gorgeous" courtyard; the "decent" food, though, plays rather a supporting role. / Details: www.oldparsonage-hotel.co.uk; 10.30 pm. Accommodation: 30 rooms, from £200.*

**Pierre Victoire** £43 ❷❸❸
Little Clarendon St OX1 2HP
(01865) 316616
*The most prominent surviving branch of a chain that was once famous nationally for its "very informal" Gallic-bistro formula – it attracts lots of reports, of which the worst say it's a "solid stand-by, offering good-value set deals"! / Details: www.pierrevictoire.co.uk; 11 pm, 10 pm Sun; no Amex.*

**Quod**
Old Bank Hotel £46 ④❸❸
92-94 High St OX1 4BJ (01865) 799599
*A "bustling" city-centre spot, hailed by some reporters as a "good non-chain choice"; as ever, though, critics feel it's "a bit of a waste of a great location" – "noisy", and "rather overpriced, given the quality of the food". / Details: www.oldbank-hotel.co.uk; 11 pm, Sun 10.30 pm; no booking at D. Accommodation: 42 rooms, from £137.*

**Shanghai 30s** £39 🅣
82 St Aldates OX1 1RA (01865) 242230
*Reports are surprisingly few, but this "lovely" and "atmospheric" Chinese, opposite Christ Church (in times past, home to the 'Elizabeth', RIP), is tipped for some "excellent and daring" dishes ("plus some rather bland ones"). / Details: www.shanghai30s.com; 10.30 pm; closed Mon L.*

**Sojo** **£ 40** ❶❷❸
8-9 Hythe Bridge St OX1 2EW
(01865) 202888
*Vying with My Sichuan as Oxford's best Chinese, this better-known locale impresses across the board with its "professional" approach, and its "fantastic food at a good price"; "excellent dim sum". / **Details:** www.sojooxford.co.uk; 10 pm, Sun 9 pm.*

**The Vaults**

**and Garden Cafe** **£ 17** ❿
University Church of St Mary the Virgin, Radcliffe Sq OX1 4AH (01865) 279112
*A useful tip in the heart of the city – "a large vaulted room", by the university church, offering "self-service home-cooked food in generous portions"; "views across Radcliffe Square" too. / **Details:** www.thevaultsandgarden.com; 4 pm; L only.*

| OXTED, SURREY | 3–3B |
|---|---|

**The Gurkha Kitchen** **£ 32** ❷❷❸
111 Station Road East RH8 0AX
(01883) 722621
*"A traditional family-run Nepalese that produces consistently excellent food time after time" – no wonder it's considered something of a "classic local favourite". / **Details:** 11 pm, Sun 10 pm; no Amex.*

| OXTON, CHESHIRE | 5–2A |
|---|---|

**Fraiche** **£ 78** ❶❷❷
11 Rose Mount CH43 5SG
(0151) 652 2914
*"Outstanding in every way", Marc Wilkinson's very personal restaurant offers "stunning" food – "an explosion of tastes and textures" – as well as an "excellent" wine list, and "outstanding" service; good value too – "it blew our minds, but the bill didn't!" / **Details:** www.restaurantfraiche.com; 8.30 pm, Sun 7 pm; closed Mon, Tue, Wed L & Thu L; no Amex.*

| PADSTOW, CORNWALL | 1–3B |
|---|---|

**Margot's** **£ 48** ❷❷❷
11 Duke St PL28 8AB (01841) 533441
*"By far the most intimate dining experience in town"; Adrian Oliver's "friendly", "fun" and "authentic" back street bistro receives high praise from all who comment on it. / **Details:** www.margotspadstow.blogspot.co.uk; 9 pm; D only, closed Mon & Sun.*

**Paul Ainsworth**
**at Number 6** **£ 59** ❶❷❷
6 Middle St PL28 8AP (01841) 532093
*"Forget Rick, and go here!"; reporters rated Paul Ainsworth's small, back-street townhouse-restaurant "Padstow's best" this year – no wonder it has won a huge following for his "terrific" fish and seafood, prepared with "flair and imagination"; "don't miss the puddings!" / **Details:** www.number6inpadstow.co.uk; 10 pm; closed Mon & Sun; no Amex.*

**Rick Stein's Café** **£ 42** ❶❷❸
10 Middle St PL28 8AP (01841) 532700
*"A good-value alternative to the Seafood"; the TV-chef's "fun" and "family–friendly" spin-off wins impressively consistent support for its "fresh" and "excellent" seafood – "you don't need to pay for his posh place!" / **Details:** www.rickstein.com; 9.30 pm; no Amex; Only for D. **Accommodation:** 3 rooms, from £97.*

**Rojanos** **£ 45** ❿
9 Mill Sq PL28 8AE (01841) 532796
*A "busy" institution, nearly 40 years old, that's taken on new life since being taken over by Paul Ainsworth; it's now tipped as a "really good" Italian that serves "the best pizzas going". / **Details:** www.rojanos.co.uk; 10 pm.*

**St Petroc's** **£ 56** ❷❷❷
4 New St PL28 8EA (01841) 532700
*"A worthy part of the Stein empire"; this "buzzy" and "cramped" bistro is "always busy", and its "simple food well done", with "friendly" service too, underpins a "fun" and "cosy" formula. / **Details:** www.rickstein.com; 10 pm; no Amex. **Accommodation:** 10 rooms, from £145.*

**Seafood Restaurant** **£ 73** ❷❷❷
Riverside PL28 8BY (01841) 532700
*"Super fish cooked with the lightest touch" plus "down-to-earth" staff (and a massive dose of TV celebrity) have won huge renown for Rick Stein's "unpretentious" fixture, near the quayside; it has had its ups-and-downs over the years – current performance is "excellent", but still sometimes it can seem "too expensive". / **Details:** www.rickstein.com; 10 pm; ; no Amex; booking: max 14; children: 3+. **Accommodation:** 16 rooms, from £145.*

**Stein's Fish & Chips** **£ 34** ④⑤⑤
South Quay PL28 8BL (01841) 532700
*"Customers seem blinded by the name" – this "dull café" may have "massive queues", but it "lives on Stein's reputation"; expect "good fish, not very good batter, and average chips" – "any other chippy will be as good or better, and for half the price too!" / **Details:** www.rickstein.com; 9 pm; no Amex.*

| PAXFORD, GLOUCESTERSHIRE | 2–1C |

**The Churchill Arms**  £43  ❷❸❷
GL55 6XH   (01386) 594000
*"Pub food at its best", "great beer" and "great location" too – "if only they had a few more staff", this Cotswold boozer would be pretty much perfect. / Details: www.thechurchillarms.com; off Fosse Way; 11 pm; no Amex.*
**Accommodation:** *4 rooms, from £80.*

| PEEBLES, SCOTTISH BORDERS | 9–4C |

**Cringletie House**  £58  ❷❷❷
Edinburgh Rd EH45 8PL   (01721) 725750
*A baronial-style country house hotel, where the "superb classical dining room" offers a tasting menu "in a class of its own"; it almost invariably impresses reporters across the board. / Details: www.cringletie.com; between Peebles and Eddleston on A703, 20m S of Edinburgh; 9 pm; D only, ex Sun open L & D; booking essential.*
**Accommodation:** *13 rooms, from £100.*

| PENSHURST, KENT | 3–3B |

**Spotted Dog**  £34  ❶
Smarts Hill TN11 8EE   (01892) 870253
*A "typical country gastro-pub", handy for walkers, and tipped as a "good stand-by"; "wonderful views" too. / Details: www.spotteddogpub.co.uk; near Penshurst Place; 9 pm, Sun 8 pm; closed Mon D.*

| PENZANCE, CORNWALL | 1–4A |

**The Honey Pot**  £22  ❶
5 Parade St TR18 4BU   (01736) 368686
*The "best cafe in town", tipped for "high-quality" cooking and "friendly" service; it's a handy place to know about too – "they're open later than the competition". / Details: L only, closed Sun; no credit cards.*

| PERTH, PERTH AND KINROSS | 9–3C |

**Deans at Let's Eat**  £44  ❷❸❸
77-79 Kinnoull St PH1 5EZ
(01738) 643377
*"Worth a jaunt from Edinburgh or Glasgow just for the quality of the food", says one hard-core fan of this eminent town-centre restaurant; "the atmosphere is best at busy times". / Details: www.letseatperth.co.uk; 9 pm; closed Mon & Sun; no Amex.*

| PETERSFIELD, HAMPSHIRE | 2–3D |

**JSW**  £65  ❷❷④
20 Dragon St GU31 4JJ   (01730) 262030
*"Inventive food, well-cooked and served" – amongst the very best in the county – has won many admirers for Jake Saul Watkins's "unfussy" small restaurant, which occupies a former coaching inn; "the ambience, however, lags far behind the level of the food and service". / Details: www.jswrestaurant.com; on the old A3; 8 min walk from the railway station; 9 pm; closed Mon & Sun; children: 5+ D.* **Accommodation:** *4 rooms, from £85.*

| PETWORTH, WEST SUSSEX | 3–4A |

**The Noahs Ark Inn**  £43  ❸❸❷
Lurgashall GU28 9ET   (01428) 707346
*"On a quintessential village green", this "lovely country pub" offers a "welcoming getaway" – "simple and pleasant all-round". / Details: www.noahsarkinn.co.uk; 9.30 pm, Sun 3 pm; closed Sun D.*

| PICKERING, NORTH YORKSHIRE | 8–4C |

**The White Swan**  £46  ❸④❸
Market Pl YO18 7AA   (01751) 472288
*"Accomplished", "bistro-style" food again wins high popularity for this "classic coaching inn"; its ratings, though, are undercut by a minority who find prices "hard to justify". / Details: www.white-swan.co.uk; 9 pm.*
**Accommodation:** *21 rooms, from £150.*

| PINNER, GREATER LONDON | 3–3A |

**Friends**  £50  ④❸❸
11 High St HA5 5PJ   (020) 8866 0286
*Terry Farr's "warm and friendly" venue, in a 17th-century house, is generally applauded for its "imaginative" cooking and "interesting" interior; critics can find it a touch "twee", though, and standards no more than "reasonable". / Details: www.friendsrestaurant.co.uk; 9.30 pm; closed Mon & Sun D.*

**L'Orient**  £43  ❸❷❸
58 High St HA5 5PZ   (020) 8429 8488
*"An excellent way of trying different oriental cuisines" – this "reliable" pan-Asian is back on top form, pleasing all who report on it with its "varied" dishes and "really helpful" service; "sit at the front if you can". / Details: www.lorientcuisine.com; 10 pm, Sat 11 pm, Sun 10 pm; closed Mon, Tue-Fri D only, Sat & Sun open L & D; no Amex.*

| PLEASINGTON, LANCASHIRE | 5–1B |
|---|---|

**Clog and Billycock**   £37   ❷❷❸
Billinge End Rd  BB2 6QB   (01254) 201163
*"Always a treat", say fans of this "family-friendly" gastropub – part of the Ribble Valley Inns ('Northcote') chain; no fireworks, but "reliably good pub food from local ingredients".*
/ **Details:** www.theclogandbillycock.com; 8.30 pm Mon-Thu, Fri & Sat 9 pm, Sun 8 pm.

| PLUMTREE, NOTTINGHAMSHIRE | 5–3D |
|---|---|

**Perkins**   £40   ⓣ
Old Railway Station  NG12 5NA
(0115) 937 3695
*A local restaurant sometimes tipped for its "quirky" charms; one or two reporters, though – while conceding the cooking is of "high quality" – feel that prices are "excessive".*
/ **Details:** www.perkinsrestaurant.co.uk; off A606 between Nottingham & Melton Mowbray; 9.30 pm; closed Sun D.

| PLYMOUTH, DEVON | 1–3C |
|---|---|

**The Barbican
Kitchen Brasserie**   £40   ❸❸❸
60 Southside St, The Barbican  PL1 2LQ
(01752) 604448
*"The Tanners' bistro – handily located in the original Plymouth Gin Distillery, on the historic Barbican" – is an "attractive" spot, praised for its "good-value cooking".*
/ **Details:** www.barbicankitchen.com; 10 pm.

**Chloe's
Gill Akaster House**   £59   ⓣ
Princess St  PL1 2EX   (01752) 201523
*Still not as many reports as we'd like, but the Franchet family's Gallic bistro is tipped by its small fan club as offering "a superb experience all-round".* / **Details:** www.chloesrestaurant.co.uk; 10 pm; closed Mon & Sun.

**Tanners Restaurant**   £53   ❶❷❷
Prysten Hs, Finewell St  PL1 2AE
(01752) 252001
*"They could charge twice as much for this quality!" – the Tanner brothers' stylish, small restaurant offers "outstanding" cooking "in a city otherwise barren of haute cuisine".*
/ **Details:** www.tannersrestaurant.com; 9.30 pm; closed Mon & Sun.

| POOLE, DORSET | 7–3D |
|---|---|

**Branksome Beach**   £47   ⓣ
Pinecliff Rd  BH13 6LP   (01202) 767235
*With its "great location right next to the beach", this "buzzy" spot has a "great ambience" and "reasonable prices" too (well, "considering this is Sandbanks"); fish, seafood and bread are all singled out as "excellent".*
/ **Details:** www.branksomebeach.co.uk.

**Fishy Fishy**   £46   ⓣ
18 Dolphin Quay  BH15 1HH
(01202) 680793
*In the marina, a spin-off from the Brighton establishment of the same name, and tipped for its "fabulous sustainable seafood", including fish 'n' chips.* / **Details:** www.fishyfishy.co.uk; 11 pm.

**Guildhall Tavern**   £40   ❶❶❷
15 Market St  BH15 1NB   (01202) 671717
*"A very welcoming, authentic French restaurant specialising in seafood", just a minute from the quay; reports include many hymns of praise to Frederic & Severine Grande's "brilliant" food and "superb" service.*
/ **Details:** www.guildhalltavern.co.uk; 10 pm; closed Mon & Sun; no Amex.

**Storm**   £49   ❷❷❸
16 High St  BH15 1BP   (01202) 674970
*A "rustic" going-on "basic" interior sets the scene at Pete & Frances Miles "reliable" fixture, where the star of the menu is "fish caught by the chef and his friends"; "don't miss pudding, either".*
/ **Details:** www.stormfish.co.uk; 9.30 pm, Fri & Sat 10 pm; closed Mon L, Tue L & Sun L.

| PORT APPIN, ARGYLL AND BUTE | 9–3B |
|---|---|

**Airds Hotel**   £70   ⓣ
PA38 4DF   (01631) 730236
*A comfortable hotel beside Loch Linnhe that's consistently well-rated, and tipped for its fish and seafood.* / **Details:** www.airds-hotel.com; 20m N of Oban; 9.30 pm; no jeans or trainers; children: 8+ at D; SRA-75%. **Accommodation:** 11 rooms, from £245.

| PORTHGAIN, PEMBROKESHIRE | 4–4B |
|---|---|

**The Shed**   £33   ❷❷❷
SA62 5BN   (01348) 831518
*"A highlight of a trip to Pembrokeshire!" – this "rustic" 'fish 'n' chip' bistro serves "fantastic" fish, "imaginatively cooked", right by the harbour; "the smarter à la carte menu is also very impressive" (formula price, circa £41).*
/ **Details:** www.theshedporthgain.co.uk; 9 pm; no Amex; Booking essential.

---

**PORTHLEVEN, CORNWALL**  1–4A

**Kota** £45 ❶❷❷
Harbour Head TR13 9JA (01326) 562407
*"Classy cuisine amongst the pasty-munchers!"* –
this *"beautifully-positioned"* harbourside
restaurant is rated a *"great find"* by all who
comment on it, thanks not least to its *"exciting"*
fish menu that's *"beautifully presented"*.
/ **Details:** www.kotarestaurant.co.uk; 9 pm; D only,
closed Mon & Sun; no Amex. **Accommodation:** 2
rooms, from £70.

---

**PORTMAHOMACK , HIGHLAND**  9–2C

**The Oystercatcher** £57 ❶❷❷
Main St IV20 1YB (01862) 871560
*"Short of being on the boat itself, this is as fresh
as seafood gets"* – this *"totally unexpected"*
restaurant on the harbourfront not only offers
*"beautifully-cooked"* dishes (*"with passion"*) but
*"top-quality"* wines too.
/ **Details:** www.the-oystercatcher.co.uk; 10 pm; closed
Mon, Tue, Wed L & Sun D; no Amex.
**Accommodation:** 3 rooms, from £77.

---

**PORTMEIRION, GWYNEDD**  4–2C

**Portmeirion Hotel** £62 ❷❸❷
LL48 6ET (01766) 772440
At the heart of Sir Clough Williams-Ellis's
Italianate-fantasy village, this *"romantic"* hotel
dining room enjoys one of the UK's most
*"picturesque"* locations, with *"wonderful estuary
views"*; the food mostly measures up, and is
complemented by *"an excellent range of wines
and beers"*. / **Details:** www.portmeirion-village.com;
off A487 at Minffordd; 9 pm. **Accommodation:** 14
rooms, from £185.

---

**PORTSMOUTH, HAMPSHIRE**  2–4D

**abarbistro** £40 ❹❷❸
58 White Hart Rd PO1 2JA
(02392) 811585
A bright dining room in a former pub; it can
sometimes be *"very noisy"*, but otherwise all
reports affirm that it's a *"consistent"* spot whose
*"regularly-changing"* menu offers *"good value"*.
/ **Details:** www.abarbistro.co.uk; midnight, Sun
10.30 pm.

**Le Café Parisien** £27 ❶
1 Lord Montgomery Way PO1 2AH
(023) 9283 1234
*"A first-class breakfast or lunch venue"*, in the
University Quarter, tipped for its *"excellent
snack-style plates"*; a *"lively"* spot, it benefits
from a large, sunny terrace.

/ **Details:** www.lecafeparisien.com; 8 pm; closed Sun;
no Amex.

**Loch Fyne** £42 ❶
Unit 2 Vulcan Buildings PO1 3TY
(023) 9277 8060
*"A bit of a barn, but the fish is good"* – even
detractors of this chain-outlet sometimes tip it as
*"still good value, in what's otherwise a fish
desert"*. / **Details:** www.lochfyne-restaurants.com;
10.30 pm.

**Relentless Steak &
Lobster House** £45 ❷❷❸
85 Elm Grove PO5 1JF (02392) 822888
The *"great mix of surf 'n' turf"* on offer at this
*"relaxed"* Southsea *"hidden gem"* includes some
*"fabulously fresh seafood, caught by the chef's
father"*; *"great Wednesday BOGOF offer too!"*

---

**PRESTBURY, CHESHIRE**  5–2B

**Bacchus** £48 ❸❷❸
The Village SK10 4DG (01625) 820009
*"The quality restaurant Prestbury has been
waiting for since the White House closed"*; run
by refugees from the former Moss Nook, it
*"continues the high standards with which that
restaurant was associated… but a bit cheaper!"*
/ **Details:** www.bacchusprestbury.co.uk; 9.30 pm,
Fri & Sat 10 pm; closed Mon & Sun D.

---

**PRESTON BAGOT, WARWICKSHIRE**  5–4C

**The Crabmill** £44 ❸❷❸
B95 5EE (01926) 843342
A large modern gastropub, where the food
(improved in recent times) is *"always fresh and
imaginative"*; it's *"extremely popular"* – *"arrive
early if you want a table in the bar"*.
/ **Details:** www.thecrabmill.co.uk; on main road
between Warwick & Henley-in-Arden; 9.30 pm; closed
Sun D; no Amex; booking essential.

---

**PRESTON CANDOVER, HAMPSHIRE**  2–3D

**The Purefoy Arms** £43 ❷❸❷
RG25 2EJ (01256) 389 777
*"An interesting village pub, now run by a Spanish
chef who challenges the norms"* – this *"cosy"*
and *"tastefully-decorated"* country inn delights
practically all reporters with its *"Hispanic-
influenced"* cuisine and wine list.
/ **Details:** www.thepurefoyarms.co.uk.

PRESTON, LANCASHIRE          5–1A

**Bukhara**          **£21**   **❶❷❸**
154 Preston New Rd  PR5 0UP
(01772) 877710
*"What an oasis of fresh and imaginative
cooking"; this "amazing" Indian never fails to
please with its "delicate" and "distinctive"
spicing; indeed, it's so good, "the lack of alcohol is
no hardship" – "try the lime soda".*
*/ **Details:** www.bukharasamlesbury.co.uk; 11 pm;
D only; no Maestro.*

PWLLHELI, GWYNEDD          4–2C

**Plas Bodegroes**          **£63**   **❷❷❶**
Nefyn Rd  LL53 5TH  (01758) 612363
*"A magical environment, makes for a truly
memorable occasion" – the Chowns' restaurant-
with-rooms, in a Georgian house is especially
lauded for its "beautiful" setting, but the cooking
is often hailed as "faultless" too.*
*/ **Details:** www.bodegroes.co.uk; on A497 1m W of
Pwllheli; 9.30 pm; closed Mon, Tue-Sat D only, closed
Sun D; no Amex; children: not at D.*
***Accommodation:** 10 rooms, from £130.*

QUEENSBURY, MIDDLESEX          3–3A

**Regency Club**          **£30**   **T**
19-21 Queensbury Station Pde  HA8 5NR
(020) 8905 6177
*"It's a pub Jim, but not as we know it" – "with
Hindi music, cricket and Bollywood movie songs
on the big screens", this suburban "gem" serves
"some of the tastiest kebabs and tandooris
around". / **Details:** www.regencyclub.co.uk;
10.30 pm; closed Mon L.*

QUEENSFERRY, CITY OF EDINBURGH  9–4C

**Dakota Forth Bridge**          **£48**   **T**
Ferrimuir Retail Pk  EH30 9QZ  (0870) 423
4293
*As implausibly-located as a trendy restaurant can
be (by a Tesco car park, at the south end of the
Forth Road Bridge), this ambitious operation is
still tipped as a "brilliant all-rounder".*
*/ **Details:** www.dakotaforthbridge.co.uk; 10 pm;
booking essential. **Accommodation:** 132 rooms,
from £99.*

RADLEY GREEN, ESSEX          3–2B

**The Cuckoo**          **£43**   **❷❸❸**
CM4 0LT  (01245) 248946
*It's "not a place you'd find by accident", but the
local "ladies who lunch" set their SatNavs to
seek out this "charming" small restaurant – "a
beautiful restoration of old cottages" – which
offers a "varied seasonal menu", mostly locally-
sourced. / **Details:** www.cuckooradleygreen.co.uk; On
the A14 between Ongar and Chelmsford; 8.45 pm,
Fri-Sat 9 pm; closed Mon & Sun; no Amex.*

RAMSBOTTOM, LANCASHIRE          5–1B

**Ramsons**          **£60**
18 Market Pl  BL0 9HT  (01706) 825070
*Chris Johnson has run this "quirky" restaurant
since 1985, and it has long achieved a level
rarely found in the North West (including "one
of the best Italian wine lists in the country");
however, the long-time chef left during 2012, so
a rating of the new régime will have to await
next year's survey.*
*/ **Details:** www.ramsons-restaurant.com; 9.30 pm;
closed Mon, Tue L & Sun D; no Amex.*

RAMSGATE, KENT          3–3D

**Age & Sons**          **£35**   **T**
Charlotte Ct  CT11 8HE  (01843) 851515
*"Bright and unfussy", Toby Leigh's bistro is a
"pleasant" sort of place, tipped for "interesting"
main courses, an "outstanding" cheese board
and "great" puddings too – even fans, though,
can find standards "inconsistent".*
*/ **Details:** www.ageandsons.com; 10 pm; closed
Mon & Sun D.*

**Eddie Gilbert's**          **£44**   **❷❸❸**
32 King St  CT11 8NT  (01843) 852 123
*"Tip-top fish 'n' chips" are but one attraction of
this "excellent seafood restaurant, located over a
wet fish shop", but its appeal is wide-ranging –
"gastro-tourists travel miles just for the signature
starter of soft-boiled duck egg with crispy
smoked eel soldiers!"*
*/ **Details:** www.eddiegilberts.com; off the Main Street;
9.30pm; closed Sun D; no Amex.*

RAMSGILL-IN-NIDDERDALE, NORTH
YORKSHIRE          8–4B

**Yorke Arms**          **£87**   **❶❶❷**
HG3 5RL  (01423) 755243
*"Faultless in every respect" – Frances & Gerald
Atkins's grand inn in a "tiny picturesque Dales
village" provides a "classy and comfy" destination
at the end of a "stunning drive"; true, prices are
"eye-watering", but the "classical" dishes are*

realised to an "absolutely superb" standard.
/ **Details:** www.yorke-arms.co.uk; 4m W of Pateley
Bridge; 8.45 pm; no Amex. **Accommodation:** 16
rooms, from £150.

READING, BERKSHIRE                    2–2D

**Cerise**
**Forbury Hotel**            £56    ❸❸❸
26 The Forbury  RG1 3EJ  (01189) 527770
Top tip for business entertaining – this is "one of
the better hotel restaurants" hereabouts, and the
weekday lunch, in particular, offers "very good
value for money".
/ **Details:** www.theforburyhotel.co.uk; 10 pm.
**Accommodation:** 23, 17 apts rooms, from £150.

**Forbury's**              £52    ❷❷❷
1 Forbury Sq  RG1 3BB  (0118) 957 4044
Citing "fabulous food and amazing value", most
reporters are very up on this "always-
competent" Gallic fixture, in the city-centre; it's
"quite formal in the evening", but "more relaxed
at the weekend, and very welcoming towards
children". / **Details:** www.forburys.co.uk; 10 pm;
closed Sun.

**London Street Brasserie**   £48   ❸❸❸
2-4 London St  RG1 4PN  (0118) 950 5036
A "pretty" riverside brasserie, hailed by most
reporters as the "jewel in Reading's culinary
crown", offering "fresh" and "well-executed"
dishes, at "reasonable" prices; "good menu du
jour". / **Details:** www.londonstbrasserie.co.uk;
10.30 pm, Fri & Sat 11 pm.

REIGATE, SURREY                       3–3B

**La Barbe**               £48    ❸❸④
71 Bell St  RH2 7AN  (01737) 241966
"Good ambience, good service and great
cooking… but it's not cheap" – the almost
invariable theme of the (voluminous)
commentary on this "professional" and
"buzzing" Gallic "classic", now entering its fourth
decade in business. / **Details:** www.labarbe.co.uk;
9.30 pm; closed Sat L & Sun D.

**Tony Tobin @**
**The Dining Room**        £59    ❷❷❸
59a High St  RH2 9AE  (01737) 226650
"Possibly over-hyped by the locals, but still a very
nice meal and great service" – all reports
confirm that the TV chef's cosy HQ offers food
that's "well-cooked and presented".
/ **Details:** www.tonytobinrestaurants.co.uk; 10 pm;
closed Sat L & Sun D.

REYNOLDSTON, SWANSEA           1–1C

**Fairyhill**              £64    ④❸❸
SA3 1BS  (01792) 390139
For its devotees, the cuisine at this country house
hotel, set deep in the Gower Peninsula, remains
"very good indeed" ("my only complaint after
several days, was that it's rather rich"); ratings
have headed south, though, in recent years – let's
hope for a turnaround under new chef Neil
Hollis, who arrived in 2012!
/ **Details:** www.fairyhill.net; 20 mins from M4, J47 off
B4295; 9 pm; no Amex; children: 8+ at D.
**Accommodation:** 8 rooms, from £180.

RHOSCOLYN, ANGLESEY          4–1C

**The White Eagle**        £40    ❸❷❸
LL65 2NJ  (01407) 860 267
"Worth hunting out, down a country lane leading
to the sea", this "relaxed" inn (with sea-views
from some tables, and the terrace) offers an
"extensive" and "varied" menu of "local fish and
meat"; popularity with families can make it
"noisy at weekends".
/ **Details:** www.white-eagle.co.uk; 9 pm; no Amex.

RIPLEY, SURREY                3–3A

**Drakes**                 £81    ❶❷④
The Clock Hs, High St  GU23 6AQ
(01483) 224777
"Terrific" taste-combinations have helped make
Steve Drake's village-restaurant one of the most
celebrated in the Home Counties; the dining
room has traditionally suffered from an
atmosphere "like an upmarket funeral parlour",
but some fans say it's "much improved" after a
recent face-lift!
/ **Details:** www.drakesrestaurant.co.uk; 9.30 pm;
closed Mon, Tue L & Sun; no Amex; booking: max 12.

RIPPONDEN, WEST YORKSHIRE     5–1C

**El Gato Negro Tapas**    £41    ❶❷❷
1 Oldham Rd  HX6 4DN  (01422) 823070
"Still by far the best tapas in the North of
England!" – Simon Shaw's "excellent" converted
pub is "a joy" to all who report on it; if there's a
downside, it's that it can be "too noisy".
/ **Details:** www.elgatonegrotapas.com; 9.30 pm, Fri &
Sat 10 pm, Sun 7.30 pm; closed Mon, Tue, Wed L,
Thu L, Fri L & Sun D.

## ROCK, CORNWALL      1–3B

**Dining Room**    **£52**   **T**
Pavilion Buildings, Rock Rd PL27 6JS
(01208) 862622
*"Nathan Outlaw has some competition in up-and-coming chef Fred Beedle", say fans of this "inventive" family-run spot, where "everything is made in-house" – more reports please.*
/ *Details: www.thediningroomrock.co.uk; closed Mon & Tue.*

**Restaurant Nathan Outlaw**
**The St Enodoc Hotel**    **£108**   **❶❷❸**
Rock Rd PL27 6LA   (01208) 863394
*"Nathan Outlaw must surely be the child of a mermaid!" – how else to explain the "simply phenomenal and exquisitely presented" fish cuisine at this "smart but unassuming-looking" venue, nowadays one of England's top dining rooms; it has "amazing" views of the Camel estuary too. / Details: www.nathan-outlaw.co.uk; 9 pm; D only, closed Mon & Sun; no Amex; no shorts; Essential; children: 12+ D. Accommodation: 20 rooms, from £130.*

## ROCKBEARE, DEVON      1–3D

**Jack in the Green Inn**    **£48**   **❸❸❸**
London Rd EX5 2EE   (01404) 822240
*"Really punching above its weight", this well-known gastropub is widely hailed for food "of restaurant quality"; even some fans, though, note it "has high prices to match".*
/ *Details: www.jackinthegreen.uk.com; On the old A30, 3 miles east of junction 29 of M5; 9.30 pm, Sun 9 pm; no Amex.*

## ROMALDKIRK, COUNTY DURHAM    8–3B

**The Rose & Crown**    **£40**   **❷❸❷**
DL12 9EB   (01833) 650213
*"A lovely village pub in a pretty setting", by the village green, that's "handy for a half-way break on the way to Scotland"; it provides "amazing local produce, cooked to perfection, at sensible prices". / Details: www.rose-and-crown.co.uk; 6m NW of Barnard Castle on B6277; 9 pm; no Amex; children: 6+ in restaurant. Accommodation: 12 rooms, from £150.*

## ROSEVINE, CORNWALL      1–4B

**Driftwood Hotel**    **£65**   **❶❷❶**
TR2 5EW   (01872) 580644
*"Spectacular views and food" – all of many reports confirm that this clifftop hotel dining room offers a "truly exceptional" dining experience; "over a week, we tried everything on the menu, and there was simply nothing which could be called a disappointment".*
/ *Details: www.driftwoodhotel.co.uk; off the A30 to Truro, towards St Mawes; 9.30 pm; D only; booking: max 6; children: 10+. Accommodation: 15 rooms, from £195.*

## ROWDE, WILTSHIRE      2–2C

**The George & Dragon**    **£43**   **❷❷❸**
High St SN10 2PN   (01380) 723053
*"Don't judge this pub by its exterior!" – it may look "a bit run down", but almost all reporters applaud its "interesting" fish-centric menu and "excellent choice of wines" too; let's hope, though, that a couple of "below-par" meals this year aren't the beginning of a trend.*
/ *Details: www.thegeorgeanddragonrowde.co.uk; on A342 between Devizes & Chippenham; 10 pm; closed Sun D; no Amex. Accommodation: 3 rooms, from £65.*

## ROWHOOK, WEST SUSSEX      3–4A

**Chequers Inn**    **£48**   **T**
RH12 3PY   (01403) 790480
*A pretty 15th-century village inn, on the Surrey/Sussex borders, tipped for "very good" food at "keen prices".*
/ *Details: www.chequersrowhook.com; 9 pm; closed Sun D; no Amex.*

## ROWSLEY, DERBYSHIRE      5–2C

**The Peacock**    **£73**   **❷❷❷**
Bakewell Rd DE4 2EB   (01629) 733518
*"Interesting menu combinations", "beautifully presented", earn high approval for this "fabulously-located" inn; there is still a minority, though, for whom the cooking is "too clever for its own good".*
/ *Details: www.thepeacockatrowsley.com; 9 pm, Sun 8.30 pm; children: 10+ at D. Accommodation: 16 rooms, from £155.*

## RYE, EAST SUSSEX      3–4C

**The Ambrette at Rye**    **£41**   **❶❶❷**
24 High St TN31 7JF   (01797) 222 043
*"My lunch compared favourably with what you might find at Benares or Tamarind!" – the "deftly spiced" and "very refined" cuisine on offer at this "outstanding" Indian is, on all accounts, "exquisite"; prices are "reasonable" too.*
/ *Details: www.theambrette.co.uk; L only; closed Mon.*

**George Hotel**    **£47**   **T**
98 High St TN31 7JT   (01797) 222114
*An "old faithful" to its fans, this ancient hotel still also inspires the odd "never again" report – let's hope the reporter who says, "at last, the George is finally getting its act together, after years of*

being profoundly disappointing", has got it right!
/ **Details:** www.thegeorgeinrye.com; 10 pm; no Amex.

**Landgate Bistro**            **£39**    **❷❷❸**
5-6 Landgate  TN31 7LH   (01797) 222829
"Creative cuisine of a consistently high standard"
makes this small and "friendly" coastal bistro
popular with all who comment on it – "great
flavours, beautiful presentation, and excellent
value for money too".
/ **Details:** www.landgatebistro.co.uk; 9 pm Sat
9.15 pm; closed Mon, Tue, Wed L, Thu L, Fri L & Sun D;
no Amex.

**Tuscan Kitchen**            **£41**    **❷❸❸**
8 Lion St  TN31 7LB   (01797) 223269
A "wonderful personal welcome" and "Tuscan
home-cooking at excellent prices" earn many
warm reviews for this "individual" two-year-old;
"good selection of wines by the glass" too.
/ **Details:** www.tuscankitchenrye.co.uk; 11.30 pm;
closed Mon, Tue, Wed, Thu L & Sat L.

**Webbe's at**
**The Fish Cafe**            **£43**    **❷❸④**
17 Tower St  TN31 7AT   (01797) 222226
"Fresh fish, just how it should taste" (from a
menu "with some old favourites, and some more
original dishes too") helps make Paul Webb's
town-centre venture a notably "enjoyable"
destination; "good dishes for carnivores" too.
/ **Details:** www.thefishcafe.com; 9.30 pm.

SALISBURY, WILTSHIRE            2–3C

**Anokaa**            **£41**    **❶❷❷**
60 Fisherton St  SP2 7RB   (01722) 414142
"Immensely creative", "delicately flavoured",
"beautifully presented" – this large, town-centre
Indian wins consistent rave reviews for its
"amazingly good" cooking; the lunch deal offers
"excellent value" too. / **Details:** www.anokaa.com;
10.30 pm; no shorts.

**Jade**            **£36**    **T**
109a Exeter St  SP1 2SF   (01722) 333355
Tipped for "very well prepared Chinese food"
("with steamed bass a speciality"), this
"standard-looking" operation is "probably better
than anywhere else of its type in the
Salisbury/Bournemouth/Shaftesbury region".
/ **Details:** www.jaderestaurant.co.uk; 11.30 pm; closed
Sun; no Amex.

SALTAIRE, WEST YORKSHIRE            5–1C

**Salts Diner**            **£32**    **❸❸❷**
Salts Mill, Victoria Rd  BD18 3LA
(01274) 531163
Hockney prints set the scene at this "lovely airy

diner", in a "beautiful" converted mill (part of a
World Heritage site) – a perennially popular and
"bustling" destination, offering very dependable
pizza, burgers and so on.
/ **Details:** www.saltsmill.org.uk; 2m from Bradford on
A650; L & afternoon tea only; no Amex.

SALTHOUSE, NORFOLK            6–3C

**Cookies Crab Shop**            **£21**    **❷④④**
The Grn, Coast Rd  NR25 7AJ
(01263) 740352
"Excellent fish in a shed on a road – sounds bad,
but the fish more than makes up for it!"; this
"quirky" ("absolutely nuts") '50s hang-over
serves "seafood that's simply divine, at
unbelievable prices"; "you're shoe-horned in"
however, and service is "brusque".
/ **Details:** www.salthouse.org.uk; on A149; 7 pm;
no credit cards.

SANDSEND, NORTH YORKSHIRE            8–3D

**Estbek House**            **£57**    **❶❷❷**
East Row  YO21 3SU   (01947) 893424
This "delightful" restaurant-with-rooms, "right on
the seafront", inspires stellar reports – "superb
in every way", it offers "beautiful fish dishes,
cooked to perfection", and a "very good wine
list" too. / **Details:** www.estbekhouse.co.uk; 9 pm;
D only; no Amex. **Accommodation:** 4 rooms,
from £125.

SAPPERTON, GLOUCESTERSHIRE            2–2C

**The Bell at Sapperton**    **£47**    **T**
GL7 6LE   (01285) 760298
A pretty Cotswold gastropub, still sometimes
tipped for its "laid-back" charms; it's nowhere
near as highly rated as once it was though.
/ **Details:** www.foodatthebell.co.uk; from Cirencester
take the A419 towards Stroud, turn right to Sapperton;
9.30 pm, Sun 9 pm; no Amex; children: 10+ at D.

SAWLEY, LANCASHIRE            5–1B

**The Spread Eagle**            **£39**    **T**
BB7 4NH   (01200) 441202
Oddly little feedback this year on this old
coaching inn, in the famously pretty Ribble Valley;
it's tipped, though, for its "lovely" location, its
"temptingly wide" menu, and its "tastefully-
appointed" dining room.
/ **Details:** www.spreadeaglesawley.co.uk; 9.15 pm, Sun
7.15 pm. **Accommodation:** 7 rooms, from £80.

SCARBOROUGH, NORTH YORKSHIRE 8–4D

**Lanterna**            **£47**    **❸❸④**
33 Queen St  YO11 1HQ   (01723) 363616
"Excellent fish in a friendly environment" – that's

the formula that's kept this "cramped" trattoria in business for nearly two decades; there have been up-and-down reports of late, though, and one reporter notes that "even though it's very popular with the regulars, it's not consistent". / **Details:** www.lanterna-ristorante.co.uk; 9.30 pm; D only, closed Sun; no Amex.

| SEER GREEN, BEACONSFIELD , BUCKINGHAMSHIRE | 3–3A |

**The Jolly Cricketers**    **£47**    ❸④④
24 Chalfont Rd  HP9 2YG   (01494) 676308
"I can't praise this village pub highly enough" – the majority view on this "warm and buzzing" hostelry, praised for its "excellent food at reasonable prices"; sceptics, though, put it somewhere round the "reasonable stand-by" level. / **Details:** www.thejollycricketers.co.uk; 11.15 pm, Fri & Sat midnight; closed Mon & Sun D.

| SEVENOAKS, KENT | 3–3B |

**The Vine**    **£50**    ❸④❸
11 Pound Ln  TN13 3TB   (01732) 469510
"Easily the best dining in Sevenoaks"; near the eponymous cricket ground, this "airy" and "pleasant" spot is hailed for its "good and varied" cuisine; Sunday lunch attracts particular praise. / **Details:** www.vinerestaurant.co.uk; 9.30 pm; closed Sun D; no Amex.

| SHALDON, DEVON | 1–3D |

**Ode**    **£54**    ❶❷❸
Fore St  TQ14 0DE   (01626) 873977
"A proper little jewel in a lovely seaside town" – this "intimate" and "romantic" spot is universally praised by reporters for cooking of a "very high standard". / **Details:** www.odetruefood.co.uk; 9.30 pm; closed Mon, Tue L, Wed L, Sat L & Sun; no Amex; booking essential; SRA-88%.

| SHEFFIELD, SOUTH YORKSHIRE | 5–2C |

**Artisan**    **£47**    ❶
32-34 Sandygate Rd  S10 5RY   (0114) 266 6096
Richard Smith's "buzzing" bistro is tipped by its fans as a "firm favourite for any occasion"; the odd local sceptic, though, does sense drift in recent times. / **Details:** www.artisansheffield.co.uk; 9.30 pm; no Amex.

**The Cricket Inn**    **£43**    ❷❸❷
Penny Ln  S17 3AZ   (0114) 236 5256
"Superb pub grub" – "not too fussy or smart" – wins only very positive reports on this "great local", next to the cricket ground; it makes "a great relaxed destination for all the family".

/ **Details:** www.relaxeatanddrink.co.uk; Mon-Sat 9.30 pm, Sun 8 pm; no Amex.

**The Milestone**    **£41**    ❸❸④
84 Green Lane At Ball St  S3 8SE
(0114) 272 8327
"It's a real find", say fans of this "high-quality" gastropub, which is the type of place that's "simply fantastic" for a "laid-back" brunch; the occasional critic, though, does fear it's a touch "over-rated". / **Details:** www.the-milestone.co.uk; 10 pm, Sun 9 pm; no Amex.

**Moran's**    **£48**    ❷❷❷
289 Abbeydale Road South  S17 3LB
(0114) 235 0101
"A little gem… despite appearing to be located in a bike shop!" – this "small and classy" Abbeydale venture (sharing an entrance with the afore-mentioned store) offers "outstandingly good food and wine at very sensible prices"; "unsurprisingly, it's very popular". / **Details:** www.moranssheffield.co.uk; 9 pm, Fri & Sat 9.30 pm; closed Mon, Tue-Fri L & Sun D; no Amex.

**Nonna's**    **£43**    ❷❷❷
535-541 Eccleshall Rd  S11 8PR   (0114) 268 6166
"The place to be seen queuing for!" – all of the many reports confirm that this "consistently great and vibrant" Eccleshall Italian "favourite" maintains "high standards"; it now has a Chesterfield spin-off too. / **Details:** www.nonnas.co.uk; 9.30 pm, Sat & Sun 9.45 pm; no Amex.

**The Old Vicarage**    **£86**    ❶
Ridgeway Moor, Ridgeway  S12 3XW
(0114) 247 5814
A "flowery" quarter-centenarian we include primarily because it might seem odd to exclude somewhere that's long boasted a Michelin star – survey feedback suggests it is "good, but well past its prime", and "overpriced" too. / **Details:** www.theoldvicarage.co.uk; 9.30 pm; closed Mon, Sat L & Sun; no Amex.

**Rafters**    **£52**    ❷❷❸
220 Oakbrook Rd, Nether Grn  S11 7ED
(0114) 230 4819
"Maintaining high standards", this Ranmoor fixture continues to offer a "quiet and intimate dining experience" which pleases all who comment on it. / **Details:** www.raftersrestaurant.co.uk; 10 pm; D only, closed Tue & Sun.

**Silversmiths**    **£35**    ④❺❸
111 Arundel St  S1 2NT   (0114) 270 6160
In the city-centre's 'Cultural Quarter', this "lively"

bar/restaurant is perhaps "the most 'individual' of the establishments", and wins praise for its "fantastic value" (especially midweek); the British scoff "lacks consistency", though, and service can be "amateurish beyond belief". / **Details:** www.silversmiths-restaurant.com; 11.30 pm, Fri & Sat midnight; D only, closed Sun; no Amex.

**Wasabisabi** £31 **T**
227A, London Rd  S2 4NF   (0114) 258 5838
This large Japanese restaurant continues to be strongly tipped for "very good food", served "with flair and imagination"; "great sushi" too.
/ **Details:** www.wasabisabi.co.uk; 11 pm; no Amex.

**Black Horse at Ireland** £48 ❷❷❷
Ireland  SG17 5QL   (01462) 811398
"Very popular, and you can see why!" – this beamed former boozer is now a restaurant, offering "unfussy but high quality pub grub, imaginatively and beautifully cooked".
/ **Details:** www.blackhorseireland.com; 9.30 pm, Fri & Sat 10 pm; closed Sun D. **Accommodation:** 2 rooms, from £55.

**Three Acres** £56 ❸❸❷
Roydhouse  HD8 8LR   (01484) 602606
Over 40 years in the same ownership, this "quaint" inn is an ambitious sort of place to find out on't moors – "so relaxed, yet so special", and offering "superb" game dishes, and so on; even fans however are increasingly inclined to note that it's "getting very pricey".
/ **Details:** www.3acres.com; 9.30 pm; no Amex. **Accommodation:** 16 rooms, from £125.

**The Green** £51 ❷❸❸
The Green  DT9 3HY   (01935) 813821
"A pleasant spot in this pretty market town" – praised for food that's "always sound"; when the owners are absent, though, service can be "lacking". / **Details:** www.greenrestaurant.co.uk; 9 pm; closed Mon & Sun.

**King's Arms** £44 **T**
Charlton Horethorne  DT9 4NL
(01963) 220281
Just outside the town, this 'country pub and hotel' is tipped for "outstanding" food of a quality that's "always consistent", and an "interesting wine list" too. / **Details:** www.thekingsarms.co.uk; ?; no Amex. **Accommodation:** 10 rooms, from £105.

**Kinghams** £50 ❸❸❸
Gomshall Ln  GU5 9HE   (01483) 202168
With its "good food", "cottage-atmosphere" and "cheerful service", this 20-year-old establishment is still probably "the best local restaurant"; for critics, though, it is rather "stuck in a time warp". / **Details:** www.kinghams-restaurant.co.uk; off A25 between Dorking & Guildford; 9 pm; closed Mon & Sun D.

**The William Bray** £50 ❹❹❸
Shere Ln  GU5 9HS   (01483) 202 044
In a "beautiful village", this posh gastropub inspires quite a few reports; most reporters applaud "a good experience all-round", although doubters can find results a little "bland".
/ **Details:** www.thewilliambray.co.uk; 10 pm; no Amex.

**L'Ortolan** £92 ❸❷❸
Church Ln  RG2 9BY   (0118) 988 8500
Alan Murcheson's "cutting-edge" cuisine is part of a "first-class-all-round formula" that makes his former rectory a "real treat" for most who report on it; it's kept back from the survey's very front rank, though, by an undertow of feedback saying it's "good but not outstanding".
/ **Details:** www.lortolan.com; 8.30 pm; closed Mon & Sun.

**The Chaser Inn** £39 ❷❸❸
Stumble Hill  TN11 9PE   (01732) 810360
"Cosy pub"… "winter lunch treat"… "always busy" – there are lots of reports on this "lovely" rural inn, all of which suggest it's "always reliable"! / **Details:** www.thechaser.co.uk; 9.30 pm, Sun 9 pm.

**Orwells** £55 ❸❸❹
Shiplake Row  RG9 4DP   (0118) 940 3673
Hailed by many reporters as a "real foodie find", this "restaurant in the middle of nowhere" is consistently praised for its "fantastic" cuisine; it can seem "expensive" though, and – for the occasional reporter – "not nearly as good as it thinks it is". / **Details:** www.orwellsatshiplake.co.uk; 9.30 pm; closed Mon & Sun D; no Amex.

**Aagrah** £30 ❷❸❸
4 Saltaire Rd  BD18 3HN   (01274) 530880
"The original branch and still the best", say fans – this "swish" home base of a leading local

Indian chain still offers a "winning" formula, and "great value" too. / **Details:** www.aagrah.com; 11.30 pm; closed Sat L.

---

SKENFRITH, MONMOUTHSHIRE          2–1B

**The Bell at Skenfrith**     £51    ❸④④
NP7 8UH    (01600) 750235
"Amazing creative food from local producers" and a "huge and interesting" wine list inspire a good number of very positive reports on this remote inn; too many incidents of "inattentive" and "ill-informed" service, however, contribute to an impression in some quarters of standards "well down" on their past best.
/ **Details:** www.skenfrith.co.uk; on B4521, 10m E of Abergavenny; 9.30 pm, Sun 9 pm; no Amex; children: 8+ at D. **Accommodation:** 11 rooms, from £110.

---

SLEAT, HIGHLAND          9–2B

**Kinloch Lodge**     £80    ❷❷❸
IV43 8QY    (01471) 833333
"The top gastronomic experience in the north western Highlands" – the ancestral home of the Macdonald of Macdonald is, on almost all accounts, a "first-class" destination all-round.
/ **Details:** www.kinloch-lodge.co.uk; 9 pm; no Amex. **Accommodation:** 15 rooms, from £150.

---

SMALL HYTHE, KENT          3–4C

**Swan at Chapel Down**     £49
Tenterden Vineyard  TN30 7NG
(01580) 761616
In the heart of an "enterprising winery", the restaurant formerly branded under the name of Richard Phillips was relaunched as a thoroughly British restaurant in 2012 – too late, sadly, to attract any survey commentary; given standards at the other 'Swans', though, it should be a handy destination. / **Details:** www.loveswan.co.uk; 9.30 pm; closed Mon, Tue D, Wed D & Sun D.

---

SNAPE, SUFFOLK          3–1D

**The Crown Inn**     £39    ❷④❷
Bridge Rd  IP17 1SL    (01728) 688324
Near the Maltings, this "delightful typical Suffolk pub" is a "warm and welcoming" operation, with a great line in "local produce, well prepared" (especially fish). / **Details:** www.snape-crown.co.uk; off A12 towards Aldeburgh; 9.30 pm, Sat 10 pm, Sun 9.30 pm; no Amex. **Accommodation:** 2 rooms, from £90.

---

SONNING-ON-THAMES, BERKSHIRE    2–2D

**The Bull Inn**     £45    ❸❷❶
High St  RG4 6UP    (0118) 969 3901
"A delightful medieval inn, in a beautiful Thames-side village" – it has "no gastropub pretensions", but its "properly-cooked English pub-food" ("plus the odd Gallic bistro classic") helps make it a perennially "popular" destination.
/ **Details:** www.bullinnsonning.co.uk; off A4, J10 between Oxford & Windsor; 9.30 pm.
**Accommodation:** 7 rooms, from £99.

**The French Horn**     £80    ❷❷❷
RG4 6TN    (0118) 969 2204
"A good dose of '70s glamour" still permeates this "gloriously-located" riverside "classic", whose "traditional" appeal seems largely unaffected by the passing of the years; it helps that the food is generally "of high quality", and service is "friendly" and "professional" too… but "you do need deep pockets".
/ **Details:** www.thefrenchhorn.co.uk; 9.30 pm; booking: max 10. **Accommodation:** 21 rooms, from £160.

---

SOUTH SHIELDS, TYNE AND WEAR    8–2B

**Colmans**     £33    ❶❷❸
182-186 Ocean Rd  NE33 2JQ    (0191) 456 1202
"Best fish (non-sticky) 'n' chips (non-greasy) this side of the Toon!" – and "excellent" personal service too – make this "large-scale" chippy (est. 1926) well "worth the drive".
/ **Details:** www.colmansfishandchips.com; L only; no Amex.

---

SOUTHAMPTON, HAMPSHIRE    2–3D

**Coriander Lounge**     £27    ❷❷❸
130-131 High St  SO14 2BR
(02380) 710888
This 'high street Indian' is a "welcoming and relaxing" establishment, praised for food that's consistently "better than average".
/ **Details:** www.corianderlounge.com; 11pm, Sun 10pm; booking essential on weekends.

**Kuti's**     £31    ❶
37-39 Oxford St  SO14 3DP    (023) 8022 1585
In a city with little in the way of obvious restaurant culture, this popular Indian has long been tipped as "a cut above average"; a "good-value" place, it offers "pleasant views out over Southampton Water" too.
/ **Details:** www.kutis.co.uk; 11 pm.

**Simons at Oxfords**     £41    ❶
35-36 Oxford St  SO15 3DS    (023) 8022 4444
A handily-located city-centre bistro-restaurant, tipped for its "great prices" and its suitability for anything from "Sunday brunch at its best" to a

*"special night out"; more reports please!*
*/ Details: www.simonsatoxfords.com; 10 pm, Fri & Sat 10.30 pm, Sun 9 pm; no shorts.*

**White Star**  £ 47  🇹
28 Oxford St  SO14 3DJ   (023) 8082 1990
A *"pleasant"* city-centre pub, tipped for *"very good"* food – of some ambition – served in *"pleasant"* surroundings.
*/ Details: www.whitestartavern.co.uk; 9.45 pm.*
**Accommodation:** 13 rooms, from £85.

SOUTHPORT, MERSEYSIDE       5–1A

**Gusto Trattoria**  £ 34  🇹
58-62 Lord St  PR8 1QB   (01704) 544 255
*"Intimate and very friendly"*, a trattoria tipped not just for *"excellent, large, thin pizzas"*, but for *"good specials, and wines"* too.
*/ Details: www.gustotrattoria.co.uk; 10 pm; closed Mon.*

**The Vincent Hotel**  £ 41  🇹
98 Lord St  PR8 1JR   (01704) 883800
The restaurant of this *"stylish"* hotel offers *"a mixture of well-presented British and Italian dishes"*, and is tipped as *"a great place for a coffee, lunch, afternoon tea or dinner"; "the weekday supper menu is very good value for money"*. */ Details: www.thevincenthotel.com; 10 pm.*
**Accommodation:** 60 rooms, from £93.

SOUTHROP, GLOUCESTERSHIRE       2–2C

**The Swan at Southrop**  £ 45
GL7 3NU   (01367) 850205
This prominent Cotswold gastroboozer changed hands after our survey for the year had concluded; let's hope for the best under its new régime – they have quite a lot to live up to!
*/ Details: www.theswanatsouthrop.co.uk; 10 pm; closed Sun D; no Amex.*

SOUTHWOLD, SUFFOLK       3–1D

**The Crown**
**Adnams Hotel**  £ 54  ④❸❷
90 High St  IP18 6DP   (01502) 722275
This *"bustling"* inn – owned by famous local brewery, Adnams – is *"always crowded"*; the *"traditional"* cooking can be *"very good"*, but it's often just *"solid"* – the wine list, on the other hand, is *"superb"*.
*/ Details: www.adnams.co.uk/stay-with-us/the-crown; 9 pm.* **Accommodation:** 14 rooms, from £130.

**Sutherland House**  £ 51  ❷❸❸
56 High St  IP18 6DN   (01502) 724544
*"The glorious Tudor ceiling complements the excellent food"*, says one of the fans of Peter &

Anna Banks's *"very sound"* restaurant, which has *"a lovely location in this superb coastal town"*.
*/ Details: www.sutherlandhouse.co.uk; 9.30 pm; closed Mon (winter).* **Accommodation:** 3 rooms, from £140.

**The Swan**  £ 51  ④④❸
The Market Pl  IP18 6EG   (01502) 722186
*"The Adnams flagship"* – this well-known hotel has the undoubted plus of the brewery's formidable wine list; its *"classically-styled"* dining room is, say fans, *"ideal for a special occasion"*, but critics, noting that it's *"not cheap"*, say it needs *"livening up"*.
*/ Details: www.adnams.co.uk/stay-with-us/the-swan; 9 pm; no jeans or trainers; children: 5+ at D.*
**Accommodation:** 42 rooms, from £150.

SOWERBY BRIDGE, WEST YORKSHIRE 5–1C

**Gimbals**  £ 40  🇹
76 Wharf St  HX6 2AF   (01422) 839329
*"A very pleasant bistro"*, with slightly *"quirky"* decor; all reports confirm that it's a *"cosy"* and *"comfortable"* sort of place where the puddings, in particular, are *"inspired"*.
*/ Details: www.gimbals.co.uk; 9.15 pm; D only, closed Sun; no Amex.*

SPARSHOLT, HAMPSHIRE       2–3D

**The Plough Inn**  £ 44  ❸❸❷
SO21 2NW   (01962) 776353
*"A lovely old country pub, where high-quality food is served by charming staff"; it's "always full"*. */ Details: www.theploughsparsholt.co.uk; 9 pm, Sun & Mon 8.30 pm, Fri & Sat 9.30 pm; no Amex.*

SPELDHURST, KENT       3–4B

**George & Dragon**  £ 45  ❸❷❷
Speldhurst Hill  TN3 0NN   (01892) 863125
*"Always consistent"*, this *"very popular"* inn, in a pretty village, is widely applauded by reporters for its *"good use of local produce"*; even fans, though, may have a slight feeling that the place *"trades on its reputation"*.
*/ Details: www.speldhurst.com; 9.30 pm; closed Sun D; no Amex.*

ST ALBANS, HERTFORDSHIRE       3–2A

**Barrissimo**  £ 14  🇹
28 St Peters St  AL1 3NA   (01727) 869999
*"Bellissimo!"; looking for an "excellent coffee and homemade fresh pastries and paninis"?* – this Italian café is the top tip locally.
*/ Details: 5.30 pm, Sun 4 pm; L only; no credit cards.*

**Cock**  **£44**  🅣
48 St Peters St  AL1 3NF  (01727) 854 816
*With its roaring fires and ancient decor, a "really cute pub", between the cathedral and the river; it can be a bit "noisy" and the food's not ambitious, but it's still "better than at most pubs in the area".*
/ **Details:** *www.thecockinstalbans.co.uk.*

**Darcy's**  **£49**  ❷❷❸
2 Hatfield Rd  AL1 3RP  (01727) 730777
*"A very safe place to eat in a culinary desert"; Ruth Hurren's consistent fixture is an all-round crowd-pleaser, especially with kids – "the menu has some nice twists to traditional dishes (how can kangaroo steaks be so good!), and is evidently carefully prepared".*
/ **Details:** *www.darcysrestaurant.co.uk; 9 pm, Fri & Sat 10 pm.*

**Lussmanns**  **£43**  ④❷❸
Waxhouse Gate, High St  AL3 4EW
(01727) 851941
*"Akin to Ask! or PizzaExpress in decor" – this "family-friendly" fixture, right next to the Abbey, is a "lively and modern" brasserie, whose "commendable" and wide-ranging menu helps make for a "consistently pleasant" experience.*
/ **Details:** *www.lussmanns.com; 10 pm, Fri & Sat 10.30 pm, Sun 9 pm; SRA-65%.*

**The Waffle House**

**Kingsbury Water Mill**  **£21**  🅣
St Michael's St  AL3 4SJ  (01727) 853502
*Looking for a snack that's "quirky and cute"? – with its "vast array of waffles, both savoury and sweet", this pretty old mill is a local institution (est. 1981), tipped for its "never-failing" charms.*
/ **Details:** *www.wafflehouse.co.uk; 6 pm; L only; no Amex; no booking.*

**Seafood Restaurant**  **£64**  ❷❷❷
The Scores, Bruce Embankment  KY16 9AB
(01334) 479475
*A "glass box practically in the sea"; it provides a "magnificent setting overlooking the bay", and is a destination that "takes some beating", thanks not least to its "amazing" fish and seafood.*
/ **Details:** *www.theseafoodrestaurant.com; 10 pm; children: 12+ at D.*

**Vine Leaf**  **£46**  ❷⓿❷
131 South St  KY16 9UN  (01334) 477497
*"Standards have never slipped… over a quarter of a century!" – this recently refurbished bistro offers a "good-value and wide" menu of "old favourites with a twist".*

/ **Details:** *www.vineleafstandrews.co.uk; 9.30 pm; D only, closed Mon & Sun.*

**Cwtch**  **£43**  ❸❷❸
22 High St  SA62 6SD  (01437) 720491
*This town-centre spot is, on most reports, a "surprisingly excellent and popular small restaurant in a bit of a foodie desert" – there's some suggestion, though, that the stress can show at peak times.*
/ **Details:** *www.cwtchrestaurant.co.uk; 9.30 pm; D only.*

**Warpool Court**

**Warpool Court Hotel**  **£50**  🅣
SA62 6BN  (01437) 720300
*"A very old-fashioned hotel", tipped for its "splendid view", and its "modern and precise cooking" too; "our booking confirmation contained the most extraordinary prohibition on submitting disparaging reviews to online or other guides… but luckily I liked the place!"*
/ **Details:** *www.warpoolcourthotel.com; 9 pm.*
**Accommodation:** *22 rooms, from £140.*

**Alba Restaurant**  **£42**  ❸❷❸
The Old Life Boat Hs, Wharf Rd  TR26 1LF
(01736) 797222
*"Book an upstairs window table if you can", if you dine at this "friendly" harbourside venue; even fans can find it "a bit pricey", but it mostly wins praise for its "consistently strong" cooking, "with an accent on fish".*
/ **Details:** *www.thealbarestaurant.com; 10 pm; D only.*

**The Black Rock**  **£41**  🅣
Market Pl  TR26 1RZ  (01736) 791911
*"A relatively hidden gem!" – this "unpretentious" open-kitchen bistro is tipped for "a limited menu from local produce that beats other better-known establishments nearby"; closed Oct-Feb.*
/ **Details:** *www.theblackrockstives.co.uk; 9 pm; D only, closed Sun; no Amex; max. table size 8 in summer.*

**Porthgwidden Beach**  **£41**  ❸❷⓿
Porthgwidden Beach  TR26 1SL
(01736) 796791
*"Arrive early, as it gets mobbed!" – this "relaxed" café – "in a fantastic location, overlooking a small beach", and with "divine sunset views" – offers "simple, hearty dishes", especially fish; top breakfasts too.*
/ **Details:** *www.porthgwiddencafe.co.uk; 10 pm; no Amex; booking: max 10.*

**Porthmeor Beach** £33 🅣
Porthmeor Beach TR26 IJZ
(01736) 793366
"Dogs, surfers, beach parties, Tate-visitors… all
are welcome", at this "wonderful" beach café,
which is tipped for "breakfast, lunch, dinner, light
snacks and gorgeous pastries too!"
/ **Details:** www.porthmeor-beach.co.uk; 9 pm; D only.
Closed Nov-Mar.; no Amex.

**Porthminster Café** £45 ❶❷❶
Porthminster Beach TR26 2EB
(01736) 795352
"Amazing views of the sea" ("ask for a window
seat") and "beautifully inspired" seafood "with
an Asian twist" win "a score of 10/10 all-round"
for this "lively" and mega-popular all-day
beachside restaurant; the empire is growing –
they now have their own fish 'n' chip shop too.
/ **Details:** www.porthminstercafe.co.uk; 10 pm;
no Amex.

**The Seafood Café** £37 ❷❷❸
45 Fore St TR26 IHE (01736) 794004
"Incredibly tasty" fish – which you select at the
counter, along with its cooking style – is the
mainstay of this "clean and bright" operation,
which "continues to impress, year-after-year".
/ **Details:** www.seafoodcafe.co.uk; 10.30 pm;
no Amex.

**Tate Cafe**

**Tate Gallery** £33 🅣
Porthmeor Beach TR26 ITG
(01736) 796226
Tipped for its "wonderful panoramic views
across St Ives and the sea beyond", the café
perched on top of the gallery is much better
than the usual cultural-centre dross – it makes
"a very good venue for light lunches, drinks and
snacks". / **Details:** www.tate.org.uk; L only; no Amex.

ST LEONARDS-ON-SEA, EAST SUSSEX 3–4C

**St Clement's** £44 ❸④④
3 Mercatoria TN38 0EB (01424) 200355
"Fish bought directly from the boats and cooked
without fuss" – that's the formula that makes
Nick Hales's "intimate" bistro popular with
practically all who report on it.
/ **Details:** www.stclementsrestaurant.co.uk; 10 pm;
closed Mon & Sun D; no Amex.

ST MAWES, CORNWALL 1–4B

**Hotel Tresanton** £63 ❷❷❶
27 Lower Castle Rd TR2 5DR
(01326) 270055
"The most romantic setting, overlooking St

Mawes bay" sets the scene at Olga Polizzi's
"stunning" hotel (where the best tables are al
fresco, on the cascading terraces); the food is
"pricey" but "excellent", helping make a meal
here a "memorable" experience.
/ **Details:** www.tresanton.com; 9.30 pm; booking:
max 10; children: 6+ at dinner.
**Accommodation:** 31 rooms, from £245.

ST MONANS, FIFE 9–4D

**Craig Millar**

**@ 16 West End** £60 🅣
16 West End KY10 2BX (01333) 730327
"A warm welcome, and superb fish and seafood"
("perfectly cooked", and with "intense flavours")
– that's the gist of all the (limited) commentary
on Craig Millar's elegant seaside dining room,
which enjoys fine harbour-views.
/ **Details:** www.16westend.com; 9.30 pm; closed
Mon & Tue; children: 5+.

STAMFORD, LINCOLNSHIRE 6–4A

**The George Hotel** £68 ❸❷❷
71 St Martins PE9 2LB (01780) 750750
"A lovely place in an attractive town" – this
famous coaching inn offers "solid" fare in its old-
fashioned dining room, with "theatrical service of
splendid beef from the trolley" a highlight; the
food's "not exciting", though, and prices are high
– locals tend to seek out the "sociable" (read
cheaper) Garden Room.
/ **Details:** www.georgehotelofstamford.com; 10 pm;
jacket and/or tie; children: 8+ at D.
**Accommodation:** 47 rooms, from £150.

STANLEY, PERTHSHIRE 9–3C

**The Apron Stage** £39 ❷❷❸
5 King St PH1 4ND (01738) 828888
"Small it may be" ("just 19 covers!"), but this
"tiny" gaff "packs an impressive culinary
punch!"; run by a team from Let's Eat (Perth), its
"innovative" cooking ("with a strong Scottish
flavour") is "to a standard far above what you
would expect in a small village"; note very limited
opening hours.
/ **Details:** www.apronstagerestaurant.co.uk; 9.30 pm;
closed Mon, Tue, Wed L, Thu L, Sat L & Sun..

STANTON, SUFFOLK 3–1C

**Leaping Hare Vineyard** £44 ❷❸❷
Wyken Vineyards IP31 2DW
(01359) 250287
"A haven of good, well-prepared food in the
middle of Suffolk"; as you might hope, this
"wonderfully-converted" barn offers some
"brilliant" wines from the estate too, all available

by the glass. / **Details:** www.wykenvineyards.co.uk; 9m NE of Bury St Edmunds; follow tourist signs off A143; 5.30 pm, Fri & Sat 9 pm; L only, ex Fri & Sat open L & D.

---

STATHERN, LEICESTERSHIRE          5–3D

**Red Lion Inn**          **£37**   ❷④❸
2 Red Lion St  LE14 4HS   (01949) 860868
The "less 'gastro' but arguably more enjoyable sibling of the famous Olive Branch at Clipsham" – a fine pub near Belvoir Castle with "an attractive and characterful dining area"; it offers "a wide and interesting selection of beers and wines" too. / **Details:** www.theredlioninn.co.uk; 9.30 pm; closed Sun D; no Amex.

---

STOCKBRIDGE, HAMPSHIRE          2–3D

**Clos du Marquis**          **£52**   ❷❷❷
London Rd  SO20 6DE   (01264) 810738
"Even the dog is called 'Cassoulet'!" – if you're looking for "very French food in a very Gallic atmosphere", you're unlikely to do much better than Germain Marquis's "fun", "interesting" and "reliable" country inn.
/ **Details:** www.closdumarquis.co.uk; 2m E on A30 from Stockbridge; 10 pm; closed Mon & Sun D.

**Greyhound**          **£56**   ❸❸❸
31 High St  SO20 6EY   (01264) 810833
"Always an interesting menu, and everything beautifully prepared" – pretty much unanimously the tenor of reports on this rural gastropub; for a place which was once quite a 'destination', though, it attracts relatively few reports.
/ **Details:** www.thegreyhound.info; 9 pm, Fri & Sat 9.30 pm; closed Sun D; no Amex; booking: max 12.
**Accommodation:** 7 rooms, from £95.

---

STOCKCROSS, BERKSHIRE          2–2D

**The Vineyard
at Stockcross**          **£101**   ❸❷❸
RG20 8JU   (01635) 528770
The "overwhelming" list of wines (1500 bins majoring in US vintages) is the headline feature at Sir Peter Michael's grand California-style operation; Daniel Galmiche's cuisine is, say fans, "superb" too, but there are also a few critics, for whom "it's not quite as cutting-edge as you might expect, given the prices".
/ **Details:** www.the-vineyard.co.uk; from M4, J13 take A34 towards Hungerford; 9.30 pm; no jeans or trainers; SRA-62%. **Accommodation:** 49 rooms, from £125.

---

STOCKPORT, LANCASHIRE          5–2B

**Damson**          **£38**   ❷❷❸
113 Heaton Moor Rd  SK4 4HY
(0161) 4324666

Fans of this Heaton Moor "hidden gem" extol its "assured" cooking and "carefully chosen" wines as "hands-down, the best around Manchester"; non-locals are a tad more reserved, but all reports attest to its consistent "high standards". / **Details:** www.damsonrestaurant.co.uk; 9.30 pm, Fri & Sat 10 pm; closed Mon L & Sun D.

---

STOKE HOLY CROSS, NORFOLK          6–4C

**The Wildebeest Arms**          **£45**   ❷❸❸
82-86 Norwich Rd  NR14 8QJ
(01508) 492497
A "little village pub", of rather more note than usual, thanks to its "ambitious" menu which is "cooked with some flair", and "value-for-money" too; "avoid tables by the bar, as it can get rather crowded". / **Details:** www.animalinns.co.uk; from A140, turn left at Dunston Hall, left at T-junction; 9 pm.

---

STOKE ROW, OXFORDSHIRE          2–2D

**The Crooked Billet**          **£53**   ❷❷❷
Newlands Ln  RG9 5PU   (01491) 681048
"Worth a journey down a stony track", this "posh, picturesque pub", in the Chilterns, makes a "charming find" and has become very well known, thanks to its "professional" staff and its "lovely" cooking ("more gastro than pub").
/ **Details:** www.thecrookedbillet.co.uk; off the A4130; 10 pm, Sat 10.30 pm.

---

STOKE-BY-NAYLAND, SUFFOLK          3–2C

**The Crown**          **£42**   Ⓣ
Park St  CO6 4SE   (01206) 262346
"A great location, delicious food and a varied wine list" – one reporter neatly summarises the attractions of this "satisfying" and "enjoyable" country inn (with rooms, and lovely courtyard); wine shop attached. / **Details:** www.crowninn.net; on B1068; 9.30 pm, Fri & Sat 10 pm, Sun 9 pm.
**Accommodation:** 11 rooms, from £80.

---

STOKESLEY, NORTH YORKSHIRE          8–3C

**Howards**          **£41**   Ⓣ
30 College Sq  TS9 5DN   (01642) 713391
A "value-for-money" tip, this smart village-diner offers some "good" and "unusual" dishes; dining room too busy for you? – you can take-away.
/ **Details:** www.howards-eatery.co.uk; Mon-Weds 8 pm, Thu-Sun 9 pm; closed Sun D.

---

STONE IN OXNEY, KENT                    3–4C

**Crown**                        **£39**  🅣
TN30 7JN   (01233) 758302
*"All in all, a great village pub", tipped not least
for its "consistently delicious" cuisine (and in
"good portions" too); "also a nice place to stay".*

---

STONEHAVEN, ABERDEENSHIRE            9–3D

**Marine Hotel**                 **£43**  ❷❸❶
Shorehead  AB39 2JY   (01569) 762155
*"Food and beer just like you'd hope for in a
Scottish harbourside bar"; "superb seafood" is, of
course, the menu highlight, and there are "great
views" too.*
/ **Details:** www.marinehotelstonehaven.co.uk; 9 pm;
no Amex. **Accommodation:** 6 rooms, from £110.

---

STOW ON THE WOLD, GLOUCESTERSHIRE
2–1C

**The Old Butchers**             **£44**  ❷❷❸
Park St  GL54 1AQ   (01451) 831700
*"Imaginative and eclectic food, well executed and
at a reasonable price" – that's the deal that
makes this town-centre brasserie quite a
"Cotswold find" for almost all of the many
reporters who comment on it.*
/ **Details:** www.theoldbutchers.com; on the main road
heading out of Stow on the Wold towards Oddington;
9.30 pm, Sat 10 pm; Max 12.

---

STRACHUR, ARGYLL AND BUTE            9–4B

**Inver Cottage**                **£37**  🅣
Stracthlachlan  PA27 8BU   (01369) 860537
*"A perfect day out" – this croft on the shore of
Lachlan Bay is tipped for its "very competent
cooking, attractively presented", and its
"charming" service.*
/ **Details:** www.invercottage.com; 8.30 pm; closed
Mon & Tue; no Amex.

---

STRATFORD UPON AVON, WARWICKSHIRE
2–1C

**Lambs**                        **£45**  ❹❷❸
12 Sheep St  CV37 6EF   (01789) 292554
*With its "beautiful beamed dining room", this
Tudor building seems "just right for pre-theatre
dining"; it makes a good choice at any time,
though, if you're just looking for a decent steak
'n' chips, or similar "gastropub-style" fare.*
/ **Details:** www.lambsrestaurant.co.uk; 9.30 pm;
closed Mon L & Tue L; no Amex.

**The Oppo**                     **£37**  ❹❷❷
13 Sheep St  CV37 6EF   (01789) 269980
*"Always reliable and good-value"; this "lovely"*

*spot does a "very good pre-theatre meal" (which
is what inspires most survey commentary), but
fans insist that the à la carte menu is very good
too.* / **Details:** www.theoppo.co.uk; 10 pm, Sun
9.30 pm; closed Sun L; no Amex; booking: max 12.

**Rooftop, Royal
Shakespeare Theatre**            **£45**  ⑤⑤❸
Waterside  CV37 6BB   (01789) 403449
*A "great location", but it "fails to star!" – why oh
why do famous arts institutions keep making
such a hash of their restaurants?;
"unwelcoming", "rushed", "tiny portions",
"overpriced", "inept"… – the litany of
complaints goes on and on.*
/ **Details:** www.rsc.org.uk/eat; 9.45 pm; no Amex.

**The Vintner**                  **£39**  🅣
4-5 Sheep St  CV37 6EF   (01789) 297259
*A "quirky" and "attractive" spot tipped, as ever,
for its "excellent-value pre-theatre menu";
tourists and theatregoers NB – 'lunch' is served
all afternoon.* / **Details:** www.the-vintner.co.uk;
9.30 pm, Fri & Sat 10 pm, Sun 8.30 pm; no Amex.

---

STUCKTON, HAMPSHIRE                  2–3C

**The Three Lions**              **£55**  ❷❸④
Stuckton Rd  SP6 2HF   (01425) 652489
*"London prices, but producing dishes at a level to
which few places in the New Forest aspire" – the
Womersleys' "warm" and "welcoming"
restaurant can come as something of a
"surprise" to first-time visitors.*
/ **Details:** www.thethreelionsrestaurant.co.uk; off the
A338; 9 pm, Fri & Sat 9.30 pm; closed Mon & Sun D;
no Amex. **Accommodation:** 7 rooms, from £105.

---

STUDLAND, DORSET                     2–4C

**Shell Bay**                    **£41**  ❸④❶
Ferry Rd  BH19 3BA   (01929) 450363
*"Great for fish, and the views are brilliant" – this
"shabby-chic" watersider has a "wonderful
location", and won all-round praise this year.*
/ **Details:** www.shellbay.net; near the Sandbanks to
Swanage ferry; 9 pm.

---

SUNBURY ON THAMES, SURREY            3–3A

**Indian Zest**                  **£32**  ❷❷❸
21 Thames St  TW16 5QF   (01932) 765 000
*Manoj Vasaikar's suburban subcontinental
occupies a large, rambling villa, decorated in
colonial style; it wins consistent praise for its
"excellent variations on old favourites".*
/ **Details:** www.indianzest.co.uk; 12.00 pm.

7m W of Ely, signposted off B1381 in Sutton; 9 pm, Sat 9.30 pm, Sun 8.30 pm. **Accommodation:** 4 rooms, from £79.5.

---

| SUNNINGDALE, BERKSHIRE | 3–3A |

**Bluebells**  **£64**  ❷❷❷
Shrubs Hill  SL5 0LE   (01344) 622 722
*It's not just the "incredible bargain" of a weekday set lunch which inspires a good number of reports on this often-"packed" roadside fixture – a "cheerful and competent" sort of place, it's a real all-rounder.*
/ **Details:** www.bluebells-restaurant.com; 9.45 pm; closed Mon & Sun D.

---

| SUNNINGHILL, BERKSHIRE | 3–3A |

**Jade Fountain**  **£39**  ❶
38 High St  SL5 9NE   (01344) 627070
*"In business for over two decades, and still setting the highest standards" – all reporters are impressed by the cooking at this long-running Chinese. /* **Details:** *2m from Ascot, on A329; 10.30 pm.*

---

| SURBITON, SURREY | 3–3A |

**The French Table**  **£53**  ❶❷④
85 Maple Rd  KT6 4AW   (020) 8399 2365
*"Too good for Surbiton!" – this "diamond of the suburbs" has made a huge name for its "strong" and "interesting" Gallic cooking ("occasionally flawed, occasionally unbalanced, but basically very good"); the styling of the "noisy" interior, though, is just a bit too "neighbourhood-restaurant" for some tastes.*
/ **Details:** www.thefrenchtable.co.uk; 10.30 pm; closed Mon & Sun D.

**Joy**  **£31**  ❶
37 Brighton Rd  KT6 5LR   (020) 8390 3988
*Living up to its name, on most reports, an establishment tipped for its "nice modern take on Indian cuisine"; of late, however, feedback has been a touch uneven.*
/ **Details:** www.joy-restaurant.co.uk; 11.30 pm.

**Red Rose**  **£28**  ❶
38 Brighton Rd  KT6 5PQ   (020) 8399 9647
*A suburban curry house, again tipped for its "consistently good" food and its "happy" service.*
/ **Details:** www.redroseofsurbiton.com; 11.30 pm.

---

| SUTTON GAULT, CAMBRIDGESHIRE | 3–1B |

**The Anchor**  **£44**  ❸❷❸
Bury Ln  CB6 2BD   (01353) 778537
*"In a rather isolated location in the Fens", an inn that's of particular note for its "friendly" and "efficient" service; some, but not quite all, reporters, say the "varied menu" is "worth a detour" too. /* **Details:** *www.anchorsuttongault.co.uk;*

---

| SWANSEA, SWANSEA | 1–1C |

**Didier And Stephanie**  **£38**  ❷❷❷
56 Saint Helen's Rd  SA1 4BE
(01792) 655603
*Not far from Brangwyn Hall, this "great little French restaurant" is a fairly traditional and "romantic" sort of place, which fans proclaim a real "treasure"; its ever-changing menu wins a consistent thumbs-up from reporters.*
/ **Details:** 9.15 pm; closed Mon & Sun; no Amex; booking essential.

**Morgans**

**Morgans Hotel**  **£34**  ❶
Somerset Pl  SA1 1RR   (01792) 484848
*A boutique-hotel dining room, tipped for its "wholesome" cuisine; it has an "atmospheric" setting too, in the old harbour trust building.*
/ **Details:** www.morganshotel.co.uk; 9.45 pm; children: 12+. **Accommodation:** 42 rooms, from £100.

---

| SWINBROOK, OXFORDSHIRE | 2–2C |

**Swan**  **£42**  ❸❸❷
OX18 4DY   (01993) 823339
*"Allegedly David Cameron's gastropub of choice", this "atmospheric" inn is of most interest because it's owned by Debo Mitford, youngest of the celebrated sisters, and decorated with family memorabilia; fans say the food is "better than your standard gastropub" too.*
/ **Details:** www.theswanswinbrook.co.uk; 9 pm, Fri-Sat 9.30 pm.

---

| TAPLOW, BERKSHIRE | 3–3A |

**The Terrace**
**Cliveden House**  **£91**
Cliveden Rd  SL6 0JF   (01628) 668561
*This very grand and famous (Astor/Profumo) country house hotel was bought out of the Von Essen administration just as our survey for this guide was getting under way; it's too early for a rating, but the new owners (who also own Chewton Glen) have promised great things – fingers crossed! /* **Details:** *www.clivedenhouse.co.uk; 9.30 pm; no trainers.* **Accommodation:** 38 + cottage rooms, from £240.

---

| TAUNTON, SOMERSET | 2–3A |

**Augustus**  **£38**  ❷❶❸
3 The Courtyard, St James St  TA1 1JR
(01823) 324 354
*"Front of house, Cedric, has made a real mark on Taunton's dining scene", at this "really*

*friendly" bistro run by refugees from the (now defunct) Castle Hotel dining room; the cooking is of "high quality" too, although the interior is not a highlight – when weather permits, sit in the "charming" courtyard.*
/ *Details:* www.augustustaunton.co.uk; 9.30 pm; closed Mon & Sun; no Amex.

**The Willow Tree**          **£46**   ❷❸❸
3 Tower Ln  TA1 4AR   (01823) 352835
*"A beacon in Taunton's gastronomic desert"; Darren Sherlock's "wholesome" restaurant – with its "nice view of a pond" – continues to be a general crowd-pleaser.*
/ *Details:* www.thewillowtreerestaurant.com; 9.15 pm; D only, closed Sun & Mon; no Amex; Essential, max. 6.

---

TEDDINGTON, SURREY          3–3A

**Imperial China**          **£39**   ⓣ
196-198 Stanley Rd  TW11 8UE   (020) 8977 8679
*A "surprisingly good" Chinese restaurant, often recommended by reporters as "a great place for lunchtime dim sum"; "and in Surrey, too – who'd have thought it?"*
/ *Details:* www.imperialchinalondon.co.uk; 11 sun 10 pm.

---

TENDRING, ESSEX          3–2D

**The Fat Goose**          **£32**   ⓣ
Heath Rd  CO16 0BX   (01255) 870060
*Still less feedback than we would like on this "friendly" and "efficient" gastropub; all of it confirms, however, that – "in spite of the large number of customers" – quality remains "impressive".* / *Details:* www.fat-goose.co.uk.

---

TENTERDEN, KENT          3–4C

**The Raja Of Kent**          **£35**   ❸❷④
Bibbenden Rd  TN30 6SX   (01233) 851191
*"All the usual Bangaldeshi suspects, plus lots of game and seafood choices too" – this "attractive" establishment offers "a much more interesting range of subcontinental dishes than average".* / *Details:* www.therajaofkent.com; midnight.

---

TETBURY, GLOUCESTERSHIRE          2–2B

**Calcot Manor**          **£66**   ❸④❸
GL8 8YJ   (01666) 890391
*All agree the main dining room of this famously child-friendly country house hotel is a "lovely" venue; service, though, can be "patchy", and food that's "always good" to fans is, to more sceptical reporters, "unmemorable, given the prices".*
/ *Details:* www.calcotmanor.co.uk; junction of A46 &

*A4135; 9.30 pm, Sun 9 pm.* **Accommodation:** *35 rooms, from £260.*

**Gumstool Inn**

**Calcot Manor**          **£44**   ⓣ
GL8 8YJ   (01666) 890391
*The less formal, pub-style restaurant of this child-friendly country house hotel, tipped for its "well-presented" food, and its "reliable" standards overall; "beware the local Hoorays though!"*
/ *Details:* www.calcotmanor.co.uk; crossroads of A46 & A41345; 9.30 pm, Sun 9 pm; no jeans or trainers; children: 12+ at dinner in Conservatory.
**Accommodation:** *35 rooms, from £240.*

---

THORNBURY, GLOUCESTERSHIRE          2–2B

**Ronnie's**          **£45**   ❷❸❸
11 St Mary St  BS35 2AR   (01454) 411137
*"A delightful venue, in a delightful backwater" – Ronnie Faulkner's "friendly" and "professional" operation in a 17th-century barn offers "well-presented" dishes that "never disappoint"; "good set-price meals" too.*
/ *Details:* www.ronnies-restaurant.co.uk; 930 tue thur 1030 thur -sat; closed Mon & Sun D; no Amex.

---

THORNHAM, NORFOLK          6–3B

**The Orange Tree**          **£46**   ❷❷❷
High St  PE36 6LY   (01485) 512 213
*A top gastropub "on a coast full of them!" – its "intricate" menu offers surprisingly "complex" dishes, which not only have "great presentation", but which "generally hit the mark" too.*
/ *Details:* www.theorangetreethornham.co.uk; 9.30 pm; no Amex. **Accommodation:** *6 rooms, from £89.*

---

THORPE LANGTON, LEICESTERSHIRE  5–4D

**Bakers Arms**          **£41**   ⓣ
Main St  LE16 7TS   (01858) 545201
*A cosy, slightly old-fashioned rural inn in a cute village location, tipped for its dependable comfort food (and good range of puds).*
/ *Details:* www.thebakersarms.co.uk; near Market Harborough off A6; 9.30 pm; D only, ex Sat open L & D & Sun open L only, closed Mon; no Amex; children: 12+.

---

TIMBLE, NORTH YORKSHIRE          5–1C

**The Timble Inn**          **£41**   ⓣ
LS21 2NN   (01943) 880530
*"An excellent country pub", in the Dales, tipped for "really good food"; only problem? – "just wish the opening hours were a bit more extensive".*
/ *Details:* www.thetimbleinn.com; 9.30 pm; closed Mon & Tue; no shorts.

**TITLEY, HEREFORDSHIRE**  2–1A

**Stagg Inn**  £49  ❷❸❷
HR5 3RL  (01544) 230221
"Consistency personified" – this "country pub-turned-restaurant" is hard to fault, thanks to Steve Reynold's "expert, beautiful, fresh, locally-sourced dishes" (starring a "divine" bread 'n' butter pudding), and the "mellow" style too.
/ **Details:** www.thestagg.co.uk; on B4355, NE of Kington; 9 pm; closed Mon & Sun D.
**Accommodation:** 6 rooms, from £85.

**TOBERMORY, ISLE OF MULL, ARGYLL AND BUTE**  9–3A

**Café Fish**  £40  ❷❸❷
The Pier  PA75 6NU  (01688) 301253
"Overlooking the harbour, so you can watch the boats go by from the nice terrace" – a "small but lovely family-run fish-restaurant (in former ferry company offices) in this truly picturesque town"; it really impresses most reporters, but the odd let-down is not unknown.
/ **Details:** www.thecafefish.com; 10 pm; Closed Nov-Mar; no Amex; children: 14+ after 8 pm.

**TOPSHAM, DEVON**  1–3D

**Darts Farm Café**  £32  ❸④④
Clyst St George  EX3 0QH  (01392) 878201
Brace yourself for a "Boden set stomping ground", but this large 'farm shop' – "retail therapy, massage, and stroking a pig, all under one roof!" – is popular locally for its "fabulous" breakfasts, "divine fish 'n' chips" and other "cracking" dishes. / **Details:** www.dartsfarm.co.uk; M5 Junction 30, A376 towards Exmouth; L only; no Amex.

**The Galley**  £48  ❶
41 Fore St  EX3 0HU  (01392) 876078
"A lovely menu, beautifully served" – the upshot of all feedback on this quirky fish restaurant, on this seaside town's main street.
/ **Details:** www.galleyrestaurant.co.uk; 9.30 pm; closed Mon & Sun; booking essential; children: 12+.

**La Petite Maison**  £51  ❷❷❸
35 Fore St  EX3 0HR  (01392) 873660
"A real gem"; this "intimate" and "charming" venue is hailed by all reporters for "consistent" cooking with "flair", and "great" service too.
/ **Details:** www.lapetitemaison.co.uk; 9.30 pm; D only, closed Mon & Sun; no Amex; booking essential at L.

**TORCROSS, DEVON**  1–4D

**Start Bay Inn**  £33  ❷❸❷
TQ7 2TQ  (01548) 580553
"Amazingly consistent" fried fish ("the chips are

not quite so good") are part of the formula that ensures a constant crush at this beachside boozer; "you can wait a long time for a table, though". / **Details:** www.startbayinn.co.uk; on beach front (take A379 coastal road to Dartmouth); 10 pm; no Amex; no booking.

**TORQUAY, DEVON**  1–3D

**Elephant**  £71  ❷❸④
3-4 Beacon Ter, Harbourside  TQ1 2BH  (01803) 200044
Simon Hulstone cooks with "imagination, skill and flair" at his town-centre "gem", which offers "pretty views across the bay" from the upstairs bar (with restaurant next door, and brasserie downstairs); there's the odd fear, though, that it's "not quite as good as he does more media".
/ **Details:** www.elephantrestaurant.co.uk; 9.30 pm; closed Mon & Sun; children: 14+ at bar.

**TOTNES, DEVON**  1–3D

**Willow**  £33  ❶
87 High St  TQ9 5PB  (01803) 862605
Top tip in these parts for "absolutely delicious vegetarian food"; look out for 'special' nights – 'live music' and 'Indian' both have their fans.
/ **Details:** 9.30 pm; closed Mon D, Tue D, Thu D & Sun; no credit cards.

**TREEN, CORNWALL**  1–4A

**Gurnards Head**  £41  ❸❷❶
TR26 3DE  (01736) 796928
An "amazing" seaside location, "perched on the windswept cliffs of west Cornwall" ensures a steady fan club for this "remote" but "cosy" coastal pub; most (if not quite all) reports laud its "hearty fare" too, some claiming that it's "upped its game considerably in recent times".
/ **Details:** www.gurnardshead.co.uk; on coastal road between Land's End & St Ives, near Zennor B3306; 9.30 pm; no Amex. **Accommodation:** 7 rooms, from £90.

**TRING, HERTFORDSHIRE**  3–2A

**Olive Limes**  £35  ❷❶❸
60 High St  HP23 5AG  (01442) 828283
If you're looking for a "friendly" and "elegant" Indian restaurant, this fixture overlooking Tring Park is the top tip locally – "fresh local ingredients, and fresh herbs" are used to create "nice clean tastes". / **Details:** www.olivelimes.co.uk; 11 pm, fri & sat 11.30 pm.

---

TROUTBECK, CUMBRIA 7–3D

**Queen's Head** £42 ❸❷❷
Townhead LA23 1PW (01539) 432174
"A great country pub for a cold day!" – with its "hearty" fare and its "fine selection of ales", this "remote" inn is, on most accounts, "worth seeking out"; it must be said, however, that the food does not always quite convince.
/ **Details:** www.queensheadhotel.com; A592 on Kirkstone Pass; 9 pm; no Amex.
**Accommodation:** 15 rooms, from £120.

---

TRURO, CORNWALL 1–4B

**Indaba** £44 ❷❷❸
Tabernacle St TR1 2EJ (01872) 274 700
A recently-expanded restaurant that's "getting better as it gets bigger" – the menu is "not all fish, but that's what they do best".
/ **Details:** www.indabafish.co.uk.

---

TUDDENHAM, SUFFOLK 3–1C

**Tuddenham Mill**
**Tuddenham Mill Hotel** £62 ❹❹❸
High St IP28 6SQ (01638) 713 552
"The location, building and food all have the wow factor", say fans of this "gorgeous" property, who cite Paul Foster as a chef "certainly destined for greatness"; there are almost as many critics, though, who find the whole approach "pretentious", and service far below the standard expected. / **Details:** www.tuddenhammill.co.uk.

---

TUNBRIDGE WELLS, KENT 3–4B

**The Black Pig** £47 ❸❹❸
18 Grove Hill Rd TN1 1RZ
(01892) 523030
Handiness for the station and the leading local department store adds to the appeal of this "popular" gastropub; standards are a bit up-and-down, especially on the service front, but the food generally pleases. / **Details:** 9 pm, Fri & Sat 9.30 pm; no Amex.

**Hotel du Vin et Bistro** £41 ❹❸❸
Crescent Rd TN1 2LY (01892) 526455
As so often, "variable" food is a gripe at this potentially very atmospheric outpost of the hotel/bistro chain – those who remember "how good it used to be" are most likely to find it "overpriced" nowadays.
/ **Details:** www.hotelduvin.com; 10 pm, Fri & Sat 10.30 pm; booking: max 10. **Accommodation:** 34 rooms, from £120.

---

**Thackeray's** £64 ❷❷❸
85 London Rd TN1 1EA (01892) 511921
Occupying an "elegant" Regency villa, Richard Philips's popular fixture wows its many fans, who acclaim it as a "romantic" destination with "perfectly pitched service, and food to match"; those who enjoyed the "tremendous-value" set lunch are the most upbeat.
/ **Details:** www.thackerays-restaurant.co.uk; 10.30 pm; closed Mon & Sun D.

---

TUXFORD, NOTTINGHAMSHIRE 5–2D

**Mussel and Crab** £42 ❶
Sibthorpe Hill NG22 0PJ (01777) 870 491
A surprisingly ambitious fish and seafood restaurant, tipped for offering "fabulous food and décor"… and a wine list that "can't be beaten" too. / **Details:** www.musselandcrab.com.

---

TYN-Y-GROES, CONWY 4–1D

**Groes Inn** £38 ❹❹❸
Nr Conway LL32 8TN (01492) 650545
"Lovely traditional food" has helped make this beautifully-located and "atmospheric" ancient inn quite a destination; this year, though, it did inspire the odd dud report. / **Details:** www.groesinn.co.uk; on B5106 between Conwy & Betws-y-coed, 2m from Conwy; 9 pm; children: 10+ in restaurant.
**Accommodation:** 14 rooms, from £105.

---

ULLSWATER, CUMBRIA 7–3D

**Sharrow Bay** £95
CA10 2LZ (01768) 486301
The UK's original country house hotel, complete with stunning lake view, was sold – for a song – by administrators of the former Von Essen group shortly before this guide went to print (to a group including Dragon's Den star James Caan); in the circumstances, we don't think a rating is appropriate. / **Details:** www.sharrowbay.co.uk; on Pooley Bridge Rd towards Howtown; 8 pm; no jeans or trainers; children: 10+. **Accommodation:** 24 rooms, from £175.

---

UPPER SLAUGHTER, GLOUCESTERSHIRE 2–1C

**Lords of the Manor** £88 ❸❹❷
GL54 2JD (01451) 820243
The dining room at this "really lovely" Cotswolds hide-away is "incredibly romantic", and most reports extol the "memorable" cuisine and "interesting, well-chosen wine list"; there is a minority, though, for whom it's "good, rather than special", and "very expensive" too.
/ **Details:** www.lordsofthemanor.com; 4m W of Stow on the Wold; 9.30 pm; D only, ex Sun open L & D;

---

*no jeans or trainers; children: 7+ at D in restaurant.*
**Accommodation:** *26 rooms, from £199.*

---

UPPINGHAM, RUTLAND      5–4D

**The Lake Isle**     **£47**   🅣
16 High Street East   LE15 9PZ
(01572) 822951
*"A really pleasant restaurant" (with rooms) at
the heart of a lovely small town – "just the place
to take your parents"; it offers a "limited" menu,
realised to a good standard, plus some "serious"
wines. / Details: www.lakeisle.co.uk; past the Market
place, down the High Street; 9 pm, Fri & Sat 9.30 pm;
closed Mon L & Sun D.* **Accommodation:** *12
rooms, from £75.*

---

VENTNOR, ISLE OF WIGHT     2–4D

**The Hambrough**    **£81**   ❶❷④
Hambrough Road   PO38 1SQ
(01983) 856333
*Robert Thompson's "cutting-edge" cuisine is
"unbelievably good", the wine list is "extensive"
and the seaside location of this hotel dining room
is a "knockout" too – shame the modern décor
is on the "sterile" side.
/ Details: www.robert-thompson.com; 9.30 pm; closed
Mon & Sun; no Amex.* **Accommodation:** *7 rooms,
from £170.*

---

VERYAN-IN-ROSELAND, CORNWALL   1–4B

**Dining Room**
**The Nare Hotel**    **£61**   ❷❸❸
Carne Beach   TR2 5PF   (01872) 501111
*Looking for a "traditional", "peaceful", and
"extremely comfortable" (if perhaps rather
"middle-aged") hotel dining room? – you're
unlikely to do much better than the one at this
"superbly-located" seaside spot.
/ Details: www.narehotel.co.uk; 9.30 pm; D only;
jacket & tie; Booking essential; children: 7+.*
**Accommodation:** *37 rooms, from £270.*

---

WADEBRIDGE, CORNWALL     1–3B

**Relish**     **£29**   🅣
Foundry Ct   PL27 7QN   (01208) 814214
*"You can't get a better cup of coffee in
Cornwall", say fans of this "real gem" of a deli-
café, tipped for its "out-of-this-world" brews, plus
"lovely" sarnies and cakes.
/ Details: www.relishwadebridge.co.uk; 4 pm; closed
Mon, Tue-Sat D & Sun; no Amex.*

---

WALBERSWICK, SUFFOLK     3–1D

**The Anchor**    **£41**   ❷④❷
Main St   IP18 6UA   (01502) 722112
*"Possibly the best restaurant in a 30-mile
radius"; this old inn – transformed by the ex-
landlord of Fulham's 'Sloaney Pony' – is praised
not just for its "fine" food, but also an "amazing"
list of wines and beers too; it's "so popular",
though – just occasionally, the service can show
the strain. / Details: www.anchoratwalberswick.com;
9 pm.* **Accommodation:** *10 rooms, from £110.*

---

WALLINGFORD, OXFORDSHIRE     2–1D

**The Partridge**    **£54**   🅣
32 St Mary's St   OX10 0ET   (01491) 825
005
*This elegantly-updated town-centre inn wins
consistent praise for its "charming" style and
"carefully presented" food.
/ Details: www.partridge-inn.com; 10 pm; closed
Sun D.*

---

WARLINGHAM, SURREY     3–3B

**India Dining**    **£38**   🅣
6 The Grn   CR6 9NA   (01883) 625905
*"I don't like Indian restaurants, but I'll make an
exception for this one!"; this "unusual"
subcontinental, emphasising its use of local
ingredients, is tipped for its "consistent" and
"well-prepared" food and its "friendly" service.
/ Details: www.indiadining.co.uk; 11 pm, Fri & Sat
11.30 pm, Sun 10.30 pm.*

**White Bear**    **£36**   🅣
Fairchildes Ln   CR6 9PH   (01959) 573166
*"A 16th-century treasure in the country lanes
round Croydon", tipped for "good hearty pub
food and lots of atmosphere"; it inspires only
very positive reports.
/ Details: www.the-whitebear.com; 9 pm, Fri-Sat
9.30 pm; no Amex.*

---

WARNINGLID, WEST SUSSEX     3–4B

**The Half Moon**    **£41**   ❷❸❸
The Street   RH17 5TR   (01444) 461227
*"Just a great-value pub and dining room";
indeed, this "busy" and "unpretentious" spot has
only one "downside" (or, some may think,
advantage) – "children are welcome only in
certain part of the property".
/ Details: www.thehalfmoonwarninglid.co.uk; 9.30 pm;
closed Sun D; no Amex.*

---

WARWICK, WARWICKSHIRE     5–4C

**The Art Kitchen**    **£43**   ❷❸④
7 Swan St   CV34 4BJ   (01926) 494303
*"Super-reliable if you like your food hot and
spicy", this "relaxed" town-centre Thai maintains
an impressively large following among reporters.
/ Details: www.theartkitchen.com; 10 pm.*

**The Saxon Mill**  £42  **T**
Coventry Rd, Guys Cliffe  CV34 5YN
(01926) 492255
*Tipped by all reporters for its riverside "location, location and location" ("it doesn't get much better than the balcony here"), this "airy" gastropub makes a "reliable" culinary pit stop, even if some would say the food is no more than "reasonable".* / **Details:** *www.saxonmill.co.uk; 9.30 pm, Fri & Sat 10 pm, Sun 9 pm.*

**Tailors**  £51  **❷❷❸**
22 market place  CV34 4SL  (01926) 410590
*"Excellent", "astonishingly good", "astounding"… – local fans don't mince their words when praising the food at this town-centre spot, housed in former shop premises.* / **Details:** *www.tailorsrestaurant.co.uk; 9.30 pm; closed Mon & Sun.*

**The Beach Hut**
**Watergate Bay Hotel**  £40  **❸❸❷**
On The Beach  TR8 4AA  (01637) 860543
*A "lovely, welcoming beach café" that's hard to beat if you're looking for some "superb post-surf grub" (using "fresh and tasty local ingredients"); generally "efficient" service too.* / **Details:** *www.watergatebay.co.uk; 9 pm; no Amex.* **Accommodation:** *69 rooms, from £105.*

**Fifteen Cornwall**
**Watergate Bay Hotel**  £80  **❸❷❶**
TR8 4AA  (01637) 861000
*The best of Jamie Oliver's restaurants – this "funky" beachside venue offers not only "stunning views from pretty much every table", but also very "satisfying" cooking, and "very friendly" service (that's "patient with kids"); "fabulous" for brunch.* / **Details:** *www.fifteencornwall.co.uk; on the Atlantic coast between Padstow and Newquay; 9.15 pm.*

**Loch Bay**  £39  **❶❷❸**
Stein  IV55 8GA  (01470) 592235
*"Sublime seafood, appropriate wine list, first-class service and a delightful setting, what more is there to say?" – this lochside bistro pleases all who comment on it.* / **Details:** *www.lochbay-seafood-restaurant.co.uk; 22m from Portree via A87 and B886; 8m from Dunvegan; 9 pm; closed Mon & Sun.*

**The Bell Inn**  £45  **T**
Binton Rd  CV37 8EB  (01789) 750353
*A 17th-century inn that makes "a lovely winter pub", and is tipped for its "superior" cooking.* / **Details:** *www.thebellwelford.co.uk; 9.30 pm.* **Accommodation:** *6 rooms, from £42.*

**Globe**  £40  **T**
The Buttlands  NR23 1EU  (01328) 710206
*Reports on food and service are a bit up-and-down, but this Adnams-run pub in a seaside town is tipped as a "classy joint in a lovely location", and its "generous" dishes generally hit their mark.* / **Details:** *www.holkham.co.uk/globe; 9 pm.* **Accommodation:** *7 rooms, from £100.*

**Goodfellows**  £53  **❷❷❸**
5 Sadler St  BA5 2RR  (01749) 673866
*"What a nice surprise!" – hidden-away behind the café of the same name, Adam Fellows' "quirky" and "genuinely good" fish restaurant; "if you think it feels cramped, you should admire the chefs for producing such excellent food in such a confined space".* / **Details:** *www.goodfellowswells.co.uk; 9.30 pm; closed Mon, Tue D & Sun.*

**Old Spot**  £44  **❷❸❸**
12 Sadler St  BA5 2SE  (01749) 689099
*It may qualify as "a real pub", but Ian Bates's town-centre venture, with its wonderful views of the cathedral, impresses everyone with its "superbly executed, good-value modern British food with solid French foundations" – the chef used to cook at Bibendum.* / **Details:** *www.theoldspot.co.uk; 9.15 pm; closed Mon, Tue L & Sun D.*

**Auberge du Lac**
**Brocket Hall**  £89  **❸❷❶**
AL8 7XG  (01707) 368888
*A "lovely" lakeside location (with many tables al fresco) makes this rural venue a "beautiful" and "romantic" destination (especially for lunch); most reports extol Phil Thompson's "fabulous" cuisine too, but critics can find it a touch "predictable", and service, though "charming", "can slip".* / **Details:** *www.brocket-hall.co.uk; on B653 towards Harpenden; 9.30 pm; closed Mon & Sun; no jeans or trainers* **Accommodation:** *16 rooms, from £175.*

**The Wellington** £44 ④④❸
1 High St AL6 9LZ (01438) 714036
*"A restaurant that thinks it's a pub, or vice-versa?" – either way, this "relaxed" destination offers an "unusual selection of Australian wines", and some "well-cooked" dishes to go with them.*
/ **Details:** www.wellingtonatwelwyn.co.uk; 10 pm; no Amex. **Accommodation:** 6 rooms, from £100.

---

WEST BRIDGFORD, NOTTINGHAMSHIRE5–3D

**Escabeche** £37 ⓣ
27 Bridgford Rd NG2 6AU (0115) 981 7010
*"A fab tapas bar", tipped for its "very good early-evening and lunch deals"; the staff are "friendly and helpful", too, contributing to "a good atmosphere, even midweek".*
/ **Details:** www.escabeche.co.uk; 10 pm; no Amex.

**Larwood and Voce** £43 ❸❷❸
Fox Rd NG2 6AJ (0115) 981 9960
*Backing on to Trent Bridge, a gastropub (part of a local chain) that offers food that's "a step up from the usual", from an "interesting, locally-sourced and well-priced menu"; "good beer" and "helpful service" too.*
/ **Details:** www.larwoodandvoce.co.uk; 9 pm, Sun 5 pm; closed Sun D.

---

WEST CLANDON, SURREY 3–3A

**The Onslow Arms** £41 ❷❸❸
The St GU4 7TE (01483) 222447
*"Good, down-to-earth cooking" and at "value-for-money" prices too – all part of the formula that's made this grand and "attractive" inn, recently refurbished, a "justifiably popular" destination.*
/ **Details:** www.onslowarmsclandon.com; 10 pm, Fri & Sat 10.30 pm; children: 18+ after 7.30pm.

---

WEST HOATHLY, WEST SUSSEX 3–4B

**The Cat Inn** £43 ❷❸❷
Queen's Sq RH19 4PP (01342) 810369
*"An unexpected find in a tiny village"; this "deservedly successful" gastroboozer, "in Bluebell Line country", offers an "enjoyable" experience all-round, and it's becoming "very popular".*
/ **Details:** www.catinn.co.uk; 9 pm, Fri-Sun 9.30 pm; closed Sun D; no Amex; children: 7+.
**Accommodation:** 4 rooms, from £100.

---

WEST MALLING, KENT 3–3C

**The Swan** £51 ④④❸
35 Swan St ME19 6JU (01732) 521910
*This "good neighbourhood restaurant" is praised by fans for its "well-cooked" and "well-presented" dishes, served in an "elegant" setting*

*(with "lovely" garden); sceptics, however, feel "you pay through the nose" – "like it was offering fine dining in a smart London postcode".*
/ **Details:** www.theswanwestmalling.co.uk; 11 pm, Sun 8 pm.

---

WEST MEON, HAMPSHIRE 2–3D

**The Thomas Lord** £42 ❷❸❸
High St GU32 1LN (01730) 829244
*"A bit shabby-chic, but the food is very good indeed" – this "charming" gastroboozer, in the South Downs National Park, continues to please all who comment on it.*
/ **Details:** www.thethomaslord.co.uk; 9 pm, Sat 9.30 pm; no Amex.

---

WEST MERSEA, ESSEX 3–2C

**The Company Shed** £26 ❶④❸
129 Coast Rd CO5 8PA (01206) 382700
*"BYO bread and wine, and bag a bargain!" – this "basic" but legendary seaside seafood shack is a "consistent joy" for all of the many reporters who comment on it, and "well worth a special trip"; arrive early to beat the queues.*
/ **Details:** www.the-company-shed.co.uk; 4 pm; L only, closed Mon; no credit cards; no booking.

**West Mersea Oyster Bar** £37 ❸❸❸
Coast Rd CO5 8LT (01206) 381600
*Offering such luxuries as booking, and being able to order a drink with your meal, this "bright", "IKEA-style" operation (think "glorified chippy") "is trying to be a sort of upmarket version of the Company Shed" – "it doesn't quite succeed, but it's nice not to have to worry about taking your own bread!"*
/ **Details:** www.westmerseaoysterbar.co.uk; 8.30 pm; Sun-Thu closed D; no Amex; no shorts.

---

WEST WITTON, NORTH YORKSHIRE 8–4B

**The Wensleydale Heifer** £55 ❷❷❸
Main St DL8 4LS (01969) 622322
*"Seafood heaven!" – this country pub may be locked-away "in the middle of the landlocked Yorkshire Dales", but it's acclaimed for its "wonderful" fish; seating is "tightly-packed", though, and the cooking outshines the other aspects of the operation.*
/ **Details:** www.wensleydaleheifer.co.uk; 9.30 pm; booking required. **Accommodation:** 13 rooms, from £130.

---

WESTCLIFF ON SEA, ESSEX 3–3C

**Toulouse** £49 ❷❷❸
Western Esplanade SS0 8FE (01702) 333731
*"Right on the seafront", this pair of former public*

conveniences (geddit?) puts an emphasis on
seafood, and is nowadays "one of the best
restaurants in the area"; there's an "eclectic
selection of wines" too; formula price is from the
'bistro' menu — you can spend more if you want!
/ **Details:** www.toulouserestaurant.co.uk; 11 pm, Sat
midnight, Sun 7 pm; closed Mon L.

---

WHALLEY, LANCASHIRE          5–1B

**Food by Breda Murphy**      £36    ❶❷❷
41 Station Rd  BB7 9RH  (01254) 823446
"Shame it's (usually) only open for lunch!" – this
Ballymaloe-trained chef's "gem" of a café/diner,
near the station, has a big name for its "always-
great simple food" (including "fab open
sandwiches" and puddings that "make you weep
for joy"); "cream teas to die for" too.
/ **Details:** www.foodbybredamurphy.com; 5.30 pm;
closed Mon & Sun, Tue-Sat D; no Amex.

**The Three Fishes**      £39    ❸❹❸
Mitton Rd  BB7 9PQ  (01254) 826888
"The original Ribble Valley Inn, and still the
best!" – this birthplace of the Northcote Manor-
inspired chain is, for its army of fans, "everything
a great pub/restaurant should be", thanks not
least to its "well-executed" cuisine; sometimes,
though, it can seem a bit pricey for what it is.
/ **Details:** www.thethreefishes.com; 8.30 pm, Fri & Sat
9 pm, Sun 8 pm.

---

WHEPSTEAD, SUFFOLK          3–1C

**The White Horse**      £43    ❷❸❸
Rede Rd  IP29 4SS  (01284) 735 760
"Superior pub food" ("local sausages are
particularly good") help make this pub in a "very
quiet" village a "very enjoyable" destination.
/ **Details:** www.whitehorsewhepstead.co.uk; 9, Sat &
Sun 9.30 pm; closed Sun D; no Amex.

---

WHITBY, NORTH YORKSHIRE          8–3D

**Greens**      £46    ❶
13 Bridge St  YO22 4BG  (01947) 600284
A "little haven" – with a downstairs bistro and
more formal dining room above – that's highly
rated by most of the reporters who comment on
it; "the fishing boat which caught that day's fish
is named on the menu".
/ **Details:** www.greensofwhitby.com; 9.30 pm, Fri &
Sat 10 pm.

**Magpie Café**      £38    ❶❷④
14 Pier Rd  YO21 3PU  (01947) 602058
"A true legend" – this "still unbeatable" (and "so
reasonable") harbour-side institution remains
widely acclaimed as "the best fish 'n' chip shop
in the UK, bar none"; it's "crowded" and "you

always have to queue", but it's "worth it".
/ **Details:** www.magpiecafe.co.uk; 9 pm; no Amex;
no booking at L.

**Trenchers**      £36    ❷❸❸
New Quay Rd  YO21 1DH  (01947) 603212
"Fabulous posh fish 'n' chips"; "forget the
competition", says the small but enthusiastic fan
club of this "stylish" spot, who feel "this is the
best"; "don't forget to check out the loos!"
/ **Details:** www.trenchersrestaurant.co.uk; 8.30 pm;
need 7+ to book.

---

WHITEBROOK, MONMOUTHSHIRE          2–2B

**The Crown at
Whitebrook**      £79    ❷❶❸
NP25 4TX  (01600) 860254
Whatever the difficulty of finding this "off-the-
beaten-track" restaurant-with-rooms, it's pretty
much invariably rewarded by "impressive"
cooking, "faultless" service and an "elegant"
ambience; some dishes can seem "fussy" though
– "maybe they're striving just a bit too hard for
that second star?"
/ **Details:** www.crownatwhitebrook.co.uk, 2m W of
A466, 5m S of Monmouth; 9 pm; children: 12+ for D.
**Accommodation:** 8 rooms, from £145.

---

WHITSTABLE, KENT          3–3C

**Birdies**      £38    ❶
41 Harbour St  CT5 1AH  (01227) 265337
"A local French-style restaurant" – "very
traditional, and offering a good range of dishes in
a lovely bistro-style atmosphere", it's tipped as a
"good safe bet"; a "very good-value set lunch
menu" is a highlight. / **Details:** 9.15 pm; closed
Mon L & Tue; no Amex.

**Crab & Winkle**      £43    ❷❷④
South Quay, Whitstable Harbour  CT5 1AB
(01227) 779377
"Great fish, even if the setting is a bit basic and
café-like"; "scenically-located" above the
harbourside fish market, this is an establishment
which "never disappoints".
/ **Details:** www.crabandwinklerestaurant.co.uk;
9.30 pm; Seasonal opening; closed Mon in winter, closed
Sun D ; no Amex.

**JoJo**      £30    ❷❷❷
2 Herne Bay Rd  CT5 2LQ  (01227) 274591
"A wonderful, relaxed dining experience"; this
'Meze, Meat & Fish Restaurant' moved a couple
of years ago to "more spacious" (but "noisy")
premises, and pleases all reporters with its
"cheap" locally-sourced tapas-style dishes,
"friendly" service and "good sea views"; licensed,
but you can BYO.

/ **Details:** www.jojosrestaurant.co.uk; 8.30 pm; closed Mon, Tue, Wed L & Sun D; no credit cards.

**Pearson's Arms**  £ 44  ❸❸❸
The Horsebridge, Sea Wall  CT5 1BT
(01227) 272005
*Branded with the name of a leading local chef (Richard Phillips), a "semi-faux-rustic" inn, just off the seafront, that's "very popular with the Down-From-Londons"; many (but not quite all) reporters rate it a "real find" – for the view, go upstairs.*
/ **Details:** www.pearsonsarmsbyrichardphillips.co.uk; 9 pm, Fri & Sat 9.30 pm, Sun 8.30 pm; closed Mon & Tue D; no Amex.

**Samphire**  £ 46  ❷❷❸
4 High St  CT5 1BQ  (01227) 770075
*"A local gem"; with its "interesting menu using locally-sourced products" and its "friendly" service, this all-day venture thrills (almost) all reporters who comment on it; it is usually "very busy". / **Details:** www.samphirerestaurant.co.uk; 10 pm; no Amex.*

**The Sportsman**  £ 49  ❶❷❷
Faversham Rd, Seasalter  CT5 4BP
(01227) 273370
*Amidst the salt marshes, Stephen Harris's "entirely pub-like" operation ("slightly scruffy, and you order at the bar") has won fame out of all proportion to its "low-key" style; for once, though, this is a place that "deserves the hype" – its "phenomenal" mix of "stunning" local seafood and "informal" style is pure "bliss".*
/ **Details:** www.thesportsmanseasalter.co.uk; 8.45 pm; closed Mon & Sun D; no Amex; children: 18+ in main bar.

**Wheelers Oyster Bar**  £ 44  ❶❸❷
8 High St  CT5 1BQ  (01227) 273311
*"Like eating sublimely-executed fish dishes in granny's front room!" – this "bizarre" and "quaint" parlour (est. 1856) may be "cosy as a teapot", but its "very ambitious"seafood is "brilliant" – some of the best in the UK; "book well ahead" for one of the (few) tables (and if you wish, you can BYO).*
/ **Details:** www.seewhitstable.com/Wheelers-Whitstable-Restaurant.html; 7.30 pm, Sun 7 pm; closed Wed; no credit cards.

**Whitstable Oyster
Fishery Co.**  £ 52  ❷❸❷
Royal Native Oyster Stores, Horsebridge
CT5 1BU  (01227) 276856
*"Really delicious oysters and every other fishy delight" make this characterful seafront institution very popular,"especially at weekends" – improved ratings tend to support the reporter*

who finds "a serious return to form after several years of under-performance".
/ **Details:** www.whitstableoystercompany.com; 8.45 pm, Fri 9.15 pm, Sat 9.45 pm, Sun 8.15 pm.

**The Fox**  £ 45  ❸❸④
SG6 2AE  (01462) 480233
*"The interior may be a little functional, but the food makes up for it", says a fan of this "busy" gastropub, whose menu includes an impressive range of fish and game; standards of late have been a bit up-and-down, however – perhaps the strain of opening a sister establishment ('Hermitage Rd', Hitchin).*
/ **Details:** www.foxatwillian.co.uk; 1 mile from junction 9 off A1M; 9 pm; closed Sun D; no Amex.

**5 North Street**  £ 65  ❶❷④
5 North St  GL54 5LH  (01242) 604566
*"Innovative and delicious" cooking from chef Marcus, and "friendly" service from wife Kate, win plaudits for the Ashenfords' restaurant in former tea-rooms – for the most part a "delightful experience", although even fans can find the space "cramped" and "slightly lacking in ambience". / **Details:** 9 pm; closed Mon, Tue L & Sun D.*

**Wesley House**  £ 47  ❷❷❸
High St  GL54 5LJ  (01242) 602366
*In a Tudor house, "a lovely 'character' restaurant", offering "good value for the quality of the cuisine" – it's "always a relaxing treat" (though perhaps one better enjoyed in the main room than in the conservatory).*
/ **Details:** www.wesleyhouse.co.uk; next to Sudeley Castle; 9 pm; closed Sun D. **Accommodation:** 5 rooms, from £90.

**Bangkok Brasserie**  £ 33  ❷❷❸
33 Jewry St  SO23 8RY  (01962) 869 966
*"Popular, for good reason"; "thoroughly enjoyable" Thai food (including some "unusual" dishes) and "bright" service inspire many upbeat reports on this "very busy" destination.*
/ **Details:** www.bangkokbrasserie.co.uk; 10.30 pm.

**The Bengal Sage**  £ 36  ❶
72-74 St George's St  SO23 8AH
(01962) 862 173
*"Innovative dishes put this a cut above the rest"; this year-old Indian – offering "light" dishes of a "high" standard – is tipped as a very "useful addition" to the city-centre's subcontinental*

*scene.* / **Details:** *www.thebengalsage.co.uk; 10.30 pm; no Amex.*

**The Black Rat** **£56** ❷❷❸
88 Chesil St SO23 0HX (01962) 844465
*"Don't be fooled by the unprepossessing exterior!" – this "quirky" former boozer is a "fabulously classy" venture and easily "the best restaurant in Winchester"; let's hope it can maintain standards now that chef Chris Bailey has moved on.* / **Details:** *www.theblackrat.co.uk; 9.30 pm; closed weekday L; children: Weekend L only.*

**The Chesil Rectory** **£51** ❸❸❸
1 Chesil St SO23 0HU (01962) 851555
*A "favourite" for some reporters – this attractively-housed city-centre "oasis" is almost invariably hailed as a "pretty good all-rounder"; "the kitchen knows what it's doing", and "local produce is always at the forefront".* / **Details:** *www.chesilrectory.co.uk; 9.30 pm, Sat 10 pm, Sun 9 pm; children: 12+ at D .*

**The Chestnut Horse** **£47** ❸❸❶
Easton Village SO21 1EG (01962) 779257
*"A warren of rooms creates a lovely atmosphere", at this "food-led pub" in an "attractive village", where the menu of "British pub classics" is "decent" and "dependable"; "the bar offers better value than the restaurant".* / **Details:** *www.thechestnuthorse.com; Junction M3 Newbury exit right hand lane; 9.30 pm, Sun 8 pm; no Amex.*

**Hotel du Vin et Bistro** **£51** ④④❸
14 Southgate St SO23 9EF (01962) 841414
*It still has its fans (not least for its "exceptionally strong", if nowadays quite "expensive", wine list), but this original branch of the Gallic hotel/bistro chain has "gone off the boil" in recent years – the ambience is still "lovely", but the "un-fancy" food can be "bland", and service "slow".* / **Details:** *www.hotelduvin.com; 9.45 pm; booking: max 12.* **Accommodation:** *24 rooms, from £145.*

**The Avenue**
**Lainston House Hotel** **£79** ④❸❸
SO21 2LT (01962) 776088
*"Lovely… but far too expensive" – a fair summary of the views on this grand country house hotel, which is lauded by most reporters for its "excellent" cuisine and "really special" ambience, but which can also seem "pretentious".* / **Details:** *www.lainstonhouse.com; 9.30 pm, 10 pm Fri & Sat.* **Accommodation:** *50 rooms, from £245.*

**The Old Vine** **£37** ❸❸❷
8 Great Minster St SO23 9HA
(01962) 854616
*Cutely located by the cathedral, this "always-busy" and "very welcoming" hostelry makes a "lovely" spot for a meal; it serves quite an "interesting" menu, realised to a very "competent" standard.*
/ **Details:** *www.oldvinewinchester.com; 9.30 pm, Sun 9 pm; children: 6+.* **Accommodation:** *5 rooms, from £100.*

**Wykeham Arms** **£47** ④④❷
75 Kingsgate St SO23 9PE (01962) 853834
*Near the College, this "lovely", old inn inspires only a modest number of reports nowadays; optimists insist it's "back on form after many years" (with steak among the better options).*
/ **Details:** *www.fullershotels.com; between Cathedral and College; 9.15 pm; children: 14+.*
**Accommodation:** *14 rooms, from £129.*

WINDERMERE, CUMBRIA 7–3D

**First Floor Café**
**Lakeland Limited** **£32** ❷❸❸
Alexandra Buildings LA23 1BQ
(015394) 47116
*The "airy" in-store dining room of this kitchen equipment retailer inspires only rave reviews for its "high-quality" food (from an ex-head chef of Le Gavroche!) and its "quick and friendly" service; "the only pity is that it's not open at night".* / **Details:** *www.lakeland.co.uk; 6 pm, Sat 5 pm, Sun 4 pm; no Amex.*

**Gilpin Lodge** **£83** ❷❷❷
Crook Rd LA23 3NE (01539) 488818
*"A true gastronomic experience, in very tasteful surroundings"; this "luxurious but unpretentious" country house hotel has much improved in recent times, and most – if not quite all – reporters now judge it "exceptional in every way".* / **Details:** *www.gilpinlodge.co.uk; 9.15 pm; no jeans; children: 7+.* **Accommodation:** *20 rooms, from £290.*

**Holbeck Ghyll** **£87** ❷❸❸
Holbeck Ln LA23 1LU (01539) 432375
*It's not just the "beautiful" lake-view that makes this 19th-century hunting lodge a destination of real note – most reporters praise "classic" cuisine that's "beautifully executed" too, although it can also seem a touch "overpriced" nowadays.* / **Details:** *www.holbeckghyll.com; 3m N of Windermere, towards Troutbeck; 9 pm; no jeans or trainers; booking essential; children: 13+ at D.*
**Accommodation:** *23 rooms, from £150.*

**Jerichos**  £50  ❷❸④
College Rd  LA23 1BX   (01539) 442522
*"Steak and chips to die for" – the stand-out menu attraction at the Blaydes' "reliable", "friendly" and "buzzy" restaurant-with-rooms. / **Details:** www.jerichos.co.uk; 9 pm; closed Mon & Thu D; children: 12+. **Accommodation:** 10 rooms, from £85.*

**Linthwaite House**  £71  ❒
Crook Rd  LA23 3JA   (01539) 488600
*Fewer reports than we'd like on this "wonderful" country house hotel dining room, set above Windermere; it's tipped as "well worth a visit", not least for its "relaxed" and "unpretentious" service. / **Details:** www.linthwaite.com; near Windermere golf club; 9 pm; no jeans or trainers; children: 7+ at D. **Accommodation:** 32 rooms, from £180.*

**The Samling**  £85  ❷❷❒
Ambleside Rd  LA23 1LR   (01539) 431922
*"A beautiful getaway, with stunning scenery"; this "romantic" lake-view country house hotel seems to have emerged from the former Von Essen empire stronger than ever – the consistency of reports that "everything is just right" is impressive. / **Details:** www.thesamlinghotel.co.uk; take A591 from town; 9.15 pm.
**Accommodation:** 11 rooms, from £190.*

WINDSOR, BERKSHIRE          3–3A

**Al Fassia**  £39  ❒
27 St Leonards Rd  SL4 3BP
(01753) 855370
*A long-running tip for "good-value" Moroccan cuisine; even fans, though, can find the ambience "nothing to write home about", and – unusually – this year saw a couple of reports of "surly" service. / **Details:** www.alfassiarestaurant.com; 10.15 pm, Fri & Sat 10.30 pm, Sun 9.45 pm; closed Mon L; Booking recommended Fri & Sat.*

**The Greene Oak**  £45  ❒
Deadworth Rd, Oakley Grn  SL4 5UW
(01753) 864294
*A tip that's "slightly off the tourist track" – a "cheerful" inn, offering quality food at prices that are "reasonable, by the standards of such a pricey area". / **Details:** www.thegreeneoak.co.uk; 9.30 pm, Sun 3.30 pm.*

WINTERINGHAM, LINCOLNSHIRE   5–1D

**Winteringham Fields**  £107  ❷❷❸
1 Silver St  DN15 9ND   (01724) 733096
*"Back to delivering truly excellent food… albeit at eye-watering prices"; this "delightful"*

restaurant-with-rooms – *"an almost surreal find in the middle of nowhere" – now seem to be well on its way back to achieving the stellar standards of yesteryear.
/ **Details:** www.winteringhamfields.co.uk; 4m SW of Humber Bridge; 9.30 pm; closed Mon & Sun; no Amex.
**Accommodation:** 11 rooms, from £180.*

WISWELL, LANCASHIRE          5–1B

**Freemasons at Wiswell**  £52  ❶❷❷
8 Vicarage Fold Clitheroe  BB7 9DF
(01254) 822218
*"In the heart of the Ribble Valley", Steven Smith's "outstanding" country inn is seen by its growing fan club as a serious competitor to nearby Northcote Manor, and for its fans offers "the best eating for about 50 miles"; perhaps the food is sometimes "over-refined and fussied up", but it's truly "very accomplished".
/ **Details:** www.freemasonswiswell.co.uk; Tue-Thu 9 pm, Fri & Sat 9.30 pm, Sun 8 pm; closed Mon; no Amex; 8+ have to pre-order.*

WIVETON, NORFOLK            6–3C

**Wiveton Bell**  £46  ❷❷❷
Blakeney Rd  NR25 7TL   (01263) 740 101
*"Enjoy a walk in North Norfolk, then get yourself to this inviting place for good, wholesome food, and you will not be disappointed" – the tenor of all reports on this child-friendly inn, in the "middle-of-nowhere".
/ **Details:** www.wivetonbell.co.uk; 9 pm.
**Accommodation:** 4 rooms, from £75.*

WOBURN, BEDFORDSHIRE         3–2A

**Paris House**  £91  ❶❶④
Woburn Pk  MK17 9QP   (01525) 290692
*"Nice views over the deer park" add interest to a visit to this "formal but friendly" outpost of Alan Murchison's '10 in 8' empire; despite the "majestic" Woburn Estate location, the dining room can seem surprisingly "stark", but otherwise "the experience is sublime from first to last". / **Details:** www.parishouse.co.uk; on A4012; 8.30 pm; closed Mon, Tue L & Sun D.*

WOBURN, BUCKINGHAMSHIRE      3–2A

**The Black Horse**  £42  ❒
1 Bedford St  MK17 9QB   (01525) 290210
*"In the lovely village of Woburn", an "extremely busy" pub tipped for its quite ambitious food.
/ **Details:** www.blackhorsewoburn.co.uk; 9.45 pm, Sun 9 pm; SRA-58%.*

| WOLVERCOTE, OXFORDSHIRE | 2–2D |
|---|---|

**The Trout Inn**  £41  🅣
195 Godstow Rd  OX2 8PN
(01865) 510930
*"Gone upmarket in recent times" ("and so has the bill") – the "extremely busy" pub made famous by Inspector Morse, with its "fantastic" riverside location, has seemed to cope better with peak times of late; it makes "a brilliant summer destination".*
/ **Details:** www.thetroutoxford.co.uk; 2m from junction of A40 & A44; 10 pm, Fri & Sat 10.30 pm, Sun 9 pm.

| WOLVERHAMPTON, WEST MIDLANDS | 5–4B |
|---|---|

**Bilash**  £46  ❶❶❷
2 Cheapside  WV1 1TU  (01902) 427762
*"Brilliant quality, in amongst the dross of the Wolverhampton dining scene!" – "even metropolitan snobs are impressed" by Sitab Khan's "excellent" Indian 30-year-old; the least enthusiastic report? – "staff try very hard, and it's always very busy".*
/ **Details:** www.thebilash.co.uk; 10.30 pm; closed Sun.

| WOODLANDS, HAMPSHIRE | 2–4C |
|---|---|

**Terravina**
**Hotel Terravina**  £57  ❷❶❸
174 Woodlands Rd, Netley Marsh, New Forest  SO40 7GL  (023) 8029 3784
*You'd expect a top master of wine to provide "an amazing wine list" and to employ an "incredibly knowledgeable" sommelier, but Gerard Basset's (and wife Nina's) "classy" hotel, "quietly located on the edge of the New Forest", also achieves "wow" status with its "fine cooking" and "amazing service".*
/ **Details:** www.hotelterravina.co.uk; 9.30 pm.
**Accommodation:** 11 rooms, from £160.

| WOODSTOCK, OXFORDSHIRE | 2–1D |
|---|---|

**The Feathers**  £69  ❷❷❷
Market St  OX20 1SX  (01993) 812291
*In this "beautiful" small town, a luxurious inn – given a "funky" makeover some time back – where the food is "good, sometimes excellent"; looking for "a totally new experience"? – try the "quirky gin-tasting menu"!*
/ **Details:** www.feathers.co.uk; 8m N of Oxford on A44; 9 pm; no jeans or trainers.
**Accommodation:** 21 rooms, from £169.

| WORSLEY, GREATER MANCHESTER | 5–2B |
|---|---|

**Grenache**  £36  🅣
15 Bridgewater Rd  M28 3JE  (0161) 799 8181
*A few miles north west of Manchester, a "very pleasant and entertaining" destination achieving high praise from all who report on it.*
/ **Details:** www.grenacherestaurant.co.uk; 10 pm, Sun 5 pm; closed Mon, Tue & Sun D.

| WORTHING, WEST SUSSEX | 3–4A |
|---|---|

**The Fish Factory**  £32  ❸❸④
51-53 Brighton Rd  BN11 3EE  (01903) 207123
*"Very fresh fish, with the option of frying in matzo meal or batter" helps win consistent praise for this "busy" spot, liked for its "family-friendly" style and "good value".*
/ **Details:** www.protorestaurantgroup.com; 10 pm.

| WRINEHILL, CHESHIRE | 5–2B |
|---|---|

**The Hand and Trumpet**  £40  ❸④❹
Main Rd  CW3 9BJ  (01270) 820048
*This "busy country pub" is part of the generally reliable Brunning & Price chain; the food, if "not spectacular", is "always consistent" (and comes in "generous portions" too).*
/ **Details:** www.brunningandprice.co.uk/hand; 10 pm, Sun 9.30 pm; no Amex.

| WYE, KENT | 3–3C |
|---|---|

**The Wife of Bath**  £49  ❷❷❷
4 Upper Bridge St  TN25 5AF  (01233) 812232
*"Better under the new ownership", this small village restaurant-with-rooms is "worth a detour", especially for the "very good-value" prix-fixe lunch.* / **Details:** www.thewifeofbath.com; off A28 between Ashford & Canterbury; 9.30 pm; closed Mon, Tue L & Sun D; no Amex. **Accommodation:** 5 rooms, from £95.

| WYKE REGIS, DORSET | 2–4B |
|---|---|

**Crab House Café**  £44  ❷❸❸
Ferrymans Way, Portland Rd  DT4 9YU  (01305) 788867
*"A local legend for ultra-fresh fish and seafood"; this "quirky" and "unpretentious" ("shack-like") seaside spot – overlooking both Weymouth Bay and Chesil Beach – makes a simply "brilliant" sunny-day destination.*
/ **Details:** www.crabhousecafe.co.uk; overlooking the Fleet Lagoon, on the road to Portland; 9 pm, Sat 9.30 pm; closed Mon & Tue; no Amex; 8+ deposit of £10 per head.

WYMONDHAM, LEICESTERSHIRE          5–3D

**The Berkeley Arms**          **£ 45**   ❷❷❷
59 Main St  LE14 2AG   (01572) 787 587
*Run by a couple who used to work at
Hambleton Hall, this is a classy inn, whose "high-
quality" cuisine and "charming" service are
winning a "growing reputation locally".
/ Details: www.theberkeleyarms.co.uk; 9 pm, Sat &
Sun 9.30 pm; closed Mon & Sun D.*

YEADON, WEST YORKSHIRE          5–1C

**Murgatroyds**          **£ 29**   ❶
Harrogate Rd  LS19 7BN  (0113) 250 0010
*"Putting the original (and nearby) Harry
Ramsden's in the shade" – this large canteen is
"unbeatable for fish 'n' chips in these parts".
/ Details: www.murgatroyds.co.uk; 9.30 pm.*

YORK, NORTH YORKSHIRE          5–1D

**Ate O'Clock**          **£ 43**   ❶
13A, High Ousegate  YO1 8RZ
(01904) 644080
*"Hidden-away down an alleyway", a "lovely"
bistro tipped for "beautiful original food in lovely
surroundings", and "good value" too.
/ Details: www.ateoclock.co.uk; 9.30 pm; closed
Mon D & Sun.*

**Bettys**          **£ 45**   ❸❷❷
6-8 St Helen's Sq  Y01 8QP   (01904) 659142
*"Fulfilling all your '20s teashop-fantasies!"; this
famous "institution" may be "highly-priced for
queueing tourists", but praise for its "reliable"
standards – not least its "Anglo-Swiss" classics
dishes – is impressive. / Details: www.bettys.co.uk;
9 pm; no Amex; no booking, except Sun.*

**The Blue Bicycle**          **£ 54**   ④❸❷
34 Fossgate  YO1 9TA   (01904) 673990
*More consistent reports of late on this "cosy
bolthole"; fans say it's "a good place for seafood
in a lovely old building overlooking the River
Foss", but there are still critics who find
standards just "not up to the prices".
/ Details: www.thebluebicycle.com; 9.30 pm, Sun
9 pm; closed Mon - Wed L; no Amex; booking: max 8
Sat D. Accommodation: 6 rooms, from £175.*

**Café Concerto**          **£ 43**   ❷❸④
21 High Petergate  YO1 7EN
(01904) 610478
*"Fresh and imaginative all-day food" – now
"discreetly refurbished" (and not before time),
this "classic" café/bistro, by the Minster, is still
better than many of the city-centre competitors.
/ Details: www.cafeconcerto.biz; 9.30 pm; booking:
max 6-8. Accommodation: 1 room, at about £175.*

**Cafe No. 8 Bistro**          **£ 45**   ❷❷④
8 Gillygate  YO31 7EQ   (01904) 653074
*It may just have a "tiny" open kitchen, but this
café/bistro near the Minster is hailed in
numerous reports for a "varied" and
"interesting" menu that's "well-executed" too.
/ Details: www.cafeno8.co.uk; 9.30 pm; no Amex.*

**City Screen
Picturehouse**          **£ 33**   ❶
Coney St  YO1 9QL   (01904) 612940
*For "good coffee, burgers and sharing dishes",
this riverside venue is a top tip locally.
/ Details: www.picturehouses.co.uk; 9 pm; no Amex;
no booking.*

**Delrio's**          **£ 41**   ❷❸❷
10-12 Blossom St  YO24 1AE
(01904) 622695
*An atmospheric cellar restaurant and bar, with al
fresco dining in fine weather, where the Italian
cooking can be "really excellent"; it's a "popular"
place, though ("best to book"), and service can
be "spasmodic" at busy times.
/ Details: www.delriosrestaurant.com; 10.30 pm;
D only, closed Mon.*

**Hotel du Vin et Bistro**          **£ 51**   ❶
89 The Mount  YO24 1AX   (01904) 557350
*Still sometimes tipped for its "great wine list",
this outpost of the hotel/bistro chain cannot
otherwise be regarded as a 'safe'
recommendation – far too many meals of late
have been "run-of-the-mill".
/ Details: www.hotelduvin.com; 9.45 pm, Fri & Sat
10.15 pm. Accommodation: 44 rooms, from £110.*

**Il Paradiso Del Cibo**          **£ 35**   ❷❸❷
40 Walmgate  YO0 1TJ   (0190) 461 1444
*"A fantastic small restaurant", praised by all
reporters for its "inexpensive but delicious"
Italian fare; "it looks nothing from the outside,
but the food is wonderful".
/ Details: www.ilparadisodelcibo.com; 10 pm.*

**J Baker's**
**Bistro Moderne**          **£ 49**   ❶④④
7 Fossgate  YO1 9TA   (01904) 622688
*York's most commented-on destination, and*
*some would argue its best; it's Jeff Baker's*
*"tremendous", "innovative" cooking that makes it*
*of note, though – the setting has "all the charm*
*of an IKEA showroom", and the "studentish"*
*service can be "dire". / **Details:** www.jbakers.co.uk;*
*9.30 pm; closed Mon & Sun.*

**Le Langhe**                **£ 46**   ❶④❸
The Old Coach Hs, Peasholme Grn  YO1
7PW   (01904) 622584
*Octavio Bocca's "lovely little restaurant, plus*
*Italian deli" has the added boon of a "great*
*courtyard" for the summer; it offers a "limited*
*but high-quality" menu of "wonderfully*
*authentic" North Italian dishes (including*
*"fabulous" pasta), plus "interesting" wines (which*
*he imports). / **Details:** www.lelanghe.co.uk;*
*midnight; closed Mon-Thu D & Sun; no Amex.*

**Little Betty's**           **£ 43**   ❶
46 Stonegate  YO1 8AS   (01904) 622865
*A "cosy" outpost of the famous tea house chain,*
*of particular note for its "charming" location –*
*"this is our favourite of all the Bettys, because of*
*its setting in a medieval building".*
*/ **Details:** www.bettys.co.uk; 5.30 pm; L only; no Amex.*

**Melton's**                 **£ 43**   ❷❷❸
7 Scarcroft Rd  YO23 1ND   (01904) 634
341
*"Quietly ploughing its furrow in what's fast*
*becoming a fashionable inner suburb", Michael*
*Hjort's "comfortable" restaurant of long standing*
*still produces "imaginative" food, accompanied by*
*a wine list that's "well-chosen" and "well-priced".*
*/ **Details:** www.meltonsrestaurant.co.uk; 9.30 pm;*
*closed Mon & Sun; no Amex.*

**Melton's Too**             **£ 37**   ④④④
25 Walmgate  YO1 9TX   (01904) 629 222
*This well-known "York stalwart" – a more*

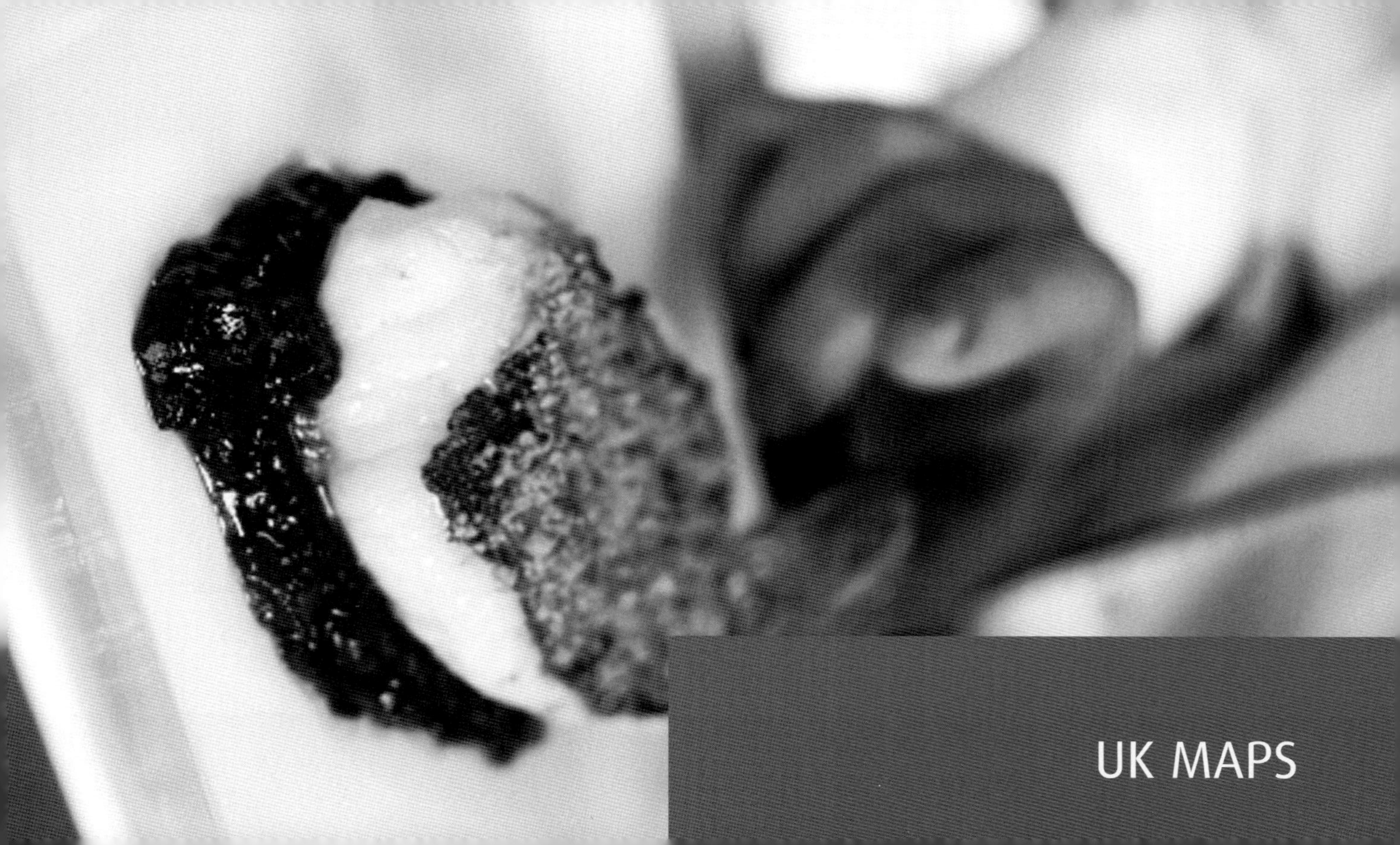

# UK MAPS

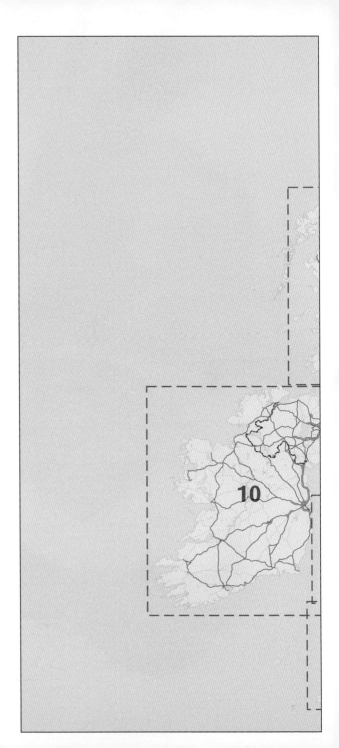

10

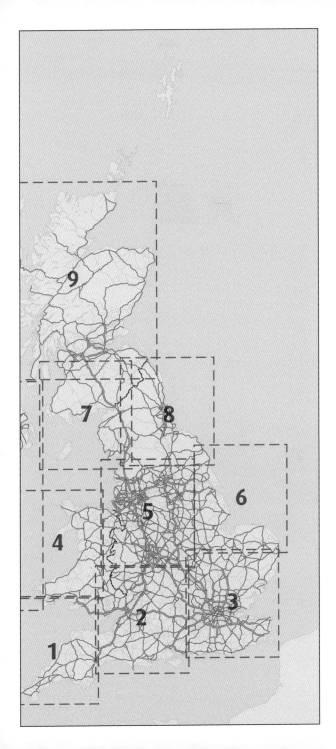

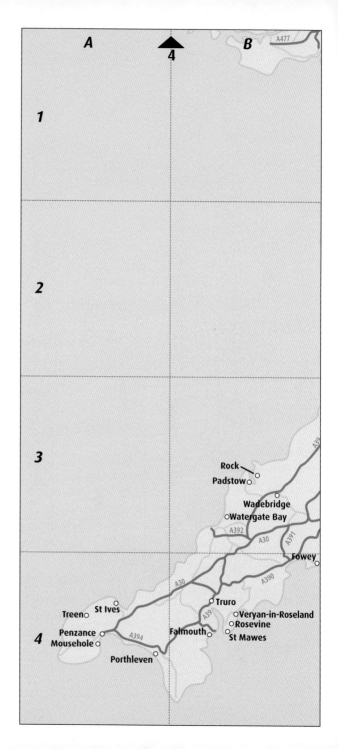

MAP 1

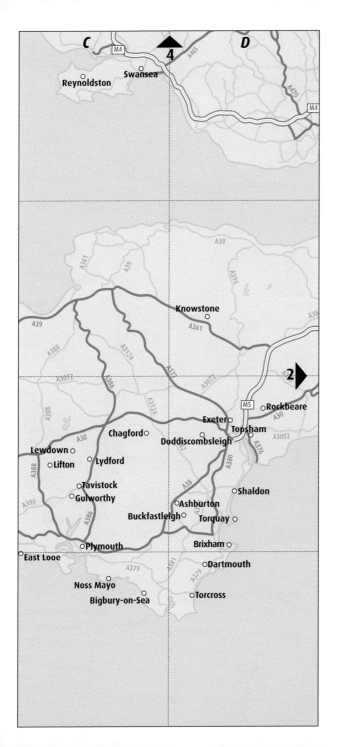

MAP 1

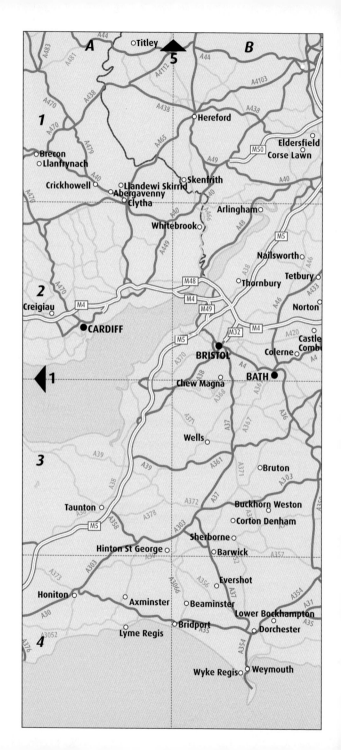

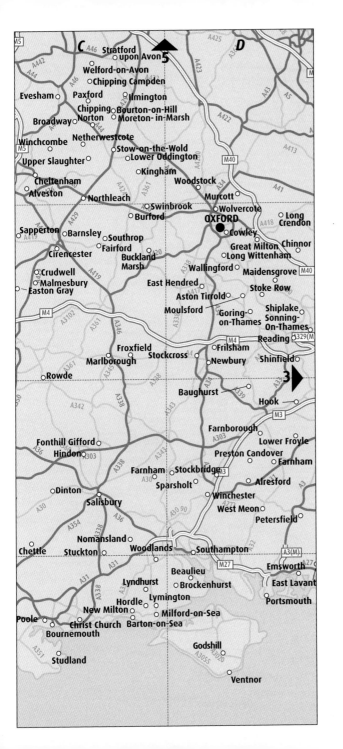

MAP 3

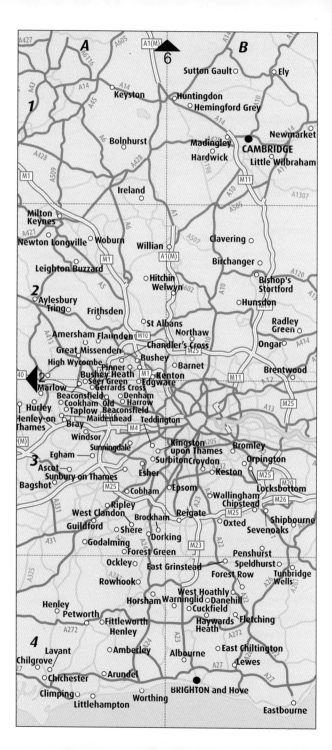

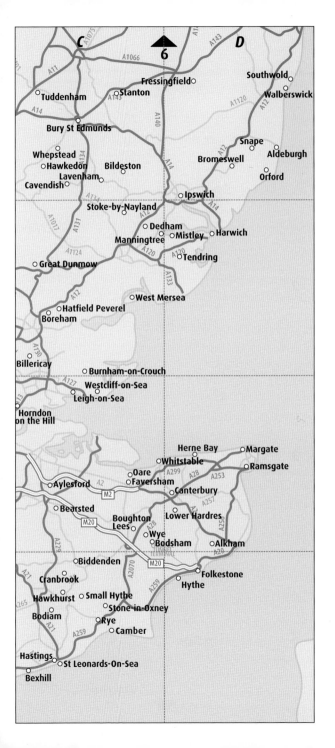

MAP 3

MAP 4

|   | **A** | **B** |
|---|-------|-------|
| **1** | | |
| **2** | | |
| **3** | | |
| **4** | St Davids | Porthgain  Newport  Broad Haven |

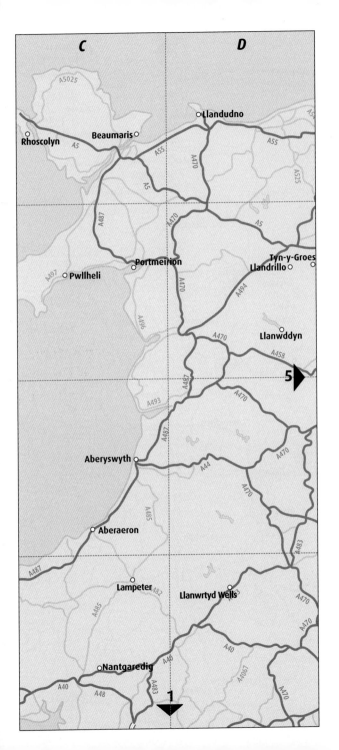

MAP 4

**C**

**D**

A5025

○ Llandudno

○ Rhoscolyn

Beaumaris ○

A5

A55

A470

A55

A55

A5

A487

A470

A5

A525

Tyn-y-Groes

○ Pwllheli
A497

Portmeirion ○

Llandrillo ○

○

A470

A494

A496

A470

Llanwddyn ○

A458

**5**

A487

A470

A493

A487

A470

Aberyswyth ○

A44

A470

A485

○ Aberaeron

A483

A487

Lampeter ○
A482

Llanwrtyd Wells ○

A470

A485

A470

○ Nantgaredig
A40

A40

A40

A4067

A470

A48

A483

**1**

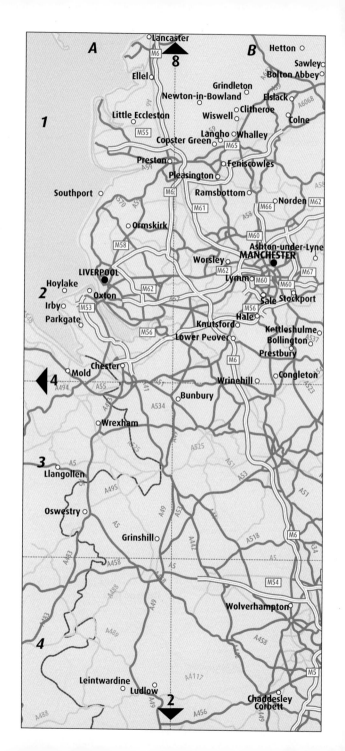

MAP 5

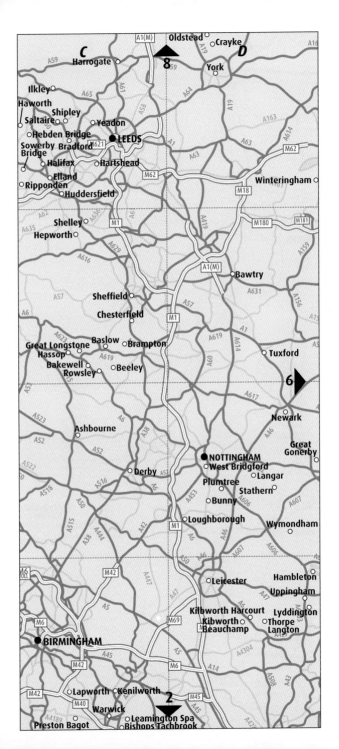

MAP 6

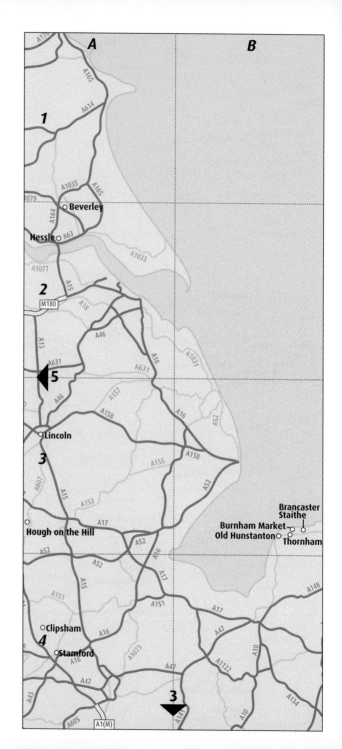

MAP 6

C   D

Holkham
Morston
Wiveton
Salthouse
Letheringsett   Holt
Wells-next-the-Sea

A148

A140

A1067

A149

A47
Norwich   Brundall   A47

A11

A146

Stoke Holy Cross
3

A140   A143

A143

MAP 7

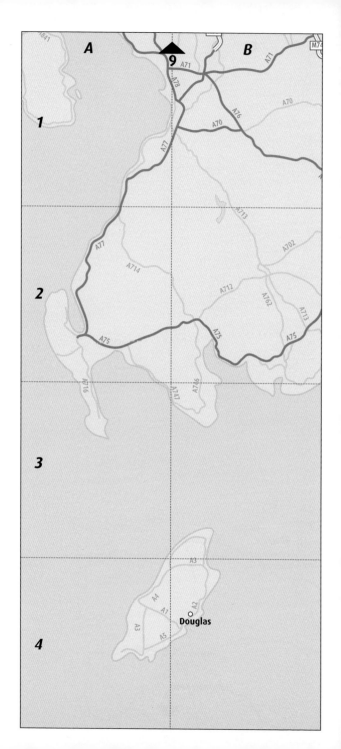

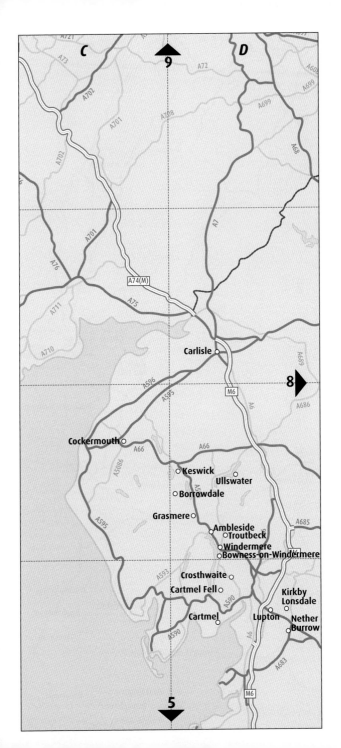

MAP 7

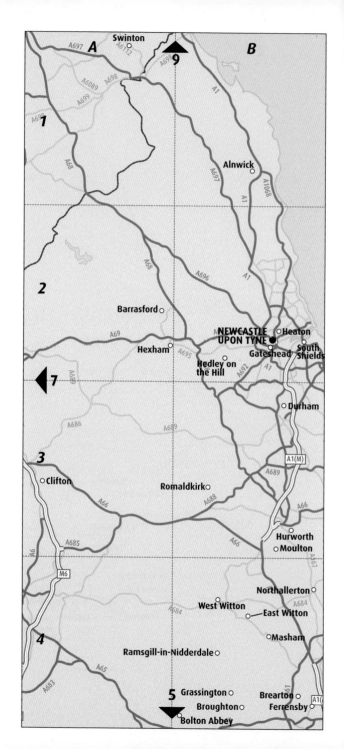

MAP 8

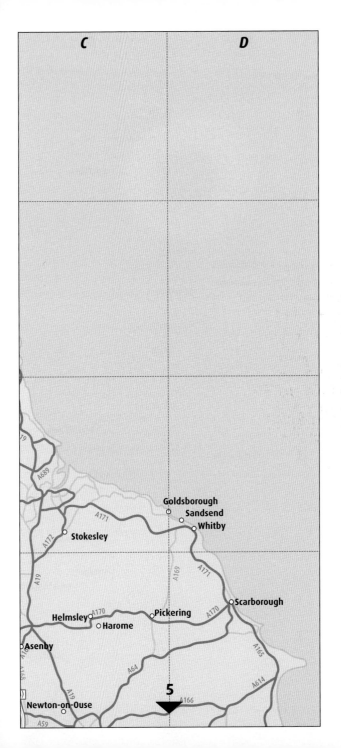

MAP 8

C
D

Goldsborough
Sandsend
Whitby
Stokesley
A171
A171
A169
A171
A172
A19
A689
79
Scarborough
Helmsley A170 Pickering A170
Harome
A165
Asenby
A64
A614
5
A166
Newton-on-Ouse
A59
A19

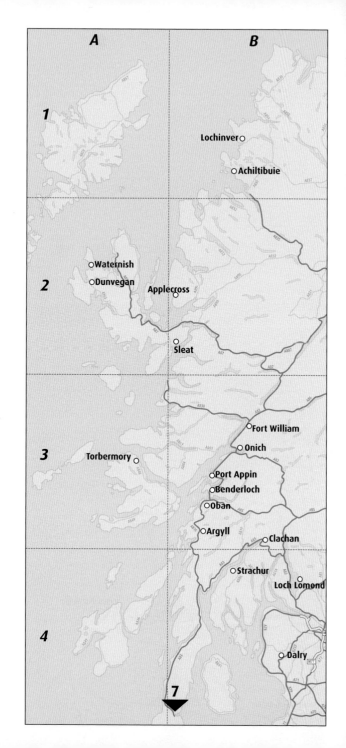

MAP 9

MAP 9

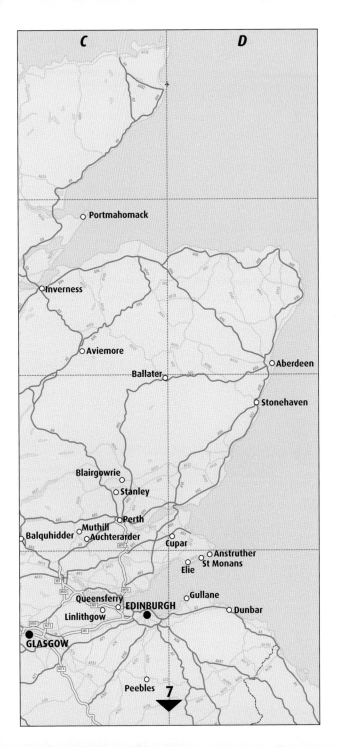

C   D

Portmahomack

Inverness

Aviemore

Ballater   Aberdeen

Stonehaven

Blairgowrie

Stanley

Perth

Muthill
Balquhidder   Auchterarder

Cupar

Anstruther
St Monans
Elie

Queensferry   Gullane

EDINBURGH   Dunbar

Linlithgow

GLASGOW

Peebles   7

MAP **10**

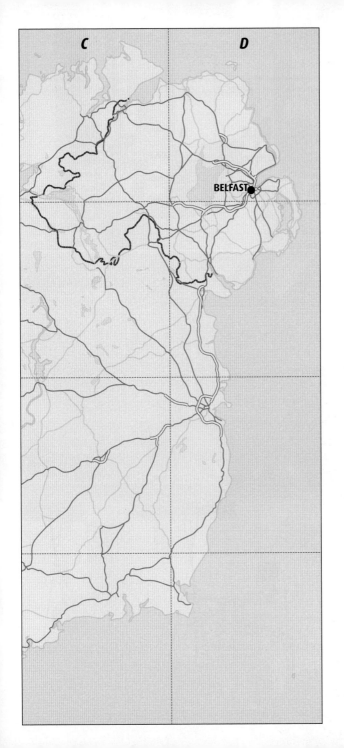

MAP 10

BELFAST

C

D

Alimentum, Cambridge

Jesmond Dene House, Newcastle

Woods Brasserie, Cardiff

# ALPHABETICAL INDEX

# ALPHABETICAL INDEX

# ALPHABETICAL INDEX

# ALPHABETICAL INDEX

# ALPHABETICAL INDEX

# ALPHABETICAL INDEX

# ALPHABETICAL INDEX